The Beatitudes Path

An Interfaith Exploration of Sacred Blessings

By

Kevin L. Meyer

The Beatitudes Path: An Interfaith Exploration of Sacred Blessings

Copyright © 2025 by Kevin L. Meyer

All rights reserved. No part of this publication may be reproduced, distributed, or transmitted in any form or by any means, including photocopying, recording, or other electronic or mechanical methods, without the prior written permission of the publisher, except in the case of brief quotations embodied in critical reviews and certain other noncommercial uses permitted by copyright law.

Bhavana Press
Morro Bay, California

ISBN: 979-8-9996276-0-5

First Edition

Scripture quotations marked NRSV are from the New Revised Standard Version Bible, copyright © 1989 National Council of the Churches of Christ in the United States of America. Used by permission. All rights reserved worldwide.

Printed in the United States of America

Contents

Part I – Introduction and Context
Introduction 1
The Context of the Beatitudes 9

Part II - The Beatitudes in Depth
Blessed Are the Poor in Spirit: A Foundation for Living 21
Blessed Are Those Who Mourn: Finding Comfort in Grief 29
Blessed Are the Meek: Reclaiming a Misunderstood Virtue 39
Blessed Are Those Who Hunger for Righteousness 49
Blessed Are the Merciful: The Power of Compassion 59
Blessed Are the Pure in Heart: The Vision That Transforms 69
Blessed Are the Peacemakers: Active Reconciliation 81
Blessed Are Those Who Are Persecuted for Righteousness 93
Blessed Are You: The Personal Turn in the Ninth Beatitude .. 103

Part III - Global and Interfaith Perspectives
Blessed Beyond the Canon 115
Earth and Spirit: Indigenous and African Wisdoms 125
Echoes from the East: Confucian, Shinto, and Jain Wisdom .. 135
The Beatitudes Around the Global Church 145

Part IV - History and Interpretation
Makarioi: The Greek Roots of the Beatitudes 165
Two Visions of Blessing: Comparing Matthew and Luke 179

Blessing and Woe: The Ethical Tension 189

Reading the Beatitudes Through the Ages 201

The Beatitudes in Early Christian Devotional Life 211

Power, Empire, and the Politics of Blessing 227

Beyond the Canon: Q, Apocrypha, and Early Wisdom 239

Part V - Applied Beatitudes

Saints of the Beatitudes: Living Witnesses to a Radical Way .. 255

Living the Beatitudes in Daily Life 273

Part VI - Conclusion and Resources

Conclusion & Reflection 289

Research Methodology 295

Notes by Chapter 305

Bibliography 343

Further Reading 367

Index 385

An 8-Week Journey of Reflection and Practice 387

About the Author 445

Other Books by Kevin Meyer 447

Part I

Introduction and Context

Introduction

Every year, I challenge myself to learn something completely new. Not a casual hobby, but an intentional, reflective, deep dive—the kind that changes how you see things.

Early on, these adventures were physical. I trained for and ran my first marathon, learned to scuba dive, picked up windsurfing, skied five countries in Europe. Later, they became more complex: a complete house remodel (which also taught me about patience), a deep dive into Buddhism that took me to Bhutan, writing and publishing a book, even learning to grow cannabis legally and well.

In 2015, my project was exploring the history of the Bible itself—not as devotional study, but as historical inquiry. The politics surrounding which texts would be included in the canon turned out to be stories of power and intrigue that would make for an excellent Netflix series. The compounding translation issues across languages and centuries revealed how much interpretation shapes what we think we're reading. It was fascinating and humbling to discover how much human decision-making went into what many consider divine revelation.

This year's project combines two interests: the Beatitudes from Matthew 5, and artificial intelligence as a research tool. It's been fascinating to see how AI can augment human curiosity without replacing the essential work of thinking and meaning-making.

Questions That Won't Go Away

As I settle into early retirement, I keep returning to the same questions: What does it mean to live well when you're no longer climbing career ladders? How do you maintain integrity and purpose outside organizational structures? What kind of person do I want to become when nobody's watching my performance metrics?

These questions led me back to a passage I've always found very compelling but never deeply explored: the Beatitudes. Eight short statements Jesus made at the beginning of his most famous sermon. Simple words that have somehow shaped Western civilization's understanding of virtue.

Blessed are the poor in spirit...
Blessed are those who mourn...
Blessed are the meek...

I'm curious: What if these aren't just religious platitudes but practical wisdom about human flourishing? What if they offer insights not just for personal meaning but for how we lead and live together?

Why This Matters Now

Though I was raised in and remain predominantly within the Christian faith—something deeply influential in my daily life though I generally keep it very private—I've become increasingly troubled by how Christian principles (and those of many other religious traditions) are being coopted for power, political and otherwise. In today's chaotic world, the very teachings that should call us toward humility, mercy, and justice are often twisted to justify their opposites.

For me, the Beatitudes have always represented the foundation of what living as a Christian really means. Not the culture war version or the prosperity gospel distortion, but the radical, challenging, transformative vision of human flourishing that Jesus outlined on that hillside. But I wondered: Are these insights uniquely Christian, or do they point toward something universal about how humans thrive together?

For this exploration, I've deliberately strived to be tradition-neutral, approaching these teachings not as religious doctrine but as wisdom that might belong to all of us, even as they find particular expression in Christian scripture.

What I'm Really Wondering About

My career has revolved around leadership, specifically servant leadership, and the more I've studied and practiced it over the years, the more I notice how its core principles echo these ancient teachings. Leaders who listen more than they speak. Who build others up rather than themselves. Who find strength in acknowledging their limitations. Who lead through influence rather than authority.

But I'm also curious about something broader: How do these insights appear in other wisdom traditions? Buddhism certainly talks about ego and compassion. Islam emphasizes mercy and humility. Hinduism teaches about surrendering false pride.

Indigenous traditions honor community over individual achievement.

Are the Beatitudes uniquely Christian, or do they articulate something universal about how humans flourish together? And if there are parallels across traditions, what might that tell us about our shared humanity?

An Unexpected Discovery

What I didn't expect was how often these core teachings feel forgotten—not just within Christianity, but across religious traditions. We seem drawn to the prescriptive rules that can be easily politicized or conveniently ignored when they conflict with power or personal advantage. Meanwhile, the deeper teachings about compassion, humility, and service—the ones that actually transform how we treat each other—get pushed aside.

Christians quote the Ten Commandments more than the Beatitudes. Muslims debate law more than mercy. Buddhists can get caught up in doctrine while missing compassion. It's as if every tradition risks losing its own heart in favor of easier, more controllable external markers.

Meanwhile, our culture seems hungry for exactly what these teachings offer: authentic leadership, genuine community, ways of engaging conflict that don't destroy relationships, models of strength that don't require dominating others.

What I've Learned (And Am Sharing)

This book is the collection of what I've discovered—one Beatitude at a time. There's no commercial intent here, just a desire to share what I've learned and perhaps learn even more through dialogue with others.

Each exploration includes:

- What the original languages actually convey (the English translations sometimes miss important nuances)

- The Jewish wisdom tradition that shaped these teachings

- How similar insights appear across world traditions—with honest attention to both parallels and differences

- What this might mean for leadership, relationships, and simply getting through our days with integrity

This isn't devotional writing, though you might find it meaningful. It's not academic theology, though it draws on serious scholarship. Think of it as one person's honest exploration of wisdom that might belong to all of us.

A Different Kind of Learning

I'm approaching this the same way I've tackled previous projects: read widely, find good teachers, try things out, share what seems useful. But I'm also aware that these aren't just intellectual puzzles to solve. They're invitations to a way of being that challenges pretty much everything our culture teaches about success and influence.

The Beatitudes suggest that strength comes through acknowledging weakness, that leadership emerges from service, that security grows from letting go of control. They point toward a kind of radical humility that looks like weakness but might actually be wisdom.

While my focus is primarily on personal transformation and moral living, my background in servant leadership does surface occasionally in brief reflections on how these teachings might inform how we lead and influence others. But the heart of this exploration is about becoming more fully human—individually and in community.

An Invitation to Wonder

Whether you're wrestling with retirement transitions, leadership questions, or simply wondering if there might be better ways to be human together, I think you'll find something worthwhile in this exploration.

This isn't about converting anyone to anything. It's about wondering together: What if these ancient observations are true? What if there really are patterns to human flourishing that transcend religious boundaries? What if the wisdom we need for our fractured world has been hiding in plain sight, waiting for us to rediscover it beneath the layers of institutional interpretation and political manipulation?

Come along if you're curious. Come along if you're skeptical. The Beatitudes have been quietly shaping lives for two thousand years. Maybe there's something here worth rediscovering.

Apocalyptic Vision and the Kingdom of Heaven: The Context of the Beatitudes

The Beatitudes are often read as timeless spiritual teachings, floating above history—beautiful, poetic, and morally inspiring. But to hear them as Jesus' first listeners did, we must step into their original context: a world charged with expectation, unrest, and longing for divine intervention.

The Beatitudes are not general life advice. They are apocalyptic proclamation—the opening salvo of a new kingdom breaking into history.

The World Behind the Words

First-century Galilee was a land under pressure. Rome occupied Judea through a complex web of client rulers, military presence, and economic extraction. Local rulers, like Herod Antipas, aligned themselves with imperial power, taxing the people heavily to fund construction projects and appease Caesar. The magnificent cities of Sepphoris and Tiberias rose from peasant labor and taxes, visible symbols of a system that concentrated wealth upward while most lived at subsistence level.

The vast majority of the population were subsistence peasants, often in debt, often hungry, caught between Roman taxation and traditional religious obligations.[1] Many had lost ancestral lands to debt or imperial confiscation. Temple authorities in Jerusalem were viewed by some as corrupt or complicit with the occupying power, having made accommodations that many saw as compromising Israel's covenant identity.

This was not merely economic hardship—it was a crisis of meaning. For a people who understood themselves as God's chosen nation, foreign domination raised profound theological questions: Had God abandoned the covenant? Were they being punished for unfaithfulness? When would the promises be fulfilled?

Amid this backdrop, Jewish communities clung to apocalyptic hope—the belief that God would soon intervene in history, overturn injustice, and establish a new era of peace and righteousness.[2] This hope was deeply rooted in Israel's prophetic tradition, from Daniel's visions of God's kingdom superseding earthly empires to Ezekiel's promises of restoration and renewal.

Understanding "Apocalyptic"

Before proceeding, we must clarify what "apocalyptic" means. In popular usage, the term conjures images of catastrophe and world-ending destruction. But in its original context, "apocalyptic" comes from the Greek *apokalypsis*, meaning "unveiling" or "revelation"—the disclosure of hidden divine purposes and the true nature of reality.[3]

Apocalyptic literature and thought in Second Temple Judaism was not primarily about cosmic catastrophe but about divine vindication—God's intervention to set right what had gone wrong, to reveal justice where injustice seemed to triumph, and to establish the divine kingdom that would restore Israel and bless the nations. It involved radical social transformation, often through divine action that would overturn existing power structures.

This hope was not just about the end of time. It was about a radical reversal of the present—a world where the lowly would be lifted up, the mighty brought down, and the poor vindicated. When Jesus says *"Blessed are the poor in spirit, for theirs is the kingdom of heaven,"* he is not offering comfort in abstract suffering. He is announcing that the long-awaited divine reversal is arriving—and arriving in the most unexpected places.

Jewish Roots and Prophetic Continuity

The apocalyptic vision Jesus proclaimed was not foreign innovation but the flowering of Israel's own prophetic tradition. From Moses' promises in Deuteronomy to the visions of Isaiah, Jeremiah, and Ezekiel, Hebrew scripture pulsed with expectation of God's ultimate intervention in history. The Jubilee traditions of Leviticus 25, with their vision of debt forgiveness, land restoration, and economic reset, provided practical models for what God's kingdom might look like.[4]

The Beatitudes echo most powerfully the language of Isaiah 61, a passage associated with liberation, justice, and jubilee:

"The Spirit of the Lord God is upon me, because the Lord has anointed me to bring good news to the poor; he has sent me to bind up the brokenhearted, to proclaim liberty to the captives, and the opening of the prison to those who are bound..."—Isaiah 61:1-2

This very text is what Jesus reads in the synagogue in Luke 4—announcing that it is fulfilled in their hearing.[5] The connection is unmistakable: Jesus saw his ministry not as general inspiration, but as the embodied fulfillment of Israel's apocalyptic longing.

The Dead Sea Scrolls reveal how widespread these expectations had become. The Qumran community spoke of the "poor in spirit" (*anawim*) as those whom God would vindicate, and their blessing formulas share striking similarities with Jesus' Beatitudes.[6] Texts like 4Q525 ("Beatitudes") show that Jesus was working within established Jewish traditions of apocalyptic blessing, even as he transformed them.

Like many Jewish teachers of his time, Jesus believed that God's kingdom was about to be revealed—not through violence or political revolution, but through a community of humility, mercy, justice, and sacrificial love that would demonstrate God's character and attract the nations.[7]

Political Challenge and Imperial Resistance

The Beatitudes were not politically neutral. In a world where Rome promised *Pax Romana* through military might and economic domination, Jesus announced an alternative kingdom based on radically different values.[8] Where Rome celebrated conquest, Jesus blessed peacemakers. Where the imperial cult demanded worship of Caesar's power, Jesus proclaimed blessing for the poor and persecuted.

This was subversive politics, though not violent revolution. The Beatitudes present a systematic challenge to both Roman imperial ideology and its local collaborators—including temple authorities who had accommodated themselves to foreign rule. By announcing blessing for the poor, the mourning, and the persecuted, Jesus was effectively declaring that God's favor rested not with the powerful but with their victims.

The economic implications were particularly pointed. In a society where wealth concentration served imperial interests, declaring the poor "blessed" and promising them the kingdom was economic heresy.[9] The vision of the meek inheriting the earth directly contradicted Roman assumptions about who deserved to rule and how power should be exercised.

Yet this political challenge operated through transformed community rather than armed resistance. Jesus was creating an alternative society that would demonstrate God's reign through its common life—a kingdom that would ultimately prove more enduring than any earthly empire.

The "Already and Not Yet" of the Kingdom

A crucial feature of Jesus' apocalyptic teaching is its tension between the present and future:

- *"Theirs is the kingdom of heaven."* (present tense)
- *"They will be comforted... they will inherit... they will be filled."* (future tense)

This mix of tenses reflects a paradox at the heart of Jesus' message: the kingdom is already present, but not yet fully manifest.[10]

New Testament scholars call this the "inaugurated eschatology" of Jesus:

- The kingdom is breaking in now—in acts of healing, forgiveness, and community formation that demonstrate God's character and power.
- But it is also coming in fullness—in a future when all wrongs are made right and God's justice fills the earth.

The Beatitudes express this tension beautifully. Those who follow Jesus are blessed now—even if they mourn, hunger, or are persecuted—because they are living into a reality that will soon be revealed to all. They are citizens of a kingdom that exists both as present experience and future hope.

This "already and not yet" structure explains how the early Christian communities could simultaneously experience joy and persecution, victory and suffering. They knew themselves to be living in the overlap of two ages—the present evil age that was passing away and the age to come that was breaking in through Jesus and his followers.[11]

The Beatitudes as Apocalyptic Announcement

Read this way, the Beatitudes are not instructions for "how to be blessed." They are declarations that the world is being turned upside down—and those who seem least powerful are already aligned with God's movement in history.[12]

They name the people already positioned in the coming kingdom:

- The poor in spirit: those who know their dependence on God rather than human systems
- The mourners: those who feel the world's pain rather than accepting injustice as normal
- The meek: those who reject domination and violence as means to power
- Those who hunger for righteousness: those who long for justice rather than personal advantage
- The peacemakers: those who resist the cycle of violence that perpetuates oppression
- The persecuted: those who stay faithful under pressure rather than compromising with corrupt systems

In a world obsessed with strength, wealth, and approval, Jesus' words are revolutionary. They echo the apocalyptic imagination of the Hebrew prophets, but go further—announcing that the future kingdom is already invading the present moment through those who embody its values.

Early Christian Reception and Embodiment

The early Christian communities understood themselves as living manifestations of this apocalyptic vision. The Book of Acts describes communities that shared goods in common, crossed ethnic boundaries, and challenged social hierarchies—practices that embodied the Beatitudes' vision of God's reversed kingdom.[13]

The willingness of early Christians to face martyrdom rather than compromise with imperial religious demands reflects their conviction that they were citizens of a higher kingdom.[14] Their acceptance of persecution for righteousness' sake was not masochistic but apocalyptic—they believed their faithfulness was participating in God's ultimate triumph over unjust powers.

Paul's letters reveal how the "already and not yet" tension shaped Christian ethics and eschatological preaching. Communities were called to live as if the kingdom had already come (sharing resources, crossing boundaries, practicing forgiveness) while waiting for its full manifestation (when death would be defeated and all creation renewed).[15]

This apocalyptic framework explains the radical social experiments of the early church—from the Jerusalem community's economic sharing to Paul's declarations that in Christ there is neither Jew nor Greek, slave nor free, male nor female. These were not progressive social policies but apocalyptic signs that the new age was breaking into the old.

Implications for Today

Understanding the Beatitudes as apocalyptic proclamation transforms how we live with them:

- They are not merely ideals for personal character, but signposts of a new world that is already breaking into our present reality.
- They challenge not only individual behavior, but collective structures of power that perpetuate injustice and inequality.
- They invite us not to retreat from the world, but to live differently within it—as citizens of a kingdom already breaking through, demonstrating alternative ways of organizing human community.
- They remind us that faithfulness to God's kingdom may bring opposition from those committed to preserving unjust systems.

The Beatitudes do not promise immediate relief from suffering or simple solutions to complex problems. They promise something bolder: that even in the midst of pain, weakness, and resistance, we are already standing on sacred ground. We are participants in a movement that began before we arrived and will continue after we depart—God's patient work of setting the world right.

Living apocalyptically means holding both realism about present suffering and hope for ultimate transformation. It means working for justice while trusting in God's ultimate vindication. It means building communities that prefigure the kingdom while acknowledging we have not yet arrived.

The Enduring Challenge

The apocalyptic vision of the Beatitudes continues to challenge every age and culture. It cannot be domesticated into mere personal piety or reduced to political program. It remains fundamentally disruptive—announcing that God's kingdom operates by different rules than any human system, and calling every generation to choose between ultimate loyalties.

In our own time of imperial power, economic inequality, and environmental crisis, the Beatitudes' apocalyptic vision remains as relevant as ever. They invite us to ask: What would it look like for God's kingdom to break into our present moment? How might we become signs of the coming transformation? Where are the poor in spirit, the mourners, the peacemakers in our world—and how might we join God's movement through their lives?

The answer, these ancient words suggest, lies not in abstract theology but in lived practice—in communities that dare to embody the kingdom's values here and now, trusting that God's future is already breaking into our present through those who have eyes to see and hearts to receive it.

Part II

The Beatitudes in Depth

Blessed Are the Poor in Spirit: A Foundation for Living

"Blessed are the poor in spirit, for theirs is the kingdom of heaven."
—Matthew 5:3

In our age of personal branding and confident opinions, the idea of being "poor in spirit" sounds like spiritual weakness. But this first Beatitude isn't praising helplessness—it's revealing the secret to genuine transformation. Unlike the Ten Commandments, which tell us what not to do, the Beatitudes show us how to be. They're not rules to follow but qualities to cultivate, starting with this paradox: the spiritually "poor" are actually the richest.

What Does "Poor in Spirit" Actually Mean?

The Greek phrase *ptōchoi tō pneumati* doesn't mean "a little short on faith." It means spiritually *destitute*—the kind of poverty that leaves you begging.[1] But here's the twist: this isn't about lacking something; it's about recognizing what you already lack and always have.

Matthew's version is unique. Luke's Gospel simply says "Blessed are you who are poor," likely referring to material poverty.[2] But Matthew adds "in spirit," making clear this is about our inner posture toward God and life itself. It's about coming to the end of our own resources and discovering that's exactly where grace begins.

The early Christian teacher John Chrysostom put it beautifully: "By the poor in spirit, [Jesus] means the humble and contrite in mind."[3] This isn't weakness—it's the strength to stop pretending we have life figured out.

The Deep Jewish Roots

Jesus wasn't inventing something new. The Hebrew Bible is full of this wisdom. The Psalms celebrate those who are "crushed in spirit" (Psalm 34:18) and declare that God's favorite sacrifice is "a broken and contrite heart" (Psalm 51:17). The prophet Isaiah promises that God esteems those who are "humble and contrite in spirit" (Isaiah 66:2).[4]

In later Jewish tradition, there was even a group called the *anawim*—the "humble poor"—who were both economically disadvantaged and spiritually dependent on God.[5] They weren't just materially needy; they were people who had learned to rely entirely on God's mercy. Sound familiar?

This tradition teaches us that being "poor in spirit" isn't about low self-esteem. It's about right-sized humility before the mystery of existence.

The Universal Human Wisdom

What's remarkable is how this insight appears across human cultures, each with its own flavor but pointing toward the same truth: transformation begins when ego ends.

Islam: The Beauty of Spiritual Poverty

In Islam, humility (*tawādu'*) is essential to faith. The Qur'an teaches that "the most noble of you in the sight of God is the most righteous" (49:13)—not the most successful or confident, but the most conscious of their need for God.[6]

The Sufi tradition goes even deeper with the concept of *faqr* (spiritual poverty). The great 13th-century poet Rumi wrote about this "radical unselfing"—emptying yourself of pride and false certainty to make room for divine love.[7] For Sufis, spiritual poverty isn't deprivation; it's preparation for divine intimacy.

The difference: While Christians receive the kingdom as pure gift, Islamic tradition emphasizes that humility leads to God's mercy and, ultimately, paradise through righteous living.

Buddhism: The Wisdom of Letting Go

Buddhism offers a fascinating parallel through its teaching on *anattā* (non-self). The Buddha taught that clinging to a fixed sense of self is the root of suffering. The *Dhammapada* warns: "The fool who thinks he is wise is a fool indeed" (63).[8]

In Mahayana Buddhism, the concept of *śūnyatā* (emptiness) teaches that all phenomena—including our sense of self—are empty of inherent existence.[9] This isn't nihilism; it's liberation. When we stop defending a false self, we discover our true nature.

The difference: Buddhist "emptiness" aims at liberation (*nirvana*) through insight, while Christian "poverty of spirit" opens us to receive God's kingdom as gift.

Hinduism: Ego's Surrender

The *Bhagavad Gita* lists humility (*amanitvam*) among the essential qualities of wisdom: "Humility, unpretentiousness, non-violence, patience... this is knowledge" (13:7-8).[10] In the devotional (*bhakti*) tradition, surrendering the ego to God is both the path and the destination.

The great teacher Ramana Maharshi taught that the question "Who am I?" dissolves the false self and reveals our true nature as one with the divine.[11]

The difference: Hindu humility often leads toward union with the divine (*moksha*) through self-realization, while Christian poverty of spirit receives relationship with God through grace.

Taoism: The Power of Lowliness

The *Tao Te Ching*, written around 600 BCE, teaches that true power comes from emptiness and non-assertion: "The highest goodness is like water... It dwells in lowly places that all disdain—this is why it is so near the Tao" (Chapter 8).[12]

The Taoist concept of *wu wei* (effortless action) suggests that forcing outcomes through ego-driven effort is less effective than flowing with life's natural rhythms. This mirrors the Christian paradox of strength through weakness.

The difference: Taoist humility seeks harmony with the natural order, while Christian poverty of spirit opens us to supernatural grace.

Comparing Approaches to Spiritual Transformation

Each tradition handles the relationship between humility and spiritual fulfillment differently:

- **Buddhism**: Emptiness leads to liberation through insight and practice
- **Hinduism**: Ego surrender enables union with the divine through realization
- **Islam**: Humility opens the path to God's mercy and paradise through righteous living
- **Taoism**: Lowliness creates harmony with the natural order through non-resistance
- **Christianity**: Spiritual poverty receives the kingdom as pure gift through grace

These aren't just theological differences—they represent different understandings of human agency, divine relationship, and the mechanics of transformation.

The Social Dimension

In Matthew's time, "the poor" weren't just economically disadvantaged—they were socially marginalized, without power or voice.[13] When Jesus blesses the "poor in spirit," he's not just talking about individual humility; he's identifying with those society overlooks.

This suggests that spiritual poverty and solidarity with the vulnerable go hand in hand. Those who recognize their own neediness are more likely to recognize and respond to others' needs. Spiritual humility creates social compassion.

A Leadership Note

It's worth noting how this ancient wisdom aligns with what we now call servant leadership. Leaders who recognize their need for others—for input, correction, support—create environments where others can flourish. The difference between leaders who enter rooms believing they have all the answers versus those genuinely curious about what they might learn is the difference between compliance and engagement, between hoarding power and multiplying it.

How to Live This Today

Being "poor in spirit" isn't about thinking less of yourself—it's about thinking about yourself less. Here's what it looks like practically:

Start with "I don't know": In conversations, lead with curiosity rather than certainty. Ask more questions than you answer.

Embrace correction: When someone points out your mistake, resist the urge to defend. Say "thank you" instead.

Practice spiritual poverty: In prayer or meditation, come empty-handed. Don't perform; just be present.

Choose vulnerability: Share your struggles, not just your successes. Let others see your real humanity.

Serve without credit: Do good work without needing recognition. Let your actions speak quietly.

Stay teachable: Assume every person and situation has something to teach you.

The Freedom of Spiritual Poverty

In a culture obsessed with confidence and control, choosing to be "poor in spirit" is revolutionary. It's the freedom to admit you don't have all the answers, change your mind when you learn something new, ask for help without shame, start over when you fail, and receive love without earning it.

This isn't weakness—it's the beginning of wisdom. It's not failure—it's the foundation of authentic success. And it's not just Christian truth—it's human truth that Christianity articulates with particular clarity.

The poor in spirit inherit the kingdom not because they're spiritually superior, but because they're spiritually honest. They've stopped pretending and started receiving. And in that receiving, they discover what every spiritual tradition knows: real strength comes from surrendering the illusion of strength.

The Ten Commandments tell us how to behave. The Beatitudes tell us how to be. And being poor in spirit—whether in the Christian sense of receiving grace or the broader human sense of embracing humility—is where transformation begins.

Blessed Are Those Who Mourn: Finding Comfort in Grief Across Traditions

"Blessed are those who mourn, for they will be comforted."
—Matthew 5:4

In our culture of constant positivity and emotional optimization, mourning feels like failure. We apologize for tears, rush through grief, and treat sorrow as a problem to solve rather than a process to honor. But this second Beatitude offers a radically different perspective: those who mourn are blessed not despite their grief, but because of what grief makes possible.

Unlike the Ten Commandments, which tell us what not to do, the Beatitudes show us how to be. They're not rules to follow but qualities to cultivate, and this one reveals a profound truth: transformation often begins in the breaking. The spiritually mature don't avoid suffering—they learn to mourn well.

What "Mourning" Actually Means

The Greek word *penthountes* doesn't refer to casual sadness or disappointment. It describes deep, soul-shaking lamentation—the kind of grief that disrupts everything.[1] In first-century Jewish culture, this mourning was dramatically public and communal. People wailed openly, tore their garments, and gathered in shared sorrow. This wasn't emotional dysfunction; it was recognized spiritual practice.

The early Christian teacher John Chrysostom understood this mourning to encompass both personal loss and what he called "holy sorrow"—grief over sin, injustice, and the world's brokenness.² Augustine similarly taught that mourning opens the heart to transformation in ways that comfort alone cannot.³

This communal dimension matters enormously. Ancient peoples understood what we've forgotten: grief shared is grief transformed. The promise of comfort isn't individual therapy—it's collective consolation.

The Deep Jewish Roots

Jesus wasn't introducing foreign concepts. The Hebrew Bible is saturated with the sacred nature of lament. The Psalms don't hide from sorrow—they dive into it:

"Those who sow in tears shall reap with shouts of joy" (Psalm 126:5).

"The Lord is near to the brokenhearted and saves the crushed in spirit" (Psalm 34:18).

The prophet Isaiah promises divine comfort: *"Comfort, O comfort my people, says your God"* (Isaiah 40:1). Even the book of Lamentations—an entire biblical book dedicated to mourning—demonstrates that grief isn't spiritual failure but spiritual honesty.⁴

Jewish mourning rituals like *shiva* embody this wisdom. For seven days, the community gathers around the grieving, not to fix their pain but to honor it.⁵ This tradition teaches that mourning is both individual experience and communal responsibility.

The Hebrew concept of the *anawim*—the humble poor—often included those whose grief had taught them dependence on God.⁶ Sound familiar? These weren't people who had given up, but people who had learned to receive comfort from sources beyond themselves.

The Universal Human Wisdom

What's remarkable is how cultures across the globe have discovered similar truths about grief's transformative power, each offering its own path through sorrow toward healing.

Islam: The Beauty of Patient Endurance

In Islam, mourning is dignified through the concept of ṣabr—patient forbearance in the face of loss. The Qur'an teaches: *"Give glad tidings to the patient—those who, when disaster strikes them, say, 'Indeed we belong to Allah, and indeed to Him we will return'"* (2:155-156).⁷

This phrase, *inna lillahi wa inna ilayhi raji'un*, is recited upon hearing of death. It's not resignation but recognition—acknowledging both the reality of loss and the greater reality of divine sovereignty. The Prophet Muhammad himself wept at his son's death, saying: *"The eyes shed tears and the heart is grieved, but we do not say anything except that which pleases our Lord."*⁎⁸

Sufi tradition goes deeper, finding in grief a kind of spiritual alchemy. The great poet Rumi wrote about how sorrow carved space in the heart for divine love.[9] In Islamic mysticism, mourning becomes preparation for deeper intimacy with the Divine.

The difference: While Christians receive comfort as pure gift, Islamic tradition emphasizes that patient endurance through grief leads to divine reward and, ultimately, paradise through faithful perseverance.

Buddhism: Suffering as the Teacher

Buddhism begins with the First Noble Truth: life contains *dukkha* (suffering, dissatisfaction). Rather than promising external comfort, Buddhism teaches that suffering itself can lead to awakening when properly understood.[10]

The *Dhammapada* states: "Hatred never ceases by hatred, but by love alone is healed. This is an ancient and eternal law"(5).[11] Buddhist mourning practices, especially in Mahayana traditions, transform personal grief into universal compassion (*karuṇā*).

The Bodhisattva ideal exemplifies this transformation—beings who vow to remain in the world of suffering until all are liberated.[12] Mourning becomes not just personal experience but recognition of interconnectedness. When we truly understand that all beings suffer, our own grief opens us to serve others.

The difference: Buddhist "comfort" comes through insight and release from attachment, while Christian comfort is received as divine consolation that doesn't require earning or understanding.

Hinduism: Grief and the Eternal Self

Hindu tradition honors mourning through elaborate funeral rites (*antyesti*) that serve both the departed and the grieving community. The *Bhagavad Gita* addresses grief directly through Arjuna's anguish at the prospect of losing his kinsmen:

"You grieve for those who should not be grieved for, yet you speak words of wisdom. The wise grieve neither for the living nor the dead" (2:11).[13]

This isn't callousness but perspective. Hindu teaching acknowledges the reality of human grief while pointing toward the eternal nature of the soul (*ātman*). Mourning becomes a stage in spiritual development—real and necessary, but not final.

In *bhakti* (devotional) traditions, grief over separation from the Divine is actually cultivated as a form of spiritual practice.[14] The pain of divine absence intensifies the longing that eventually leads to union.

The difference: Hindu comfort comes through understanding the eternal nature of the self and eventual reunion with the Divine, while Christian comfort emphasizes relationship with God through grace in the midst of temporal loss.

Taoism: The Natural Flow of Loss

The *Tao Te Ching* teaches acceptance of life's natural rhythms: *"The highest goodness is like water, which dwells in places that all disdain. This is why it is so near the Tao"* (Chapter 8).[15] Mourning is part of nature's cycle—not to be resisted but accepted.

Chapter 50 observes: *"Death is a departure"*—not punishment or tragedy, but natural transition.[16] Taoist funeral practices often celebrate the deceased's return to the source rather than focusing solely on loss. Grief is honored but not prolonged beyond its natural course.

The concept of *wu wei* (effortless action) applies here: fighting grief creates more suffering, while flowing with it allows natural healing.

The difference: Taoist comfort comes from harmony with natural order and acceptance of universal cycles, while Christian comfort promises supernatural intervention and divine presence that transcends natural processes.

Comparing Approaches to Grief and Comfort

Each tradition handles the relationship between mourning and consolation differently:

- **Buddhism**: Suffering leads to compassion and wisdom through understanding attachment and impermanence

- **Hinduism**: Grief becomes spiritual teaching about the eternal self through ritual and philosophical understanding
- **Islam**: Patient endurance through loss opens the path to divine mercy and reward through faithful perseverance
- **Taoism**: Mourning flows with natural cycles toward harmony through acceptance of universal change
- **Christianity**: Comfort comes as divine gift to those who mourn through grace and divine presence

These aren't just theological differences—they represent different understandings of suffering's purpose, comfort's source, and the relationship between human vulnerability and spiritual transformation.

The Social Dimension of Sacred Sorrow

In Matthew's time, "those who mourn" included not just the personally bereaved but those who grieved injustice, oppression, and systemic brokenness.[17] When Jesus blesses mourners, he's identifying with all who suffer—both individually and collectively.

This suggests that personal grief and social compassion go hand in hand. Those who have learned to mourn their own losses are more capable of mourning with others. Authentic grief creates authentic empathy. The person who has never allowed themselves to truly mourn will struggle to comfort others in their mourning.

Modern research confirms this ancient wisdom: people who suppress grief often become less emotionally available to others.[18] But those who learn to mourn well develop what researchers call "emotional intelligence" and "empathic capacity."

A Leadership Note

Leaders who have learned to mourn well create different kinds of environments than those who haven't. They're more likely to acknowledge mistakes, sit with difficult emotions, and create space for others to be human. The difference between leaders who can handle only success stories versus those who can navigate failure and loss with grace is often the difference between compliance and genuine trust.

Organizations led by people comfortable with grief tend to be more innovative—failure isn't devastating but informative. Teams feel safer taking risks when they know their leader won't panic at the first sign of loss.

How to Mourn Well Today

Learning to be "blessed" in mourning isn't about enjoying sadness—it's about allowing grief to do its transformative work. Here's what this looks like practically:

Don't apologize for tears: Grief is not dysfunction. It's love with nowhere to go. Honor it.

Mourn with others: Isolated grief becomes toxic. Shared grief becomes sacred. Find your community.

Grieve injustice, not just loss: Let yourself feel the weight of the world's brokenness. It's the beginning of compassion.

Create rituals: Light candles, plant trees, write letters. Give your grief tangible expression.

Practice presence over solutions: When others mourn, don't fix—just stay. Your presence is the comfort.

Allow the transformation: Grief changes you. Let it. Don't rush back to who you were before.

The Freedom of Sacred Sorrow

In a culture that pathologizes sadness and medicalizes grief, choosing to mourn deeply is revolutionary. It's the freedom to feel without apologizing, need others without shame, acknowledge that some losses can't be fixed, discover that breaking open isn't the same as breaking down, and find that comfort often comes through community, not clarity.

This isn't weakness—it's emotional honesty. It's not depression—it's engagement with reality. And it's not just Christian truth—it's human truth that Christianity articulates with particular hope.

Those who mourn are blessed not because grief is good, but because comfort is real. Not because suffering has purpose, but because love is stronger than loss. And not because mourning ends, but because it transforms—both the mourner and those who witness faithful grieving.

The Ten Commandments tell us how to behave. The Beatitudes tell us how to be. And learning to mourn well—whether in the Christian sense of receiving divine comfort or the broader human sense of allowing grief to create compassion—is essential to becoming fully human.

Blessed Are the Meek: Reclaiming a Misunderstood Virtue

"Blessed are the meek, for they will inherit the earth."
—Matthew 5:5

Of all the Beatitudes, this one might be the most widely misunderstood. In modern usage, "meek" often implies weak, passive, or submissive. Nobody puts "meekness" on a resume or celebrates it in performance reviews. But the original Greek word here, *praús*, tells a very different story—one that our achievement-oriented culture desperately needs to hear.

In classical Greek, *praús* was used to describe a wild animal that had been tamed—power under control.[1] Think of a trained war horse: capable of fierce action, but entirely responsive to its rider. The biblical use carries this same strength-with-restraint sense. Meekness is not weakness. It's the rare inner composure that comes from humility, trust, and self-mastery.

Unlike the Ten Commandments, which tell us what not to do, the Beatitudes show us how to be. They're not rules to follow but qualities to cultivate, and this third Beatitude reveals a profound paradox: in a world that rewards domination, true strength lies in restraint. The meek aren't losers—they're the ones who understand that real power serves love, not self.

What Does "Meek" Actually Mean?

The Greek *praús* in the Septuagint (the Greek Old Testament) translates the Hebrew *anav* (humble, gentle), connecting Jesus' teaching to a rich scriptural lineage.[2] This broadens the sense of meekness beyond mere self-control to include being "open to correction and receptive to God"—not self-diminishing, but right-sized before the mystery of existence.

The early Christian teacher John Chrysostom understood meekness as disciplined self-mastery grounded in humility rather than pride.[3] It's not about lacking power but about not being ruled by it. It means being strong enough to be gentle, influential enough to be quiet, and secure enough to go unnoticed.

The Deep Jewish Roots

Jesus wasn't inventing something new. The Hebrew Scriptures celebrate this quality throughout. Numbers 12:3 calls Moses "very meek, more than all people who were on the face of the earth." Yet Moses wasn't weak—he challenged Pharaoh, led a nation through the wilderness, and faced down rebellion. His meekness came not from insecurity but from his deep trust in God and refusal to exalt himself.[4]

The immediate textual backdrop to Jesus' Beatitude comes from Psalm 37:11: "The meek shall inherit the land."[5] In the Psalm's context, the Hebrew *eretz* (land) refers to Israel's inheritance, emphasizing patient trust and a refusal to advance personal power through violence or scheming. Jews of Jesus' day would have heard political resonance here—those who trust in God, rather than force, ultimately endure.

Rabbinic writings later honored humility (*anavah*) as one of the highest virtues in texts like Pirkei Avot, where the humble are granted wisdom and lasting legacy.[6] In Jewish tradition, meekness isn't about timidity; it's about refusing to grasp for power that doesn't belong to you.

The Universal Human Wisdom

This insight into strength-through-restraint is not unique to Christianity or Judaism. Versions of it appear across world religions, each casting meekness in a slightly different but resonant light.

Islam: The Honor of Humility

In Islam, true strength lies in humility before God (*tawādu'*) and in patient endurance of insult. The Qur'an praises those who "walk humbly on the earth" and respond to ignorance with peace (Surah 25:63).[7] The Prophet Muhammad is described in the Hadith as mild-tempered and forgiving even to his enemies, demonstrating *hilm* (forbearance) as a form of spiritual excellence.[8]

Sufi tradition deepens this by emphasizing *adab* (refined manners and respectful conduct) as a spiritual discipline.[9] The strong are those who restrain the ego, not those who assert it. As Rumi wrote about the inner transformation that comes from "radical unselfing"—emptying yourself of pride to make room for divine love.[10]

The difference: Islamic meekness emphasizes patient forbearance (*sabr*) and refined conduct (*adab*) as pathways to divine mercy and eventual paradise through faithful perseverance, while also serving as a model of prophetic character.

Buddhism: Power Without Aggression

Buddhism doesn't use the term "meek," but the concept lives in the ideal of *metta* (loving-kindness) and *upekkha* (equanimity). The *Dhammapada* teaches: "Victory breeds hatred; the defeated live in pain. Happily the peaceful live, giving up both victory and defeat" (15).[11]

Strength in Buddhism is measured not by dominance but by inner calm and compassionate restraint.[12] The truly strong are those who do not retaliate. This isn't about submissive meekness but about "strength through non-harm"—the ability to withstand offense without reactive anger.

The difference: Buddhist strength comes through insight into non-attachment and the cultivation of equanimity (*upekkha*), leading to liberation from the cycle of reactive anger and suffering, rather than receiving divine inheritance.

Hinduism: The Strength of Self-Control

The *Bhagavad Gita* lists *ahimsa* (nonviolence) and *damah* (self-restraint) as signs of true wisdom. Krishna praises those who are "free from pride and delusion, who have conquered the evil of attachment, who dwell in the Self, with desires extinguished" (Chapter 13).[13]

This vision of meekness demonstrates *atma-vinigraha* (self-mastery)—not being a doormat, but not needing to dominate others to feel secure.[14] In *bhakti* (devotional) traditions, humility is often idolized as the most attractive quality in a devotee, creating space for divine grace.

The difference: Hindu meekness leads toward self-realization and eventual union with the divine (*moksha*) through mastery over the ego and desires, rather than receiving earthly inheritance through grace.

Taoism: Yielding That Overcomes

The *Tao Te Ching* celebrates the paradox of yielding strength: "The soft overcomes the hard; the gentle overcomes the rigid" (Chapter 36).[15] Meekness, in Taoist thought, is a way of aligning with the Tao—the natural order of things—rather than forcing outcomes.

Chapter 8 famously likens the highest good to water, which benefits all things but never seeks status: "The highest goodness is like water... It dwells in lowly places that all disdain—this is why it is so near the Tao."[16] The meek inherit not by seizing but by flowing.

The difference: Taoist meekness seeks harmony with the natural order (*wu wei*) through flexible responsiveness to universal principles, rather than inheriting through relationship with a personal God.

Comparing Approaches to Strength and Restraint

Each tradition handles the relationship between power and humility differently:

- **Buddhism**: Strength through non-attachment and equanimity leads to liberation from reactive cycles
- **Hinduism**: Self-mastery over ego and desires enables union with the divine through realization
- **Islam**: Patient forbearance and refined conduct open the path to divine mercy through faithful perseverance
- **Taoism**: Yielding flexibility creates harmony with natural order through effortless action
- **Christianity**: Meekness receives divine inheritance as gift through trust and self-restraint

These aren't just theological differences—they represent different understandings of the relationship between personal power, ultimate reality, and the mechanics of spiritual transformation.

The Social Dimension

In a society that prizes assertiveness and control, meekness can look like irrelevance. But what if it's actually a revolutionary virtue? Meekness disrupts cycles of aggression and creates space for collaboration rather than competition.[17] It's the secret ingredient in trust-building, peace-making, and sustainable community.

In a world addicted to winning, the meek offer an alternative path: not defeat, but participation in something deeper than personal victory. Those who practice meekness often become the ones others trust with difficult conversations, leadership responsibilities, and community healing.

A Leadership Note

Modern leadership literature has often rediscovered ancient truths under new names like emotional intelligence, vulnerability, and servant leadership. Each of these aligns with the Beatitude's vision of meekness.

Leaders who don't need to dominate create environments where people feel safe to speak up. They defuse conflict rather than escalate it, and inspire trust not through charisma but through character. True leadership, like true meekness, isn't about pushing others down—it's about lifting them up.

How to Live This Today

To cultivate meekness in daily life:

Pause before reacting: Meekness gives you time to respond thoughtfully rather than react defensively. Practice the sacred pause between trigger and response.

Listen more than you speak: Especially when power dynamics are in play. True strength often lies in making space for others' voices.

Embrace correction: Meekness welcomes feedback as a path to growth rather than a threat to ego. Say "thank you" when someone points out your mistake.

Resist the need to "win": Let go of being right in favor of being wise. Choose relationship over being right.

Lead quietly: Influence without forcing. Serve without seeking credit. Let your actions speak softly.

Let strength serve love: Direct your gifts toward others' flourishing rather than your own advancement.

The Freedom of Meekness

Meekness doesn't mean lacking power—it means not being ruled by it. It means being strong enough to be gentle, influential enough to be quiet, and secure enough to go unnoticed when necessary.

In a culture that rewards domination, choosing meekness is profoundly countercultural. It's the freedom to admit you don't have all the answers, to change your mind when you learn something new, to ask for help without shame, and to receive love without earning it.

This isn't weakness—it's the beginning of wisdom. It's not failure—it's the foundation of authentic influence. And it's not just Christian truth—it's human truth that every wisdom tradition recognizes and our world desperately needs.

The meek inherit the earth not because they're spiritually superior, but because they're spiritually honest. They've stopped grasping for control and started trusting in something larger than themselves. In that trust, they discover what every tradition knows: real strength comes not from asserting power over others, but from mastering power within ourselves.

The Ten Commandments tell us how to behave. The Beatitudes tell us how to be. And meekness—when rightly understood—is not only a Christian virtue but a human one that transcends religious boundaries while maintaining its distinctly Christian promise of inheritance.

Blessed Are Those Who Hunger and Thirst for Righteousness: The Sacred Longing for Justice

"Blessed are those who hunger and thirst for righteousness, for they will be filled."
—Matthew 5:6

We live in a culture that promises to satisfy every appetite. Yet beneath our material abundance lies a deeper hunger that no amount of consumption can fill: the ache for justice, goodness, and a world made right. Jesus' fourth Beatitude speaks to this soul-deep craving—not a casual interest in ethics, but a consuming desire for righteousness that shapes how we live, work, and relate to others.

Unlike the Ten Commandments, which tell us what not to do, the Beatitudes show us how to be. They're not rules to follow but qualities to cultivate, and this fourth one reveals a profound truth: the most morally mature people aren't those who've achieved perfection, but those who remain deeply dissatisfied with injustice. Their holy hunger becomes the engine of personal transformation and social healing.

This isn't about being a little interested in doing the right thing. The Greek verbs here are vivid: "hunger" (*peinōntes*) and "thirst" (*dipsōntes*) are in the present participle, suggesting ongoing, active desire.[1] It's about craving righteousness like a starving person craves bread, like someone dying of thirst craves water.

What Does "Righteousness" Actually Mean?

The Greek word *dikaiosynē* carries both personal and social dimensions—it encompasses individual moral integrity and communal justice.[2] In Matthew's Gospel, righteousness includes not only personal virtue but restorative justice, righting relationships, and covenant faithfulness. Jesus calls his followers to a righteousness that exceeds that of the scribes and Pharisees (Matthew 5:20)—a kind of integrity that transforms both the individual and society.

The promise is equally striking. The word for "filled" (*chortasthēsontai*) was commonly used to describe animals being fed to complete satisfaction—a surprisingly earthy metaphor for spiritual abundance.[3] Those who ache for justice won't just receive a little comfort; they will feast on fulfillment.

The Deep Jewish Roots

Jesus wasn't inventing something new. The Hebrew Scriptures are saturated with this longing for righteousness. In Hebrew, *tzedek* (righteousness) intertwines with *mishpat* (justice), creating an inseparable unity of legal justice, ethical behavior, and covenantal faithfulness.[4] It's about right relationship—with God, neighbor, and community.

The Psalms overflow with this hunger:

"Blessed are those who observe justice, who do righteousness at all times!" (Psalm 106:3)

"I will behold your face in righteousness; when I awake, I shall be satisfied with your likeness" (Psalm 17:15)

The Hebrew prophets cried out for a world where righteousness flowed like a mighty stream (Amos 5:24), condemning religious rituals divorced from ethical concern.[5] Jesus stands in this prophetic tradition, affirming that hunger for righteousness isn't weakness—it's a sign of spiritual health and moral clarity.

The Universal Human Wisdom

This longing for a just and moral life transcends religious boundaries. Across traditions, we find similar hungers for rightness, though each understands the path to satisfaction differently.

Islam: Righteousness as Complete Submission

In Islam, righteousness (*birr*) encompasses belief in God, kindness to others, prayer, charity, and perseverance in hardship (Qur'an 2:177). It's not merely faith but faith expressed through action.[6] The Qur'an promises: *"Indeed, those who have believed and done righteous deeds... their Lord will guide them because of their faith"* (10:9).[7]

Islamic righteousness connects internal submission (*islam*) to external justice (*'adl*) and mercy (*rahmah*). A righteous person submits to God's will while promoting equity among people.[8]

This creates a dynamic where personal piety and social justice reinforce each other through divine law.

The difference: Islam emphasizes both internal obedience and external justice grounded in divine law, where righteous deeds paired with faith earn divine guidance and reward. The Beatitude, by contrast, offers unconditional promise of satisfaction—not as reward for performance, but as fulfillment of holy desire through grace.

Buddhism: The Noble Hunger for Liberation

Buddhism begins by diagnosing craving (*tanhā*) as the root of suffering, yet recognizes a wholesome longing—the aspiration (*chanda*) for enlightenment and liberation from suffering (*dukkha*).[9] The Eightfold Path includes right action, right speech, and right livelihood—forms of righteousness that align one with the Dharma.

Buddhist teaching transforms the hunger for truth into universal compassion (*karuṇā*). The Bodhisattva ideal exemplifies this: beings who vow to remain in the world of suffering until all are liberated.[10] Personal yearning for awakening becomes service to others' liberation.

The difference: Buddhist righteousness aims at liberation through insight and the transformation of craving itself. Satisfaction comes not from receiving a gift but from transcending the very mechanism of craving that creates spiritual hunger.

Hinduism: Yearning for Cosmic Order

In Hindu thought, *dharma* encompasses righteousness, duty, law, and cosmic order. The *Bhagavad Gita* presents Arjuna's struggle to act righteously in a morally complex world. Krishna teaches that God responds to those who seek righteousness with devotion: *"To those who are steadfast, who worship Me with love, I give the understanding by which they come to Me"* (10:10).[11]

In *bhakti* (devotional) traditions, longing for righteousness becomes divine hunger—the soul's ache for reunion with God.[12] This yearning intensifies spiritual practice and eventually leads to union with the divine.

The difference: Hindu righteousness involves aligning with eternal law (*sanatana dharma*) and fulfilling personal duty, often guided by social context. The focus is on cosmic harmony and eventual union with the divine through realization, rather than receiving justice as divine gift.

Taoism: Effortless Virtue

Taoism takes a paradoxical approach to righteousness. The *Tao Te Ching* warns against moral striving: *"When the Tao is lost, there is goodness. When goodness is lost, there is morality..."* (Chapter 38).[13] This suggests that hungering for righteousness can signal disconnection from the natural way.

Yet the Taoist sage does act justly—not from craving but in spontaneous alignment with the Tao. Chapter 8 celebrates water's virtue: it benefits all things without seeking status, dwelling in lowly places others disdain.¹⁴ True righteousness flows effortlessly when one aligns with the natural order.

The difference: Taoism values harmony over hunger, seeking righteousness through effortless action (*wu wei*) rather than passionate desire. Christian longing is future-oriented and emotional; Taoist virtue is present-oriented and spontaneous.

Comparing Approaches to Righteousness

Each tradition addresses the relationship between moral hunger and spiritual satisfaction differently:

- **Christianity**: Hunger for righteousness leads to divine satisfaction through grace and fulfillment
- **Judaism**: Yearning for justice creates covenant faithfulness through relationship with God and community
- **Islam**: Righteous pursuit via action and faith opens divine acceptance through submission and perseverance
- **Buddhism**: Aspiration for truth transforms craving into liberation through insight and compassion
- **Hinduism**: Desire for dharma enables alignment with cosmic order through devotion and realization
- **Taoism**: Natural virtue flows from harmony with universal principles through effortless action

These differences reflect distinct understandings of human agency, divine relationship, and the mechanics of moral transformation. Some emphasize receiving (Christianity), others achieving (Buddhism), still others aligning (Hinduism, Taoism) or submitting (Islam).

The Social Dimension of Sacred Hunger

This Beatitude isn't merely about personal righteousness—it blesses those who hunger for a just society where the poor are lifted up, the oppressed are freed, and all live in peace.[15] Jesus' audience included the economically and politically marginalized. This promise says to them: your longing for justice isn't foolish—it's holy.

Today, those who fight for climate justice, racial equality, economic fairness, and human dignity are, in a very real sense, hungering and thirsting for righteousness. The Beatitude blesses their longing even when fulfillment seems distant. It suggests that moral dissatisfaction with the world's brokenness is itself a form of spiritual health.

A Leadership Note

Leaders driven by hunger for righteousness differ markedly from those driven by ego or power. They ask deeper questions: What does justice require here? How do we repair what's broken? How do we lead with integrity, not just efficiency? They don't pretend to have all the answers, but they're not satisfied with injustice either. They live in the tension between what is and what should be, pressing toward a world made right.

How to Hunger Well

To cultivate this sacred longing in daily life:

Let discomfort become desire: Don't numb your awareness of injustice with distraction or cynicism. Let your discomfort with the world's brokenness grow into holy desire for change.

Act on your hunger: Vote, volunteer, protest, donate, speak up. Let your longing shape your behavior rather than remaining merely theoretical.

Practice moral imagination: Regularly ask what a just world would look like in your family, workplace, and community. Then start building it in small, concrete ways.

Connect personal and social transformation: Work on your own character while engaging systemic issues. Inner righteousness and outer justice reinforce each other.

Stay connected to others: Righteousness is never a solo project. Join others in the work of justice-making and mutual transformation.

Embrace the long view: Moral change happens slowly. Let your hunger sustain you through setbacks and partial victories.

The Freedom of Holy Hunger

We live in a world that numbs moral hunger with distraction, relativism, and indulgence. Consumer culture promises that the right purchase will satisfy our deepest longings. Political tribalism reduces complex moral questions to team loyalty. But what if our deepest hunger for justice and goodness is the holiest thing about us?

The fourth Beatitude gives us permission to crave righteousness, to ache for justice, to never settle for a world half-healed. It suggests that our moral dissatisfaction isn't a character flaw but a spiritual gift. Those who remain hungry for righteousness are those who refuse to become comfortable with compromise when justice is at stake.

This hunger transforms both the individual and community. People who genuinely ache for righteousness become sources of moral energy for others. Their refusal to accept "the way things are" becomes an invitation for others to imagine "the way things could be." Their holy dissatisfaction becomes a catalyst for collective transformation.

The promise of being "filled" doesn't mean the hunger disappears, but that it finds its proper satisfaction. Those who hunger for righteousness discover that their deepest longings aren't misplaced but prophetic—previews of a reality where justice flows like water and righteousness like a mighty stream.

This isn't just Christian truth—it's human truth that every great tradition recognizes in its own way. The desire for righteousness, justice, and moral integrity runs through every wisdom tradition because it runs through every human heart. Those who honor this hunger, rather than suppress it, are never far from the heart of what makes us most human.

Blessed Are the Merciful: The Revolutionary Power of Compassionate Action

"Blessed are the merciful, for they will receive mercy."
—Matthew 5:7

In a world that prizes efficiency, toughness, and transactional fairness, mercy can feel like weakness or even foolish indulgence. We live in a culture that asks, "What have you done for me lately?" and measures worth by performance. But Jesus' fifth Beatitude flips this logic entirely. To be merciful, he suggests, is not to give people what they deserve—but what they need. Mercy is not passive pity or soft-hearted tolerance. It is compassionate action that moves toward suffering, even when justice might allow you to stand back.

Unlike the Ten Commandments, which tell us what not to do, the Beatitudes show us how to be. They're not rules to follow but qualities to cultivate, and this fifth one reveals a profound truth: in a world addicted to keeping score, mercy breaks the cycle of retribution and creates space for restoration. The merciful don't just avoid causing harm—they actively work to heal it.

What Does "Merciful" Actually Mean?

The Greek word *eleemon* doesn't describe a feeling but an active orientation of kindness toward those in need.[1] This term is rare in classical Greek literature, but in the Septuagint and New Testament, it carries the profound connotation of divine mercy made manifest in human action. Mercy, in this sense, is love with its sleeves rolled up. It's what you offer when the world says someone has failed, and you show up anyway.

The promise is equally striking. Those who show mercy will receive mercy—not as a transaction, but as a spiritual coherence.[2] This reciprocal rhythm runs throughout biblical teaching: "With the measure you use, it will be measured to you" (Luke 6:38). "Be merciful, just as your Father is merciful" (Luke 6:36). This isn't divine scorekeeping; it's the recognition that mercy shapes the heart of both giver and receiver.

Mercy doesn't erase justice—it transfigures it. The merciful see the person behind the failure and treat them not as a problem to be solved, but a soul to be healed. They meet people where they are, not where they think they should be.

The Deep Jewish Roots

Jesus draws on a deep well of Hebrew Scripture. In Jewish thought, mercy interweaves two powerful concepts: *chesed* (steadfast lovingkindness) and *rachamim* (compassion).[3] The Psalms proclaim:

"The Lord is merciful and gracious, slow to anger and abounding in steadfast love" (Psalm 103:8).

God's *chesed* represents covenantal loyalty—not just emotion, but faithful action that maintains relationship even when the other party fails to uphold their end. Meanwhile, *rachamim* shares its root with the Hebrew word for "womb," suggesting deep, life-giving compassion that protects the vulnerable with fierce, maternal care.[4]

The prophet Micah captures this integration beautifully: *"What does the Lord require of you but to do justice, love mercy, and walk humbly with your God?"* (Micah 6:8). Notice the sequence: justice and mercy aren't opposites but partners in the work of restoration.

In rabbinic teaching, mercy is not weak sentiment but transformative power. The Talmud teaches that one who shows mercy to others brings mercy upon themselves (Shabbat 151b).[5] The "Thirteen Attributes of Mercy" from Exodus 34:6-7, repeated throughout Jewish liturgy, frame mercy as the dominant trait by which God governs creation.[6] This places Jesus' teaching squarely within his ancestral tradition.

The Universal Human Wisdom

Like the previous Beatitudes, this wisdom about mercy's transformative power resonates across human cultures, though each tradition understands the path to mercy differently.

Islam: The Divine Essence of Mercy

Two of the most frequent names of God in the Qur'an are *al-Rahman* and *al-Rahim*—the Most Merciful, the Most Compassionate. Every chapter (except one) begins with this invocation: "In the name of Allah, the Most Gracious, the Most

Merciful."[7] Mercy is not merely one of God's traits; it defines God's relationship to the world.

"My mercy encompasses all things" (Qur'an 7:156).[8]

The Prophet Muhammad taught, *"He who does not show mercy to others will not be shown mercy"* (Sahih al-Bukhari).[9] Islamic ethics frequently return to this reciprocal theme: the mercy you show is the mercy you invite. The opening formula of the Qur'an frames almost all Islamic thought and practice, making mercy central to both personal conduct and social policy.

The difference: Islamic mercy is grounded in divine nature and expressed through both personal affection and social policy, with the promise that merciful conduct opens the path to divine mercy and eventual paradise through faithful perseverance.

Buddhism: Compassion as the Path to Liberation

While Buddhism does not emphasize mercy as a divine attribute, it places *karuṇā* (compassion) at the heart of the spiritual path.[10] The Bodhisattva ideal—especially in Mahayana traditions—exemplifies this: beings who delay their own enlightenment to assist others in overcoming suffering.

Compassion in Buddhism arises from insight into the interconnectedness of all life and the universality of suffering.[11] When we truly understand that all beings suffer, our response becomes naturally compassionate. This isn't sentiment but wisdom—recognizing that separation between self and others is illusory.

The difference: Buddhist compassion flows from awakened awareness of interdependence and the universality of suffering, leading to liberation through insight and the transformation of the very mechanism that creates separation between self and others.

Hinduism: Mercy as Moral Duty and Divine Gift

Hindu texts often associate mercy with *daya* (compassion) and *ahimsa* (non-harm). The Laws of Manu instruct rulers to temper justice with mercy.[12] In the *Ramayana* and *Mahabharata*, righteous heroes show mercy to defeated enemies, even when justice would allow vengeance.

In devotional (*bhakti*) traditions, God's mercy (*kripa*) becomes the means of liberation. The *Bhagavad Gita* teaches that the soul cannot earn salvation through merit alone—it must receive grace through divine loving intervention.[13] This creates a dynamic where human mercy reflects divine mercy.

The difference: Hindu mercy operates as both moral duty (*dharma*) aligned with cosmic order and divine gift (*kripa*) that enables liberation, often guided by social context and aimed at eventual union with the divine through realization.

Taoism: Compassion as Natural Power

Laozi names compassion (*ci*) as one of the Tao's "Three Treasures":

"I have three treasures to guard and cherish: the first is compassion, the second is frugality, and the third is humility" (Tao Te Ching, Chapter 67).[14]

In Taoism, compassion is not sentimental but deeply practical. It aligns the person with the rhythms of nature, where true power comes not from force but from gentleness that flows with the Tao.[15] The sage acts mercifully not from moral obligation but from natural harmony with the universal order.

The difference: Taoist compassion seeks harmony with natural order through flexible responsiveness to universal principles, where mercy flows effortlessly from alignment with the Tao rather than being received as divine gift or earned through practice.

Comparing Approaches to Mercy and Compassion

Each tradition addresses the relationship between mercy and spiritual fulfillment differently:

- **Christianity**: Mercy is modeled after God's character and received by those who give it through divine-human reciprocity
- **Judaism**: Mercy combines covenantal loyalty (*chesed*) and maternal compassion (*rachamim*) through relationship with God and community
- **Islam**: Mercy reflects divine essence and serves as ethical imperative with reciprocal consequences through submission and faithful perseverance

- **Buddhism**: Compassion (*karuṇā*) arises from insight into suffering and interconnectedness through understanding attachment and impermanence
- **Hinduism**: Mercy (*daya*) functions as moral duty and divine gift, often tied to liberation through devotion and cosmic alignment
- **Taoism**: Compassion (*ci*) represents the root of true strength through harmony with natural order

These differences reflect distinct understandings of human agency, divine relationship, and the mechanics of moral transformation. Some emphasize receiving (Christianity), others achieving (Buddhism), still others aligning (Hinduism, Taoism) or submitting (Islam).

The Social Revolution of Mercy

Mercy isn't just a private virtue—it's a social revolution. In a punitive world, merciful people break the cycle of retribution. They refuse to let failure define worth. They insist that people are more than their worst moments.

Mercy changes families by choosing restoration over revenge. It rebuilds communities by creating space for second chances. It transforms institutions when leaders remember their own need for grace.[16] When mercy becomes cultural practice rather than individual exception, it creates environments where growth is possible because failure isn't fatal.

Modern research on restorative justice, trauma healing, and reconciliation provides real-world evidence of mercy's transforming power. Truth and Reconciliation Commissions demonstrate how communities can choose healing over punishment. Restorative justice programs show how mercy can satisfy both victims' needs and society's requirements for accountability.

A Leadership Note

Mercy in leadership means seeing people not as problems but as possibilities. It doesn't mean avoiding accountability—it means administering it with humanity. Leaders who embody mercy don't excuse harmful behavior, but they offer a path to restoration.

These are the leaders people want to follow: the ones who offer second chances, who remember their own need for grace, and who know that real strength shows up in gentleness. They understand that punishment without the possibility of redemption creates resentment, but mercy with clear expectations creates loyalty and growth.

How to Practice Mercy Today

To cultivate this revolutionary virtue in daily life:

Assume good intent before judging others' actions: Most people are doing the best they can with the resources and understanding they have. Start there.

Offer a kind word to someone who's struggling: Sometimes mercy is as simple as speaking gently to someone having a difficult day.

Let go of the need to be right in order to be kind: Choose relationship over being right. Choose understanding over winning.

Choose restoration over revenge: When someone wrongs you, ask what healing looks like rather than what punishment they deserve.

Apologize quickly and forgive freely: Practice both giving and receiving mercy. Be quick to admit your own mistakes and slow to hold grudges.

Remember how often you've needed mercy yourself: Reflect regularly on your own experience of having received grace. This cultivates the humility that makes mercy possible.

Practice mercy toward yourself: Extend to yourself the same compassion you'd offer a good friend facing similar struggles.

The Freedom of Mercy

The merciful receive mercy because they already understand how much they need it. This is not divine manipulation—it's spiritual coherence. Mercy moves us into alignment with the heart of God, the flow of the Tao, the law of karma, or the web of interconnectedness, depending on your tradition.

In a culture that pathologizes forgiveness as weakness and celebrates vengeance as strength, choosing mercy is profoundly countercultural. It's the freedom to respond to offense without reactive anger, to see failure as opportunity for growth rather than evidence of unworthiness, and to believe that people can change.

Mercy isn't weakness. It's fierce love. It's the power to stand in the gap when justice alone would walk away. It requires more strength than revenge because it demands that we override our natural impulses toward retaliation and choose the harder path of restoration.

This isn't just Christian truth—it's human truth that every wisdom tradition recognizes in its own way. The capacity for mercy runs through every great moral system because it runs through every human heart. Those who honor this capacity, rather than suppress it, discover that mercy transforms not just relationships but the entire landscape of human possibility.

In showing mercy, we open ourselves to receive it—from others, from the divine, and perhaps most importantly, from ourselves. This is the fifth Beatitude's promise: that those who choose compassionate action over just reaction will find themselves living in a world where grace is available, forgiveness is possible, and restoration always remains within reach.

Blessed Are the Pure in Heart: The Vision That Transforms Everything

"Blessed are the pure in heart, for they will see God."
—Matthew 5:8

In our age of curated online personas and strategic image management, the idea of being "pure in heart" can sound either naive or impossible. We live in a world where appearance often matters more than reality, where success depends on managing perception rather than cultivating character. But this sixth Beatitude cuts through all the performance and pretense to reveal a profound truth: what matters most is not how things appear, but who we are beneath the surface.

Unlike the Ten Commandments, which tell us what not to do, the Beatitudes show us how to be. They're not rules to follow but qualities to cultivate, and this sixth one promises something extraordinary: those with clear hearts see clearly. Not because they're perfect, but because they're whole. Their inner transparency creates outer perception that transforms everything.

This isn't about moral perfection or prudish righteousness. It's about what the ancient world called *katharos*—a heart that's undiluted, unmixed, and undivided.[1] Think of a mountain spring: not sinless, but clear. Not flawless, but whole.

What Does "Pure in Heart" Actually Mean?

The Greek word *katharos* means clean, clear, or unadulterated—free from pollution, cloudiness, or debris. When applied to the heart, it describes not sinlessness but singleness.[2] A pure heart is an undivided heart, unified in its loves and loyalties rather than fractured by competing allegiances.

In Hebrew thought, the "heart" (*lev*) encompasses far more than emotion. It's the seat of thought, will, and moral choice—the center of the entire person.[3] To be pure in heart means to have unified moral purpose, clear intention, and transparent motive. The Psalmist captures this beautifully: "Create in me a clean heart, O God" (Psalm 51:10), and "Give me an undivided heart, that I may fear your name" (Psalm 86:11).

The promise is equally striking. Those who are pure in heart "will see God"—not necessarily as visual experience, but as spiritual perception.[4] They recognize divine presence in the world, in others, and in the depths of their own experience. As the Danish philosopher Søren Kierkegaard later put it, "Purity of heart is to will one thing."[5]

The Deep Jewish Roots

Jesus draws on a rich tradition of Hebrew spirituality that connects inner purity with access to God's presence. Psalm 24:3-4 asks the fundamental question: "Who shall ascend the hill of the Lord? And who shall stand in his holy place? Those who have clean hands and a pure heart."[6]

This connection between purity and divine access runs throughout Jewish Scripture. But purity here is never merely ceremonial—it's ethical and relational. The prophets repeatedly challenge those who perform outward religious rituals while neglecting inner integrity. Isaiah condemns those who "honor me with their lips, while their hearts are far from me" (29:13).[7]

The Hebrew concept of purity involves *tahor* (clean, pure) and *tamim* (complete, whole, blameless).[8] It's about integrity in the deepest sense—the alignment of inner reality with outer expression. As Proverbs 4:23 warns, "Above all else, guard your heart, for everything you do flows from it."

In Jewish tradition, the pure heart isn't one that never makes mistakes, but one that remains teachable, honest, and responsive to God. It's the heart that desires what God desires and sees what God sees.

The Universal Human Wisdom

This insight into the relationship between inner clarity and spiritual perception appears across human cultures, each offering its own understanding of how purity leads to vision.

Islam: Sincerity as the Foundation of Spiritual Sight

Islam places extraordinary emphasis on *ikhlas* (sincerity or purity of intention) as the foundation of all spiritual practice. The Qur'an declares: "On the Day when neither wealth nor children will benefit, only one who comes to God with a sound heart" (26:88-89).[9]

The Prophet Muhammad taught that "God does not look at your forms or your wealth, but He looks at your hearts and your deeds" (Sahih Muslim).[10] In Islamic spirituality, every action's value depends entirely on the *niyyah* (intention) behind it. A heart clouded by pride, hypocrisy, or worldly attachment cannot properly perceive divine reality.

Sufi tradition deepens this understanding through the concept of *safah al-qalb* (purity of heart) achieved through remembrance (*dhikr*), service, and spiritual discipline.[11] The pure heart becomes a mirror that reflects divine light, enabling the mystic to "see" God through spiritual insight rather than physical vision.

The difference: Islam emphasizes that purity of intention (*niyyah*) before God forms the foundation of all righteous action, with spiritual vision realized fully in the afterlife for those who maintain sincerity throughout their earthly journey.

Buddhism: Clarity Through the Cessation of Mental Pollution

Buddhism understands purity as freedom from the mental pollutants (*kilesa*) that cloud clear seeing. The *Dhammapada* opens with the principle: "All things arise from mind. When the mind is pure, joy follows like a shadow that never leaves."[12]

The Buddhist path aims at purifying consciousness from greed, hatred, and delusion through meditation, ethical conduct, and wisdom.[13] This purification doesn't lead to "seeing God" but to *vipassana* (clear insight) into the true nature of reality. When mental pollution is removed, the practitioner sees clearly into the impermanent, interconnected nature of existence.

The Theravada tradition speaks of developing a mind that is *parisuddha* (completely purified), while Mahayana traditions emphasize the inherently pure nature of Buddha-mind that becomes visible when obscurations are removed.

The difference: Buddhist purity involves clearing away mental obscurations through disciplined practice, leading to awakened insight (*bodhi*) into reality's true nature rather than receiving divine vision as gift.

Hinduism: Inner Purification for Divine Vision

Hindu tradition teaches that *chitta-shuddhi* (purification of consciousness) is essential for *darshan* (vision of the Divine). The *Bhagavad Gita* explains: "When all desires that cling to the heart are surrendered, the mortal becomes immortal and attains Brahman" (15:51).[14]

Various yoga traditions offer different paths to purification: *karma yoga* (the way of action) purifies through selfless service, *bhakti yoga* (the way of devotion) through surrendered love, and *raja yoga* (the way of meditation) through disciplined consciousness.[15] Each path aims to clear away the ego's obscurations that prevent recognition of one's divine nature.

In Advaita Vedanta, the pure heart recognizes that the individual self (*atman*) and ultimate reality (*Brahman*) are one.

This isn't seeing God as separate being but realizing one's essential divine nature.

The difference: Hindu purification removes ego-based illusions through various disciplined practices, leading to realization of one's inherent divine nature (*atman-brahman unity*) rather than receiving vision from an external God.

Taoism: Simplicity and the Natural Heart

Taoism values *pu* (simplicity, the uncarved block) and *ziran* (naturalness) as expressions of heart purity. The *Tao Te Ching* teaches: "In pursuit of knowledge, every day something is added. In pursuit of the Tao, every day something is dropped" (Chapter 48).[16]

The pure heart in Taoist understanding is one freed from artificial desires, social conditioning, and forced striving.[17] Like water, it becomes clear when undisturbed by the sediment of ego and ambition. This clarity allows natural wisdom to emerge and enables harmony with the Tao.

The sage sees clearly not through accumulating knowledge but through returning to original simplicity. This isn't "seeing God" but perceiving the natural order that underlies all existence.

The difference: Taoist purity comes through returning to natural simplicity (*pu*) and releasing artificial desires, enabling harmony with the universal principle (*Tao*) rather than encountering a personal deity.

Comparing Approaches to Purity and Vision

Each tradition addresses the relationship between inner clarity and spiritual perception differently:

- **Christianity**: Purity of heart leads to seeing God through grace and divine gift in both present experience and future hope
- **Judaism**: Heart purity creates access to God's presence through covenant faithfulness and ethical integrity within community relationship
- **Islam**: Sincerity of intention (*ikhlas*) opens spiritual vision through submission to divine will and faithful perseverance
- **Buddhism**: Mental purification enables clear insight (*vipassana*) through disciplined practice and the removal of consciousness obscurations
- **Hinduism**: Consciousness purification (*chitta-shuddhi*) leads to divine realization through various yogic disciplines and ego transcendence
- **Taoism**: Natural simplicity (*pu*) creates harmony with universal order through release of artificial striving and social conditioning

These differences reflect distinct understandings of ultimate reality, the nature of spiritual vision, and the relationship between human effort and divine grace. Some emphasize receiving (Christianity), others achieving (Buddhism), still others realizing (Hinduism) or harmonizing (Taoism).

The Social Dimension

Purity of heart isn't merely private spirituality—it creates trustworthy community. Those with undivided hearts become the people others turn to for honest counsel, difficult conversations, and moral leadership.[18] They're not perfect, but they're reliable. Their transparency creates safety for others' vulnerability.

In families, pure-hearted people become the ones who can navigate conflict without hidden agendas. In workplaces, they're trusted with sensitive information and difficult decisions. In communities, they often emerge as informal leaders because their motives are clear and their care is genuine.

A Leadership Note

Leaders with purity of heart create different kinds of environments than those driven by hidden agendas or divided loyalties. They lead with integrity rather than manipulation, creating trust through consistency of character rather than performance of image. Their clarity of purpose inspires others because people sense they're not being manipulated or used.

This kind of leadership doesn't require perfection—it requires honesty about imperfection. Pure-hearted leaders acknowledge mistakes quickly, receive feedback gracefully, and maintain accountability naturally because they have nothing to hide.

How to Cultivate Purity of Heart Today

To develop this life-transforming quality:

Examine your motives regularly: Ask not just *what* you do, but *why*. Let your deeper intentions be shaped by love rather than ego, service rather than self-advancement.

Practice transparency: Let your private life and public witness align. Reduce the gap between who you are when seen and when unseen.

Simplify your desires: Notice what clutters your heart with competing loyalties. What attachments keep you from clarity? What would it mean to "will one thing"?

Choose presence over performance: Purity of heart isn't about past perfection or future achievements—it's about being fully present to what is real right now.

Embrace correction gracefully: Welcome feedback as pathway to greater clarity rather than threat to image. Say "thank you" when someone points out a blind spot.

Return to silence regularly: Stillness reveals what noise conceals. In quiet, the heart naturally clarifies and priorities reorganize themselves.

The Freedom of Clear Vision

Purity of heart isn't about being flawless—it's about being whole. It's about having nothing to hide, nothing to prove, and nothing to fear. That kind of inner freedom changes everything about how you move through the world.

When your heart is clear, you see clearly. Not because you're morally superior, but because you're no longer looking through the fog of divided loyalties, hidden agendas, and self-protective strategies. You see people as they are rather than as threats or opportunities. You recognize beauty and truth because your perception isn't clouded by ego.

This is the sixth Beatitude's revolutionary promise: those who achieve inner transparency gain outer perception. They "see God" not because they earn divine vision through moral performance, but because clarity of heart creates clarity of sight. They recognize divine presence everywhere because they're no longer blinded by the static of inner conflict.

In a world obsessed with image management and strategic positioning, choosing purity of heart is profoundly countercultural. It's the freedom to be exactly who you are, where you are, with nothing added and nothing hidden. And in that honesty, both you and those around you discover what every spiritual tradition promises: that truth really does set us free.

This isn't just Christian wisdom—it's human wisdom that Christianity articulates with particular hope. The connection between inner purity and spiritual vision runs through every great tradition because it runs through every human heart. Those who choose transparency over performance, integrity over image, and wholeness over winning discover that seeing clearly transforms not just personal experience, but entire communities.

Blessed Are the Peacemakers: Active Reconciliation Across Traditions

"Blessed are the peacemakers, for they will be called children of God."
—Matthew 5:9

In our polarized age of endless debates, tribal politics, and social media wars, genuine peacemaking can feel both naive and impossible. We live in a culture that rewards taking sides, amplifies division, and treats compromise as betrayal. But this seventh Beatitude offers a radically different vision: not peace through victory, but peace through reconciliation. Not the absence of conflict, but the transformation of it.

Unlike the Ten Commandments, which tell us what not to do, the Beatitudes show us how to be. They're not rules to follow but qualities to cultivate, and this seventh one reveals a profound truth: in a world addicted to winning, the peacemakers are those brave enough to step into the space between opposing sides. They don't avoid conflict—they transform it.

This isn't about preferring tranquility or avoiding difficult conversations. The promise isn't for peace-lovers but for peace-makers. The difference matters enormously.

What Does "Peacemaker" Actually Mean?

The Greek word *eirēnopoioi* appears only here in the entire New Testament—a compound of *eirēnē* (peace) and *poieō* (to make or do).[1] It's literally "peace-doers," a word of action rather than sentiment. This isn't about those who enjoy calm but those who actively create it, often at personal cost.

The early Christian teacher John Chrysostom understood peacemaking as demanding, costly work that mirrors God's own character.[2] Augustine similarly recognized that true peace often requires confronting injustice rather than simply maintaining quiet.[3] These weren't passive personalities but active reconcilers willing to enter hostility for the sake of healing.

The promise is equally striking: peacemakers "will be called children of God." In Hebrew thought, being called someone's child meant bearing their essential character.[4] Peacemakers resemble God not because they've earned a title, but because they mirror the divine nature—the One who makes peace with humanity through costly reconciliation.

The Deep Jewish Roots

Jesus draws on rich Hebrew traditions that see peace not as mere absence of conflict, but as *shalom*—wholeness, justice, and right relationship.[5] Psalm 34:14 commands: "Seek peace and pursue it," using active verbs that suggest energetic effort. The prophet Isaiah envisioned swords becoming plowshares (Isaiah 2:4), not through passive waiting but through active transformation.

In Jewish tradition, peacemaking isn't weakness but righteousness. The rabbis taught that Aaron, Moses' brother, was beloved because he "loved peace and pursued peace" (Pirkei Avot 1:12).[6] Rabbinic stories depict Aaron as willing to be misunderstood or take personal risks for the sake of harmony—not avoiding truth, but finding ways to speak it that create rather than destroy relationship.

This tradition teaches that *shalom* often requires confronting unjust systems rather than simply maintaining surface calm.[7] The prophets regularly challenged religious leaders who prioritized ritual over justice, understanding that true peace demands addressing root causes of conflict, not just managing symptoms.

The Universal Human Wisdom

This understanding of peace as active work rather than passive preference appears across human cultures, each offering its own approach to transforming conflict into harmony.

Islam: Peace Through Justice and Reconciliation

The very word "Islam" shares a root with *salaam* (peace), yet Islamic tradition recognizes that authentic peace requires justice.[8] The Qur'an praises reconciliation: "Reconciliation is best" (4:128), while also establishing that peace without justice enables oppression and is therefore false peace.

The Prophet Muhammad was known as a skilled mediator even before his prophetic mission, brokering truces between warring tribes.[9] Islamic law developed sophisticated concepts around *sulh* (reconciliation), which is highly esteemed in commerce, family disputes, and community relations. The Qur'an specifically addresses reconciliation among believers: "The believers are but brothers, so make settlement between your brothers" (49:9).[10]

One of God's names in Islam is *As-Salam* (The Source of Peace), making peacemaking a divine quality that humans can embody.[11] However, Islamic tradition consistently balances peace with justice—true *salaam* cannot exist where oppression continues unchallenged.

The difference: Islamic peacemaking emphasizes reconciliation grounded in divine law and justice, where believers work to restore right relationships through submission to God's guidance and faithful perseverance in pursuit of both peace and equity.

Buddhism: Inner Peace Becoming Outer Peace

Buddhist ethics root peacemaking in *ahimsa* (non-harming) and *karuna* (compassion). The *Dhammapada* teaches: "All tremble at violence; all fear death. Putting oneself in the place of another, one should not kill nor cause another to kill" (129).[12] This isn't passive but requires active intervention to prevent suffering.

Buddhist understanding recognizes that peace begins with the mind. A peaceful heart naturally creates peaceful action, while inner conflict generates outer conflict.[13] The Bodhisattva ideal exemplifies this: beings who work to relieve others' suffering, including the suffering caused by conflict and division.

In Buddhist communities, peacemaking often involves patient dialogue, careful listening, and finding ways to address underlying attachments and ego-driven positions that fuel conflict. The goal isn't victory but mutual understanding and the cessation of harm.

The difference: Buddhist peacemaking flows from inner transformation and non-attachment to views, seeking to end suffering through compassionate intervention and wisdom about the interdependent nature of conflict.

Hinduism: Peace Through Self-Realization and Duty

The *Bhagavad Gita* presents a vision of the spiritually mature person as one who remains "the same to friend and foe... calm in mind, content with whatever comes" (12:18-19).[14] This inner equanimity becomes the foundation for outer peacemaking, as only those who have mastered inner passions can effectively calm external conflicts.

Hindu tradition also emphasizes *dharma* (righteous duty) in peacemaking. Sometimes maintaining cosmic order requires confronting injustice rather than simply maintaining surface harmony.[15] The epics (*Ramayana* and *Mahabharata*) often show righteous heroes who work for peace but are willing to fight when diplomacy fails to protect the innocent.

In many Hindu communities, elder peacemakers are those who have achieved spiritual maturity through disciplined practice, enabling them to see beyond immediate positions to underlying truths and shared interests.

The difference: Hindu peacemaking combines spiritual self-discipline with cosmic duty, seeking harmony through individual realization and adherence to eternal principles of righteousness and social order.

Taoism: Peace Through Non-Force and Natural Harmony

The *Tao Te Ching* teaches that force creates resistance, while yielding overcomes rigidity: "The soft overcomes the hard. The gentle overcomes the rigid" (36).[16] Taoist peacemaking doesn't impose harmony but embodies it, trusting that alignment with natural order will influence others toward balance.

Chapter 68 celebrates the ideal general who "does not delight in victory"—not because winning is wrong, but because true victory comes through minimizing conflict rather than maximizing force.[17] The Taoist sage creates peace by understanding underlying patterns and working with them rather than against them.

This approach values patient observation, strategic non-action (*wu wei*), and finding ways to redirect energy rather than oppose it directly. Conflict is seen as imbalance that can be corrected through wise intervention that restores natural flow.

The difference: Taoist peacemaking works through flexible responsiveness to natural principles, achieving harmony by yielding strategically and aligning with universal patterns rather than imposing solutions through force.

Comparing Approaches to Peacemaking

Each tradition offers a distinct understanding of how peace is made and sustained:

- **Christianity**: Peacemaking as courageous reconciliation that reflects God's nature through grace-enabled relationship repair
- **Judaism**: Peace pursued as wholeness and justice through covenant faithfulness and community accountability
- **Islam**: Peace achieved through reconciliation and restorative justice guided by divine law and faithful perseverance
- **Buddhism**: Peace created through non-attachment to positions and compassionate intervention to end suffering
- **Hinduism**: Peace flowing from spiritual self-realization and dutiful action aligned with cosmic order
- **Taoism**: Peace arising through yielding strength and harmony with natural universal principles

These aren't contradictory but complementary approaches. Each tradition recognizes that authentic peace requires more than avoiding conflict—it demands active work to transform the conditions that create division. The differences reflect varying understandings of human agency, divine involvement, and the relationship between inner transformation and outer reconciliation.

The Social and Political Revolution of Peace

Peacemaking isn't merely personal virtue—it's profoundly political. In Jesus' time, Rome maintained the "Pax Romana" through military dominance, crucifying anyone who challenged imperial authority.[18] Jesus offers a subversive alternative: peace through reconciliation rather than coercion, restoration rather than retribution.

To bless peacemakers is to challenge systems that benefit from division. It calls out violence in all forms—not just war, but exclusion, revenge cycles, and the quiet violence of indifference. Modern peacemakers are those who mediate rather than take sides, listen to understand rather than win, and build coalitions across traditional divides.

This work rarely receives headlines, but in God's economy, it's holy. Contemporary examples include Truth and Reconciliation Commissions that choose healing over punishment, interfaith dialogue that builds understanding across religious boundaries, and community mediation programs that transform neighborhoods from within.[19]

A Leadership Note

Effective leaders don't simply avoid conflict—they transform it. They create environments where people feel heard, valued, and safe enough to disagree constructively. The best organizational peacemakers aren't always the quietest or most agreeable—they're often the most courageous, willing to name what's broken and step into the difficult space between competing interests.

Great leaders understand that sustainable progress requires the patient work of reconciliation. They know that forced agreement creates resentment, while authentic peace builds loyalty and long-term effectiveness.

How to Make Peace Today

To cultivate this vital quality in daily life:

Develop inner stillness: External peace begins with inner clarity. Practice silence, prayer, or meditation to cultivate the calm that enables wise response to conflict.

Become a bridge-builder: Actively introduce people across divides. Look for shared values and common ground, helping others discover their mutual interests.

Learn to apologize: Peacemaking often begins with humility. Practice taking responsibility for your part in conflicts, even when others share blame.

Seek justice, not just comfort: Remember that true peace sometimes requires disrupting unjust situations. Don't mistake silence for peace or harmony for health.

Stay present in conflict: When tension arises, resist the urge to flee. Remain physically and emotionally present. Listen carefully, speak thoughtfully, and model the calm you want to see.

Practice difficult conversations: Get comfortable with disagreement. Learn to discuss contentious topics without attacking persons or positions, focusing on understanding rather than winning.

Address root causes: Look beyond surface disputes to underlying needs, fears, and values that drive conflict. Work to meet legitimate needs rather than simply managing symptoms.

The Freedom of Peacemaking

Peacemaking is demanding, often thankless work that requires tremendous inner strength and spiritual maturity. But it's also profoundly liberating. It breaks cycles of vengeance that imprison communities in endless conflict. It restores dignity to all parties by insisting that everyone is more than their worst moment. It models the Kingdom of God—a realm where relationships matter more than being right.

Those who make peace will be called children of God not because they've earned divine favor, but because they resemble the peacemaking God who entered human conflict not to dominate but to heal. They embody the family characteristic of their heavenly Father, who "makes his sun rise on the evil and on the good" (Matthew 5:45).

In a world obsessed with winning, choosing to be a peacemaker is revolutionary. It's the freedom to respond to hostility with creativity rather than retaliation, to see enemies as future friends, and to believe that reconciliation is always possible even when it seems impossible. It's choosing love over control, courage over comfort, and restoration over resentment.

This isn't just Christian truth—it's human truth that every great tradition recognizes in its own way. The capacity for peacemaking runs through every wisdom tradition because it runs through every human heart. Those who honor this capacity rather than suppress it discover that making peace transforms not just relationships but entire communities.

The seventh Beatitude promises that peacemakers will be recognized as God's children—not because they're perfect, but because they're participating in the divine work of reconciliation that heals the world one relationship at a time.

Blessed Are Those Who Are Persecuted for Righteousness' Sake: The Cost of Moral Witness

"Blessed are those who are persecuted for righteousness' sake, for theirs is the kingdom of heaven."
—Matthew 5:10

We admire courage from a distance. But up close—when it threatens our safety, our status, or our comfort—we often flinch. This final Beatitude dares to name what most of us would rather avoid: that righteousness will, at times, provoke resistance. And when it does, we are not cursed—we are blessed.

Unlike the Ten Commandments, which tell us what not to do, the Beatitudes show us how to be. They're not rules to follow but qualities to cultivate, and this eighth one reveals a hard truth: in a world where injustice often goes unchallenged, choosing righteousness can cost you. Yet those who pay this price inherit something the world cannot give or take away—the kingdom of heaven itself.

This isn't a call to seek suffering for its own sake, nor an invitation to martyrdom complexes. It's a sober recognition that moral integrity sometimes puts you at odds with systems of power, cultural expectations, or even family loyalties. The blessing comes not from the suffering but from what the suffering reveals: a life aligned with something greater than personal comfort.

What "Persecuted for Righteousness" Actually Means

The Greek word for "persecute," *diōkō*, implies persistent harassment, pursuit, or oppression. It's active, not accidental.[1] The "righteousness" (*dikaiosynē*) in question encompasses both personal integrity and social justice—the Hebrew *tzedek*, which involves right relationship with God, neighbor, and community.[2]

This Beatitude forms a bookend with the first: both promise the "kingdom of heaven."[3] But here, the emphasis is sharper. It doesn't promise reward for quiet belief but blesses those who suffer for doing what's right—whether through advocacy, truth-telling, hospitality, or simply refusing to go along with harmful norms.

The early church lived this reality. Many were ostracized, imprisoned, or killed not because they were disruptive, but because their radical love, hospitality, and refusal to worship empire upended the cultural order.[4] Their righteousness was political precisely because it was personal.

The Deep Jewish Roots

Jesus' words echo the Hebrew prophetic tradition. The prophets—Amos, Jeremiah, Isaiah, Micah—were not honored in their own time. They were slandered, imprisoned, exiled, or executed for speaking uncomfortable truths about justice, idolatry, and corruption.[5]

Hebrew Scripture repeatedly links righteousness with justice:

"Seek justice, rescue the oppressed, defend the orphan, plead for the widow." (Isaiah 1:17)
"Let justice roll down like waters, and righteousness like an everflowing stream." (Amos 5:24)[6]

To be "persecuted for righteousness" is to walk in this prophetic lineage. It's to speak up for those with no voice, to side with the marginalized, to embody covenant faithfulness—even when it costs you. The Jewish concept of *kiddush hashem*(sanctification of God's name) often involved suffering for the sake of integrity, creating a legacy that outlasted immediate persecution.[7]

The Universal Human Wisdom

Across religious traditions, those who stand for truth in the face of power are often celebrated—even as they suffer in real time. Each tradition understands this paradox of courageous suffering differently.

Islam: Bearing Witness Under Pressure

The Qur'an acknowledges that standing for truth invites opposition:

"Do people think they will be left alone after saying 'We believe' without being put to the test?" (Qur'an 29:2)

"Indeed, those who say, 'Our Lord is Allah,' and then remain steadfast... they will have no fear, nor will they grieve." (Qur'an 46:13)[8]

The concept of *shahāda* (bearing witness) in Islam encompasses not just faith declaration but truthful testimony even under threat.[9] The Prophet Muhammad himself endured exile, ridicule, and military aggression. His early followers suffered torture and displacement for their commitment to monotheism and social equality.

Islamic tradition emphasizes *ṣabr* (patient perseverance) and *ṣidq* (truthfulness) as twin pillars of dignity under pressure.[10] Those who suffer for faith and justice are not abandoned by God but honored in this life and the next.

The difference: Islamic perseverance emphasizes patient endurance (*ṣabr*) and truthful witness (*shahāda*) as pathways to divine mercy and eventual paradise through faithful submission to God's will, even when society opposes such submission.

Buddhism: Compassionate Endurance

While Buddhism does not speak in terms of persecution for righteousness, it honors those who continue to act with compassion in a world that resists awakening. Bodhisattvas remain in the world of suffering to serve others, even when misunderstood or maligned.[11]

The *Dhammapada* teaches:

"Hatred is never appeased by hatred in this world. By non-hatred alone is hatred appeased. This is a law eternal." (1.5)[12]

Buddhist monastics have historically faced persecution for resisting empire or calling out societal harm. Yet their strength comes not from retaliation but from nonviolent integrity.[13] The path of compassion sometimes puts practitioners at odds with systems that profit from suffering.

The difference: Buddhist endurance flows from insight into impermanence and non-attachment to outcomes, seeking to transform suffering through compassionate action rather than receiving divine inheritance as consolation.

Hinduism: Dharma Despite Opposition

In the *Bhagavad Gita*, Arjuna resists fighting against his own kin. But Krishna reminds him that *dharma*—righteous duty—sometimes requires acting, even when it brings pain:

"Better to perish in your own dharma than to succeed in the dharma of another." (Gita 3:35)[14]

Suffering for righteousness is understood as part of karma yoga—the path of selfless action.[15] The key is detachment from outcomes and commitment to inner and outer truth. Saints like Mahatma Gandhi embodied this: embracing suffering not for its own sake, but as a cost of faithfulness to justice and nonviolence.

The difference: Hindu righteousness involves aligning with eternal law (*sanatana dharma*) and fulfilling personal duty, seeking liberation through detachment from results rather than receiving comfort from a personal God.

Taoism: Integrity Over Safety

Taoism rarely speaks of persecution, but it honors those who live with authenticity even when the world does not understand. The sage who follows the Tao may seem strange, threatening, or subversive to the powerful—because their way isn't based on manipulation or force.[16]

"When the Tao is lost, there is goodness. When goodness is lost, there is morality. When morality is lost, there is ritual."(Tao Te Ching, 38)[17]

The *Tao Te Ching* reminds us:

"The sage is not ambitious. Like a valley, content to be below." (Chapter 7)

Suffering may come not from activism, but from refusing to play along with systems of ego and control. The Taoist accepts this as natural consequence of living in harmony with the Tao.

The difference: Taoist integrity seeks harmony with natural order (*wu wei*) through authentic action, finding peace in alignment with universal principles rather than receiving divine consolation.

Comparing Approaches to Righteousness and Suffering

Each tradition addresses the relationship between moral integrity and persecution differently:

- **Christianity**: Persecution for righteousness leads to divine inheritance through grace and kingdom belonging
- **Judaism**: Prophetic suffering sanctifies God's name through covenant faithfulness and community witness
- **Islam**: Patient endurance under persecution opens divine mercy through submission and faithful perseverance
- **Buddhism**: Compassionate action despite opposition transforms suffering through insight and non-attachment
- **Hinduism**: Righteous suffering aligns with cosmic duty through detachment and adherence to eternal law
- **Taoism**: Authentic living accepts natural consequences through harmony with universal principles

These differences reflect distinct understandings of human agency, divine relationship, and the purpose of moral suffering. Some emphasize receiving (Christianity), others achieving (Buddhism), still others aligning (Hinduism, Taoism) or submitting (Islam).

The Social Dimension

This Beatitude doesn't just refer to martyrs. It includes whistleblowers, truth-tellers, advocates for the marginalized, and anyone who quietly but consistently refuses to compromise their ethics under pressure.[18] In Jesus' day, persecution might have come from empire, religious authorities, or even one's own family. Today, it may look like professional consequences, social ostracization, or internal wrestling.

The Beatitude reminds us: not all suffering is redemptive. But when it's the cost of love, integrity, or justice—it becomes sacred. Those who are willing to lose reputation, opportunity, or comfort to maintain moral clarity often become the conscience of their communities.

A Leadership Note

Leaders often face subtle forms of persecution: resistance when they challenge unethical norms, pressure to silence dissent, backlash when they prioritize justice over convenience. Those who stay grounded in righteousness—rather than approval—become trustworthy guides. The best leaders don't just manage—they embody values. That embodiment can make them targets, but it also makes them transformational.

Living This Today

To embody this Beatitude in daily life:

Refuse complicity: Don't play along with injustice just to avoid conflict. Your integrity matters more than your comfort.

Speak truth in love: Be bold, but don't become bitter. The tone matters as much as the message.

Bear rejection wisely: Not all persecution is virtuous—but when it comes for the right reasons, don't be ashamed.

Stand with others: Be the person who shows up when it's uncomfortable. Suffering shared is suffering transformed.

Keep your eyes on the kingdom: This isn't about earthly rewards. It's about aligning your life with eternal truth.

Practice moral courage: Start small. Defend someone being gossiped about. Question policies that harm the vulnerable. Build your capacity for larger stands.

The Freedom of Holy Resistance

This final Beatitude affirms a hard-won freedom: the ability to do what's right, even when it costs you. It's the courage to lose reputation, opportunity, or comfort in order to gain integrity. In a world where power protects itself and truth is often inconvenient, those who are "persecuted for righteousness" stand out.

They are not saints because they suffer—they are saints because they refuse to stop loving, even when suffering follows. The Beatitudes don't glamorize pain—but they do recognize the hidden power in moral clarity and resilient love.

The eighth Beatitude is not a call to victimhood. It's a call to non-negotiable compassion. Those who live this way may not win the world's approval. But according to Jesus—they inherit a far greater kingdom, one that no earthly power can give or take away.

This isn't just Christian truth—it's human truth that every wisdom tradition recognizes in its own way. The willingness to suffer for righteousness runs through every great moral system because it runs through every human heart capable of loving something more than itself. Those who honor this capacity rather than suppress it discover that standing for truth transforms not just personal character but entire communities.

Blessed Are You: The Personal Turn in the Ninth Beatitude

"Blessed are you when people revile you and persecute you and utter all kinds of evil against you falsely on my account."
—Matthew 5:11

The first eight Beatitudes speak in the third person. *"Blessed are the poor... the meek... the merciful."* They paint a portrait of a community shaped by divine blessing—humble, compassionate, peace-seeking, and often persecuted. But then, suddenly, Jesus turns and looks his listeners in the eye:

"Blessed are you when people revile you and persecute you and utter all kinds of evil against you falsely on my account. Rejoice and be glad, for your reward is great in heaven, for in the same way they persecuted the prophets who were before you." (Matthew 5:11-12)

It is a striking rhetorical shift—from poetic generality to direct address, from *they* to *you*. This transition transforms the entire series from beautiful ideals into lived reality, from description into direct challenge and comfort.

The Structure: Is This Really a Ninth Beatitude?

Scholars overwhelmingly agree that **Matthew 5:11-12** is structurally distinct from the eight that precede it, but most do not classify it as a separate ninth Beatitude.[1] Instead, it functions as a personalized expansion and application of the eighth. The evidence includes:

Grammatical Shifts

- Moves from third person ("those who") to second person ("you")
- Changes from simple blessing formula to extended explanation
- Uses **three specific verbs** (*revile, persecute, slander*) rather than single terms[2]

Literary Expansion

- Is significantly longer and more detailed than the others
- Adds explanation (*"falsely"*) and motivation (*"on my account"*)
- Includes a **command** (*"Rejoice and be glad"*) unique among the Beatitudes[3]

Matthean Literary Structure

The eighth and "ninth" Beatitudes create an *inclusio* with the first—all three promise "the kingdom of heaven," framing the entire series.[4] This suggests Matthew intends the persecution blessing to serve as both climax and conclusion rather than addition.

As scholar Dale Allison notes, "Verse 11 is not a ninth Beatitude. It is a restatement and elaboration of the eighth, now addressed directly to the disciples."[5] This represents the scholarly consensus, supported by commentators like Ulrich Luz, Craig Keener, and R.T. France.

Historical Context: Why the Personal Turn Matters

This personalization wasn't merely rhetorical—it was essential for Matthew's early Christian community, likely experiencing real persecution in the wake of the Temple's destruction (70 CE) and growing tensions between Jewish Christians and both traditional Jewish communities and Gentile believers.[6]

The shift from general principle to direct address acknowledges that following Jesus brings specific opposition. Matthew elsewhere emphasizes this cost:

- *"You will be hated by all because of my name"* (10:22)
- *"If they persecuted me, they will persecute you"* (John 15:20, echoed in Matthew 24:9)[7]

The personal address creates solidarity between Jesus and his followers—what happens to them has happened to him and will happen to those who follow his path.

"On My Account": The Christological Anchor

The phrase *heneken emou*—"on my account" or "because of me"—introduces a **Christological center** that distinguishes this blessing from all others.[8] While the previous Beatitudes speak of righteousness, peace, and mercy in general terms, this one specifically identifies persecution that comes because of allegiance to Jesus personally.

This represents a remarkable claim: association with this particular rabbi will bring opposition not because he teaches controversial ideas (many teachers did that), but because of who he is and what he represents.[9] The phrase appears elsewhere in Matthew (10:18, 39; 16:25; 19:29), always in contexts of costly discipleship.

This Christological focus anticipates the Gospel's conclusion, where the risen Jesus claims "all authority in heaven and on earth" (28:18). The persecution comes not from following general ethical principles but from loyalty to one who challenges fundamental power structures.

"Rejoice and Be Glad": The Paradoxical Command

Jesus adds the only **imperative** in the entire Beatitude series: *"Rejoice and be glad, for your reward is great in heaven."*[10] This command to celebrate seems counterintuitive—why rejoice in persecution?

The answer lies in what the opposition signifies: **belonging**. Persecution for Christ's sake places disciples in the lineage of Hebrew prophets who suffered for proclaiming God's truth.[11] As Jesus explains, *"for in the same way they persecuted the prophets who were before you"* (5:12).

This isn't celebration of suffering itself but celebration of:

- **Prophetic lineage**: Standing with Isaiah, Jeremiah, and others who spoke truth to power

- **Spiritual authenticity**: Opposition often indicates that one's witness is genuine and threatening to unjust systems
- **Divine vindication**: The "reward in heaven" promises ultimate justice and recognition
- **Christological solidarity**: Sharing in the rejection Jesus himself experienced[12]

The joy comes not from pain but from the meaning the pain reveals—that one's life is aligned with God's purposes even when opposed by human powers.

Comparative Insights: Suffering for Truth Across Traditions

While the Christological focus (*"on my account"*) makes this blessing uniquely Christian, the broader pattern—suffering for spiritual fidelity or justice—resonates across religious traditions:

Buddhism

Bodhisattvas willingly endure misunderstanding and hardship for others' awakening, accepting that compassionate action sometimes meets resistance from those attached to harmful patterns.[13]

Islam

The Prophet Muhammad faced persecution for proclaiming monotheism and social justice, with the Qur'an praising patience (ṣabr) under trial: *"And give good tidings to the patient,* who, when disaster strikes them, say, 'Indeed we belong to Allah, and indeed to Him we will return'" (2:155-156).[14]

Hebrew Prophets

Jeremiah, Isaiah, Amos, and others were marginalized, threatened, or killed for confronting religious and political corruption. Jesus explicitly places his followers in this tradition.[15]

Modern Examples

From Gandhi's satyagraha to Martin Luther King Jr.'s nonviolent resistance to Malala Yousafzai's advocacy for education, history demonstrates that those who challenge injustice often face opposition.[16]

The universal pattern suggests that the ninth Beatitude articulates something fundamental about moral courage: authentic witness to truth and justice often provokes resistance from systems that benefit from the status quo.

Canonical Context: Luke's Parallel

Luke's Sermon on the Plain offers a parallel that deepens our understanding:

"Blessed are you when people hate you, and when they exclude you, revile you, and defame you on account of the Son of Man. Rejoice in that day and leap for joy, for surely your reward is great

in heaven; for that is what their ancestors did to the prophets" (Luke 6:22-23).[17]

Luke's version is even more physical (*"leap for joy"*) and explicitly mentions social exclusion, suggesting that early Christians faced not just verbal opposition but social ostracism. Both Gospels agree on the prophetic lineage and the call to joy, reinforcing that this teaching was central to Jesus' message about discipleship's cost.

Why Some Traditions Count Nine Beatitudes

Some older traditions, particularly in Eastern Christianity and certain Western liturgical uses, have historically counted nine Beatitudes by treating verses 11-12 as separate from verse 10.[18] This reflects different approaches to textual division rather than theological disagreement. The numbering affects liturgical recitation and artistic representation but doesn't change the fundamental meaning or structure of Jesus' teaching.

Modern biblical scholarship generally favors the eight-beatitude structure based on literary analysis, but the traditional nine-fold division highlights the importance early Christians placed on the persecution theme.

Living the Personal Challenge

The ninth Beatitude functions as a reality check for contemporary disciples. It suggests several practical implications:

Expect resistance: Living according to the Beatitudes' values—mercy, justice, peacemaking, humility—will sometimes provoke opposition from systems and individuals invested in alternative values.

Examine motivation: The blessing applies specifically to persecution "on account of" Jesus, not suffering that results from our own poor choices, abrasive personality, or unnecessary provocation.

Find community: The second person plural ("you") suggests that this persecution is communal, not individual. Disciples face opposition together and support each other through it.

Maintain joy: The command to rejoice isn't emotional manipulation but spiritual discipline—choosing to see opposition as confirmation of alignment with God's purposes rather than evidence of failure.

Remember the prophets: Connecting contemporary discipleship to the prophetic tradition provides both comfort (we're not alone) and challenge (we're called to their level of courage).

A Bridge from Vision to Reality

The so-called ninth Beatitude serves as a crucial bridge between poetic vision and lived experience. It takes the beautiful ideals of the first eight blessings and confronts readers with their real-world implications: following Jesus is costly.

But the cost comes with a promise. Those who face opposition for living according to kingdom values participate in something larger than themselves—the long tradition of prophetic witness that includes Jesus himself. Their persecution becomes a mark not of failure but of faithfulness, not of divine abandonment but of divine companionship.

The personal address (*"Blessed are you"*) makes this both intimate and immediate. These aren't abstract principles but personal promises for real people facing real opposition. In a world that often rewards compromise and punishes integrity, Jesus looks his followers in the eye and says: *"When the world rejects you for following me, you are blessed. Rejoice—you're in good company."*

This transforms the entire Beatitude series from moral philosophy into discipleship training. The nine blessings together answer the question: What does it look like to live as citizens of God's kingdom in a world that operates by different values? The answer includes both the character traits (humility, mercy, peacemaking) and the likely consequences (persecution, social opposition) of such a life.

The ninth Beatitude doesn't add to the list of blessed people—it personalizes the list for those brave enough to embody it.

Part III

Global and Interfaith Perspectives

Blessed Beyond the Canon: The Beatitudes in Abrahamic and Christian-Adjacent Traditions

Christianity didn't emerge in a vacuum. It grew from Jewish soil, interacted with Greco-Roman philosophy, and eventually birthed a range of related movements—some institutional, others mystical, some embraced by orthodoxy, others exiled to the margins. Yet many of these traditions, both ancient and modern, reflect remarkably similar values to those found in the Beatitudes.

This exploration reveals how movements adjacent to the Abrahamic faiths—Gnosticism, Sufism, Quakerism, Mormonism, Kabbalah, and the Baha'i Faith—engage with the same moral vision Jesus outlined on that Galilean hillside. What emerges is a chorus of sacred echoes, each offering a fresh angle on humility, mercy, purity, peace, and the paradoxical power of love.

Gnostic Texts: The Kingdom Within

Gnosticism represents a diverse collection of early Christian and quasi-Christian movements that emphasized esoteric knowledge (*gnōsis*) as the key to salvation.[1] Many texts discovered in the Nag Hammadi library in 1945 offer striking parallels to the Beatitudes, though in a symbolic and highly interiorized form.

The **Gospel of Thomas**, perhaps the most famous Gnostic text, begins: "Whoever finds the interpretation of these sayings will not taste death."² Its sayings include beatitude-like proclamations:

"Blessed is the lion which becomes man when consumed by man." (Saying 7)
"Blessed are the solitary and elect, for you will find the kingdom." (Saying 49)³

These aren't ethical commands but spiritual koans—provocations meant to awaken deeper awareness. The Gnostic "kingdom" isn't a future reward but an inner reality already present, veiled only by ignorance.⁴ Many Gnostic communities faced marginalization or outright condemnation by emerging orthodox Christianity, adding poignancy to their alternative vision of blessedness found through hidden wisdom rather than institutional belonging.

How it resonates: Gnosticism shares the Beatitudes' paradoxical tone—blessedness where we least expect it—but emphasizes awakening through esoteric knowledge rather than trustful humility. Both call for the dismantling of ego and the discovery of truth within, though they differ on whether this truth comes through revelation or realization.

Sufism: The Path of the Heart

Sufism, the mystical dimension of Islam, speaks a language that resonates deeply with the spirit of the Beatitudes while remaining firmly grounded in Qur'anic revelation and prophetic example.[5]

Rumi, the 13th-century Persian mystic, captured this beautifully:

"Be like a tree and let the dead leaves drop."
"The wound is the place where the Light enters you."[6]

His verses celebrate spiritual poverty (*faqr*) and brokenness that open us to divine intimacy. The Sufi path involves intense ego purification through practices of humility, remembrance (*dhikr*), and surrender.[7] Al-Ghazali wrote extensively on balancing mercy, humility, and divine justice—concerns that mirror the Beatitudes' integration of personal transformation with social ethics.

Like Jesus' Beatitudes, Sufi wisdom exalts the lowly and finds God meeting us where we are most undone. The mystical station of *fana* (self-annihilation) parallels the "poor in spirit," while the Sufi emphasis on a "broken heart" echoes the blessing on those who mourn.[8]

How it resonates: Where the Beatitudes promise divine reward for those who mourn, hunger, or make peace, Sufism sees these states as doorways to union with God. The language differs, but the heart beats the same: God meets us in our vulnerability and transforms suffering into sacred intimacy.

Quakerism: The Strength of Silence

The Religious Society of Friends (Quakers), emerging in 17th-century England, took Jesus' teachings to radical depths.[9] They abandoned hierarchical church structures, rejected violence, and centered their gatherings on silence—waiting for the "Inner Light" to speak.

For Quakers, **meekness isn't passive**—it's spiritually powerful. Refusing to retaliate became both ethical principle and political witness.[10] Early Friends were often persecuted for righteousness' sake, fitting squarely into the eighth Beatitude. Yet they endured with quiet strength that eventually transformed entire societies' approaches to criminal justice, slavery, and war.

Their belief in **"that of God in everyone"** echoes the Beatitudes' democratic spirit: blessedness isn't reserved for the elite or learned but is accessible to all who live with sincerity, humility, and love.[11] Quaker discernment—seeking the Inner Light through communal silence—mirrors the Beatitudes' call to spiritual authenticity and the priority of inward transformation over outward conformity.

How it resonates: Quakerism lives out the Beatitudes in public life through peacemaking, simplicity, humility, and mercy. It represents the Beatitudes made into a social ethic, not just spiritual aspiration. Their historic witness against slavery, for women's rights, and toward restorative justice demonstrates how personal transformation flows naturally into social reform.

Mormonism: Eternal Perspective, Present Compassion

The Church of Jesus Christ of Latter-day Saints (LDS), founded in 19th-century America by Joseph Smith, represents a modern Christian offshoot with distinctive cosmology that frames familiar ethics within an expanded temporal vision.[12]

The **Book of Mormon** includes its own version of the Sermon on the Mount (3 Nephi 12), nearly identical to Matthew's—but with the expanded context of Jesus teaching in the Americas after his resurrection.[13] This suggests the Beatitudes' universal applicability across cultures and continents.

LDS theology emphasizes **eternal progression**, positioning meekness, mercy, and purity of heart not just as moral ideals but as conditions for spiritual advancement.[14] The Mormon concept of "**Zion**"—an ideal just society—represents the Beatitudes' vision lived out communally, where economic equality and spiritual unity create a foretaste of divine society.

The LDS principle of **agency** (freedom to choose) makes ethical formation central.[15] The Beatitudes function both as divine promise and personal challenge, with grace and effort coexisting in the journey toward exaltation.

How it resonates: Mormonism aligns with the Beatitudes in form and value but frames them within a cosmic journey toward deification. Blessedness becomes both gift and discipline, with eternal consequences flowing from temporal choices. The vision extends beyond individual transformation to encompass the building of sacred community.

Kabbalah: The Mystical Humility of the Jewish Soul

Though firmly within the Jewish tradition, **Kabbalah** introduces mystical interpretations that harmonize remarkably with the interior logic of the Beatitudes.[16]

Tzimtzum—the idea that God "contracts" to make space for creation—models divine humility.[17] Human beings are likewise called to "contract the ego" to allow God's presence to flow through them. This cosmic humility echoes the "poor in spirit" who make room for God's kingdom.

The ten **sefirot** (emanations of God) include *chesed* (loving-kindness) and *gevurah* (discipline/strength)—a balance that mirrors the Beatitude understanding of meekness as power under control.[18] The Zohar teaches that the **"broken vessel"** is more useful to God than the perfect one, directly echoing the blessings on those who mourn and the poor in spirit.

The Lurianic Kabbalistic concept of **tikkun olam** ("repairing the world") connects personal spiritual work with cosmic restoration, paralleling how the Beatitudes link individual transformation with social healing.[19]

How it resonates: Kabbalah doesn't frame these ideas as beatitudes per se, but the parallels are vivid: interior humility enables divine presence, spiritual maturity comes through surrender, and personal transformation serves universal restoration. The "blessed" become vessels for divine light in a broken world.

Baha'i Faith: Unity Through Righteousness

The Baha'i Faith, founded in 19th-century Persia by Bahá'u'lláh, teaches the oneness of all religions and the progressive unfolding of divine revelation throughout history.[20]

The Baha'i writings call for the **elimination of extremes of wealth and poverty**, **peaceful global governance**, and **compassionate service**—all consistent with the values embedded in the Beatitudes.[21] Bahá'u'lláh writes:

"O Son of Man! Humble thyself before Me, that I may graciously visit thee."

And:

"The best beloved of all things in My sight is Justice."[22]

Like the Beatitudes, the Baha'i vision blesses humility, peace, and purity, but extends the lens globally—framing these not just as personal virtues but as **planetary necessities**. Baha'i universalism extends the Beatitudes' blessings to all humanity, transcending religious exclusivism while maintaining the call to transformation.

How it resonates: The Beatitudes are reframed as stepping stones to world unity, with spiritual transformation and global justice as inseparable goals. Personal character development serves the emergence of a peaceful, just planetary civilization. Righteousness becomes both individual achievement and collective responsibility.

A Broader Sacred Symphony

Despite doctrinal differences, these traditions share a central insight: **true blessedness doesn't come from grasping for power but from surrendering to love, truth, and transformation.** Whether through mystical surrender, ethical action, or spiritual refinement, each echoes the Beatitude logic in its own idiom.

- **Gnosticism** reminds us that the kingdom is within, accessible through awakened consciousness
- **Sufism** invites us into broken-hearted love that becomes divine intimacy
- **Quakerism** teaches the power of quiet integrity lived out in social witness
- **Mormonism** lifts our eyes to eternal horizons where present choices shape cosmic destiny
- **Kabbalah** unveils the mystery of divine presence flowing through human humility
- **Baha'i** ties our personal transformation to the emergence of global peace and justice

What emerges is not theological uniformity but spiritual resonance—a recognition that the Beatitudes articulate something universally true about the human condition and divine response. They represent not just Christian teaching but a spiritual grammar that transcends religious boundaries while maintaining its particular power and beauty.

These traditions demonstrate that the paradoxical logic of the Beatitudes—finding strength in surrender, blessing in brokenness, kingdom in humility—speaks to something fundamental about spiritual reality itself. Whether framed as gnosis, fana, Inner Light, eternal progression, divine emanation, or global unity, the core insight remains: authentic spiritual life requires the dismantling of ego and the embrace of transformative love.

In our fragmented world, these convergent witnesses suggest that the Beatitudes offer more than historical curiosity or sectarian doctrine. They articulate a way of being that crosses boundaries, builds bridges, and points toward the possibility of human flourishing grounded not in domination but in the sacred vulnerability that opens us to divine blessing.

Earth and Spirit: Indigenous and African Wisdoms on the Beatitudes

The Beatitudes speak with startling clarity about inner posture—meekness, purity, mercy, peacemaking. While rooted in the teachings of Jesus, these virtues are not exclusive to Christianity. Many Indigenous and African spiritual traditions embody the same values, often with a stronger emphasis on community, land, and right relationship with all of creation.

This exploration reveals how the heart of the Beatitudes echoes through the wisdom of Indigenous peoples—from the Great Plains to the Amazon, from the San of southern Africa to the Yoruba of Nigeria. These aren't footnotes to world religion—they are profound and distinct worldviews that speak to the same human longings for peace, justice, and spiritual integrity. What emerges is not mere parallel but profound wisdom that often anticipates and exceeds modern ecological and relational ethics, revealing dimensions of the Beatitudes we might otherwise miss.

Holiness Rooted in the Land

In many Indigenous traditions, sacredness is not abstract—it's geographical. The land itself is imbued with spirit, story, and responsibility.[1] To be "pure in heart" isn't just to have clean intentions—it's to walk rightly in relationship with the land, ancestors, and community.

In Lakota spirituality, the principle of *Mitákuye Oyás'iŋ*—"all my relatives"—expresses radical interconnectedness with all beings.² Mercy, then, includes how we treat animals, plants, and ecosystems. To harm another is to harm oneself. A "peacemaker" in this context is one who restores balance—not just between people, but between all parts of creation.

The **Sun Dance** and **sweat lodge** ceremonies embody these principles in lived ritual.³ Participants enter these sacred spaces not for personal enlightenment alone but for the healing of the entire community and the renewal of right relationship with all life. The suffering undertaken in these ceremonies parallels the Beatitudes' recognition that righteousness sometimes comes at personal cost—but always serves the whole.

In the Andean traditions of South America, among the Quechua and Aymara peoples, *ayni* (sacred reciprocity) governs life.⁴ It's not a transaction but a mutual flow of giving, receiving, and returning—to the land, to others, to the spirit world. The **despacho** ceremonies, where offerings are made to Pachamama (Mother Earth), demonstrate this reciprocal relationship. It resonates deeply with the Beatitudes' call to mercy and meekness, but does so in a relational rather than legal or doctrinal framework.

African Spiritual Traditions: Right Relationship as Righteousness

In many African traditional religions, the equivalent of righteousness (*orun rere, ubuntu, ma'at*) is rooted in maintaining right relationship—with ancestors, with the divine, with neighbors.[5] These systems don't rely on scripture as much as story, ritual, and lived wisdom. But the moral architecture is strikingly aligned with the Beatitudes.

Among the **Yoruba**, the orisha Obatala is associated with peace, wisdom, and mercy.[6] Devotees seek to live in harmony and show compassion—especially through *iwa pele*, a gentle and balanced character. A meek person is not passive but steady and composed, avoiding rash action and promoting peace in the home and community. The annual festivals honoring Obatala become communal celebrations of these virtues, where the entire community participates in rituals of purification and peace.

In **Zulu** culture, the concept of *ubuntu*—"I am because we are"—captures a communal ethic that aligns with "Blessed are the merciful" and "Blessed are the peacemakers."[7] Mercy here isn't a private virtue but social glue. It insists on dignity for all, including the stranger and the enemy. Importantly, in African religious philosophy, transgressing harmony through greed, arrogance, or violence has communal, not just personal, consequences. Thus, restoration becomes a public, embodied act involving the entire community.

In ancient **Egyptian** spirituality, the concept of *ma'at* governed both moral and cosmic order.[8] To live in *ma'at* was to be in harmony with truth, justice, balance, and righteousness. The "pure in heart" were those who upheld *ma'at*, and their hearts were weighed against a feather in the afterlife—only those whose hearts were light with truth could pass into eternal life. The echo of "they shall see God" is palpable in this ancient wisdom.

The Role of Elders and Wisdom-Keepers

Unlike hierarchical religious structures, many Indigenous and African traditions preserve moral teachings through oral transmission—songs, proverbs, ritual dances, initiation rites.[9] Elders function as both memory and conscience for the community. Their lives embody the Beatitudes without necessarily naming them.

Consider the **Kalahari San**, whose trance dances aren't entertainment but healing rituals for the whole community.[10] The healer enters altered states not for personal enlightenment but for the restoration of others—echoing "Blessed are the merciful" in embodied form. These all-night ceremonies involve the entire community, with women singing healing songs while men dance around the fire until they achieve the healing trance that can draw illness from community members.

Among the **Navajo**, *Hózhó* (harmony, beauty, balance) isn't a goal but a daily discipline.[11] To live in *Hózhó* is to live in such a way that your very presence promotes peace. The elaborate **Blessing Way** ceremonies restore individuals and communities to this state of harmony, involving days of ritual, song, and communal participation. Sound familiar?

In many **Aboriginal Australian** traditions, the **Dreamtime** stories and **songlines** map both geographic and moral landscapes.[12] Elders who know these songs don't just preserve culture—they maintain the spiritual geography that keeps community and land in right relationship. Walking the songlines becomes a form of prayer that honors ancestors, tends the land, and maintains peace between peoples.

Ritual as Living Beatitude

These traditions offer something often missing from individual spiritual practice: they embed Beatitude virtues in communal ceremonies that create and sustain moral community.

Potlatch ceremonies among Pacific Northwest peoples demonstrate radical generosity—chiefs gain status not by accumulating wealth but by giving it away, echoing the "poor in spirit" who understand that true wealth flows through sharing, not hoarding.[13]

Yam festivals among West African peoples celebrate the first harvest with community-wide thanksgiving, where the bounty is shared with everyone, including strangers and enemies.[14] This embodies both mercy and peace-making in ritual form.

Talking circles and **council fire** practices provide structured ways for communities to address conflict, make decisions, and restore harmony through patient listening and consensus-building rather than domination or punishment.[15]

Comparing Wisdom Traditions

Beatitude	Indigenous/African Parallel	Embodied Example
Blessed are the meek	*Iwa pele, ubuntu, hózhó*	Leadership by elders; humility in ritual; consensus decision-making
Blessed are the merciful	*Ayni*, healing dance, honoring all life	Restorative ceremonies; communal care; inter-species respect
Blessed are the pure in heart	*Ma'at*, ritual purity, harmony with spirit and land	Heart-weighing judgment; daily disciplines; ceremonial purification
Blessed are the peacemakers	Elder mediation, consensus, storytelling resolutions	Conflict councils; reconciliatory rites; talking circles
Blessed are the persecuted	Cultural survival, ancestor veneration	Songlines preservation; ceremonies for resistance; honoring martyred ancestors

What Makes These Traditions Distinctive

While the Abrahamic traditions often ground virtue in covenant with God, Indigenous and African systems tend to root it in **relationship with all that is**—visible and invisible, living and ancestral, human and other-than-human.[16] The Beatitudes call us inward; these traditions call us both inward and outward, especially to land and community.

This doesn't diminish the Christian vision—it deepens it. What if "the kingdom of heaven" includes the wisdom of those who lived harmoniously with creation long before the term was coined? What if meekness means ecological humility? What if purity of heart includes decolonizing the soul from systems that separate us from our place in the web of life?

These traditions also reveal that many Indigenous wisdoms persist and adapt despite centuries of colonialism, modernity, and pressure to assimilate.[17] Contemporary Indigenous theologians like George Tinker and scholars like Vine Deloria Jr. continue to articulate how these ancient wisdoms offer vital insights for addressing modern crises of meaning, community, and environmental destruction.

A Leadership Note

In many of these traditions, true leaders aren't those with titles but those with wisdom. The elder who speaks least may hold the most influence. The healer doesn't dominate the room—they listen for what's unspoken. Leadership emerges through service, patience, and the ability to maintain harmony. Meekness and mercy are qualifications for leadership, not disqualifiers. This challenges modern assumptions about authority and success, suggesting that authentic power serves the whole rather than advancing the self.

Living This Wisdom Today

To integrate these earth-honoring insights into daily life:

Listen to the land: Treat nature not as scenery but as teacher. Walk gently. Pay attention to seasons, weather, the voices of more-than-human beings.

Honor the ancestors: Whether biological or spiritual, remember those who shaped you. Learn their stories. Carry forward their wisdom.

Value community over self: Ask regularly, "How does this decision affect the whole?" Consider seven generations when making choices.

Practice reciprocity: Give back wherever you receive—time, wisdom, resources. Understand yourself as part of ongoing cycles of exchange.

Be slow to judge: Elders don't rush to conclusion. Neither should we. Patient observation often reveals what quick judgment misses.

Heal in relationship: Don't pursue wholeness alone. Healing is communal work that involves the entire web of relationships.

Learn from conflict: See disagreement as opportunity for deeper understanding rather than battle to be won.

The Freedom of Earth-Based Wisdom

The Beatitudes are a spiritual map, but they don't require paved roads. They speak as clearly under a starlit sky or by a riverbank as they do from a pulpit. When we listen to the earth-honoring voices of Indigenous and African traditions, we discover something deeper: these values are not just moral—they're ecological, communal, embodied.

To be blessed is not to rise above—it is to live rightly within. It is to understand ourselves as part of the sacred web of relationships that includes all life. It is to recognize that our personal transformation serves not just individual salvation but the healing of the world.

These traditions suggest that what global Christianity—and perhaps all religious traditions—most needs to learn is not just comparison but genuine dialogue. What would it mean for contemporary spiritual seekers to learn from, not just about, these earth-rooted wisdoms? How might the Beatitudes themselves be deepened and expanded when viewed through the lens of traditions that never separated spirit from land, individual from community, or human from more-than-human creation?

The answer, these traditions suggest, lies not in abstract theology but in lived practice—in ceremonies that heal, stories that teach, and ways of life that honor the sacred in all its forms. The Beatitudes, seen through these eyes, become not just individual spiritual practices but invitations to participate in the ongoing work of maintaining harmony between earth and spirit, community and cosmos.

Echoes from the East: Confucian, Shinto, and Jain Wisdom in Light of the Beatitudes

The Beatitudes often feel like a uniquely Christian vision. But when we expand our gaze eastward—toward Confucian, Shinto, and Jain traditions—we discover surprising harmonies. These traditions don't always use the same metaphysical language or share the same view of God. Yet each offers profound insight into living with integrity, humility, and compassion—the very qualities the Beatitudes elevate.

This is not an effort to equate all religions. But it is a way of tracing humanity's shared moral imagination across diverse landscapes, where virtue is rooted in discipline, relationship, and respect for all life. The Beatitudes may use different symbols, but their music echoes in these Eastern traditions, often with emphases on practice over belief and community flourishing over individual reward.

Confucianism: Harmony Through Virtue

In Confucianism, the good life is about cultivating *de* (virtue) through ritual, respect, and relational responsibility.[1] *Ren* (humaneness or benevolence), not wealth or power, is the true measure of a noble person.

While Confucius does not speak in terms of "blessing" or divine grace, there is a Beatitude-like ethos in his vision of the *junzi*—the "noble person" who exemplifies humility, moral restraint, and care for others.[2] This mirrors the meek, the peacemakers, and those who hunger for righteousness.

One resonant passage comes from the *Analects*:

"The Master said: The noble person is not a vessel."[3]

In other words, we are not tools for status or function—we are moral beings shaped by inner discipline and social harmony. The *junzi* practices *shu* (reciprocity)—not returning harm for harm but responding with understanding and restraint.[4] This echoes the merciful who receive mercy.

The Confucian vision elevates forgiveness, patience, and compassion—virtues closely aligned with mercy and peacemaking. Confucian *li* (ritual propriety) creates communal spaces where these virtues are practiced collectively, much like how the Beatitudes envision transformed communities.[5] But instead of divine inheritance, Confucianism emphasizes harmonious relationships and a flourishing society as the fruit of virtue.

How it resonates: Confucian ethics are grounded not in the promise of divine reward but in the restoration of moral order (*li*) and harmony (*he*) through right relationship. Both traditions understand that personal virtue serves communal flourishing, though they differ on whether the ultimate horizon is the kingdom of heaven or social harmony.

Shinto: Purity, Reverence, and Living in Alignment

Shinto, the indigenous spirituality of Japan, is less focused on moral commandments than on *kami*—the divine forces in nature—and our harmonious relationship with them.[6] Central to Shinto practice is the pursuit of *makoto* (sincerity), *wa*(harmony), and *kegare* (purity from defilement).

While Shinto lacks an explicit set of Beatitude-like teachings, it cultivates many of the same dispositions: reverence, humility, purity of heart, and respect for life.[7] The ritual cleansing (*misogi*) recalls Jesus' emphasis on inner purity: "Blessed are the pure in heart, for they shall see God."

Shrines aren't just sacred spaces—they are ethical landscapes, reminding us that the spiritual and natural realms are intertwined.[8] Living rightly means living with gratitude, care, and sincerity—not for future reward, but because it honors the divine embedded in all things.

Regular participation in community festivals (*matsuri*) and purification rituals fosters a community-wide ethical orientation, similar to how the Beatitudes envision personal virtue contributing to collective transformation.[9] The respect for *kami* also extends to environmental ethics and care for the land, echoing both purity of heart and "peacemaking" as living in right relationship with nature.

How it resonates: Shinto's ethical orientation is more aesthetic and relational than rule-based. There's little concern with sin or salvation, but a deep attentiveness to presence, place, and sacred balance. Both traditions value purity and harmony, though Shinto grounds these in cosmic rather than covenantal relationships.

Jainism: Radical Nonviolence and the Path of Restraint

Jainism offers perhaps the most radical articulation of a Beatitude-like ethic in its commitment to *ahimsa* (nonviolence) toward all living beings.[10] This extends to thought, word, and deed. Jains strive for complete harmlessness—not only to humans, but to insects, plants, and even microorganisms.

This deep reverence for life echoes "Blessed are the merciful," but even more closely aligns with "Blessed are the pure in heart" and "Blessed are the peacemakers."[11] In Jain thought, peace is not a side effect of virtue—it *is* the virtue. The doctrine of *anekantavada* (the many-sidedness of truth) fosters intellectual humility and peaceful coexistence, paralleling the meekness that inherits the earth.[12]

Monastics take this to the extreme, wearing masks to avoid inhaling bugs and sweeping the ground as they walk. But even lay Jains are called to gentleness, honesty, and spiritual discipline through vows and meditation.[13] Jain compassion is not passive—it is enacted through daily disciplines and lifelong commitment to reducing harm.

Unlike Christianity, which emphasizes grace, Jainism is rigorously karmic: you reap precisely what you sow, and liberation (*moksha*) comes only through personal effort and purity.

How it resonates: Jainism does not rely on divine mercy or relationship with God. Instead, it teaches self-liberation through perfect nonviolence, self-restraint, and asceticism. Both traditions call for radical transformation of how we relate to others, though they differ on whether transformation comes through grace or disciplined effort.

Common Threads Across Eastern Wisdom

While each of these traditions is distinct, several shared themes resonate deeply with the Beatitudes, particularly in their emphasis on practice over doctrine and their vision of virtue serving communal harmony:

Beatitude Virtue	Confucianism	Shinto	Jainism
Humility/Meekness	Noble person (*junzi*) cultivates inner virtue and social harmony	Living with sincerity (*makoto*) and reverence for *kami*	Ego renunciation through restraint and *anekantavada*
Purity of Heart	Moral clarity through education, ritual, and character development	Ritual and spiritual cleanliness (*misogi*); aesthetic purification	Purity through nonviolence (*ahimsa*) and mental discipline
Hunger for Righteousness	Seeking moral order (*li*) and social justice through virtue	Living in alignment with *kami* and natural harmony	Lifelong ethical purification through vows and practice

Beatitude Virtue	Confucianism	Shinto	Jainism
Peacemaking	Social harmony (*he*) through ritual propriety and consensus	Reverent interdependence with all beings and nature	Active nonviolence and peaceful conduct toward all life
Mercy	Compassion (*ren*) and reciprocity (*shu*) within social relationships	Gratitude toward all beings and the *kami*	Universal compassion through deeds and self-discipline

Practice Over Belief: A Shared Eastern Emphasis

These Eastern traditions share a distinctive feature: they prioritize right action and habitual disposition over doctrinal belief.[14] In Confucianism, moral education through ritual practice shapes character. In Shinto, regular participation in purification and festival creates communal ethics. In Jainism, daily vows and disciplines gradually purify consciousness.

This practical orientation resonates with how the Beatitudes function as character-forming practices rather than abstract theological concepts. Both Eastern and Christian wisdom recognize that virtue must be embodied, practiced, and lived in community to become transformative.

Community and Individual in Balance

Another shared insight across these traditions is how individual virtue serves collective flourishing. Confucian self-cultivation aims at social harmony. Shinto personal purification contributes to communal and environmental well-being. Jain individual discipline reduces suffering for all beings.[15]

This mirrors the Beatitudes' vision where personal transformation (poverty of spirit, purity of heart) naturally flows into social engagement (peacemaking, mercy, hunger for justice). The narrow path of virtue, whether framed as the *junzi*, the ritually pure, or the perfectly nonviolent, ultimately serves the healing of the world.

Modern Resonance and Contemporary Practice

These ancient wisdoms animate contemporary movements in ways that parallel the Beatitudes' ongoing relevance. Confucian emphasis on moral education and social harmony influences peace education and conflict resolution in East Asian societies.[16] Shinto environmental ethics contribute to ecological preservation movements in Japan. Jain principles of nonviolence inspire contemporary animal rights activism and sustainable living practices.

Like the Beatitudes, these traditions offer not just historical wisdom but living practices that address modern crises of meaning, community, and environmental destruction.

A Theological Note

These Eastern paths are often less concerned with doctrine and more focused on practice. They do not always posit a personal God or heaven in the Christian sense. But they seek transformation—of self, society, and the world.

Where Christianity speaks of receiving the Kingdom through grace, these traditions teach alignment, purification, and harmony through disciplined living.[17] Yet all point toward what Jesus calls "the narrow way": a path of humility, compassion, and moral courage that requires both personal commitment and communal support.

However, it's important not to forcibly equate Christian and Eastern goals, as their metaphysical frameworks and salvation visions remain quite distinct—even as their ethical outcomes overlap significantly.

How This Expands Our Understanding

Engaging Confucianism, Shinto, and Jainism expands the moral range of the Beatitudes—not by diluting them, but by enriching them. We begin to see how these virtues are not just Christian ideals, but human ones. Not limited to creeds or churches, but embedded in how people across cultures imagine the good, the true, and the just.

Jesus' teaching remains distinct—especially in its theology of grace and divine promise. But when read alongside these Eastern traditions, the Beatitudes are not less Christian; they become more universally compelling. They articulate a way of being that crosses boundaries while maintaining their particular power to transform both heart and community.

The Beatitudes, seen through Eastern eyes, reveal themselves as part of humanity's shared moral imagination—a vision of human flourishing that transcends religious boundaries while honoring the distinctive wisdom each tradition offers. In our interconnected world, these convergent insights suggest that the path of humility, compassion, and peaceful integrity remains as vital today as it was two millennia ago, whether walked in first-century Galilee, ancient China, imperial Japan, or medieval India.

The Beatitudes Around the Global Church

The Beatitudes are often read through Western theological lenses—shaped by European scholarship, Enlightenment rationalism, and Protestant or Catholic traditions. But Christianity has always been broader, deeper, and more diverse than this. From the deserts of Egypt to the rainforests of the Amazon, from the streets of Seoul to the slums of Soweto, the followers of Jesus have heard and lived the Beatitudes in strikingly different ways.

This chapter explores how the Beatitudes have been received, interpreted, and embodied across the Global Church—particularly in Latin America, Africa, Asia, and the Middle East. In doing so, it expands our understanding of these blessings beyond Western individualism and spiritual abstraction, rooting them in stories of struggle, resilience, and communal transformation.

What emerges is not mere cultural variation but profound theological insight that challenges and enriches how we understand Jesus' words about blessing, poverty, mercy, and the kingdom of God.

Latin America: Liberation and the Cry of the Poor

In the 1960s and 70s, Catholic and Protestant theologians across Latin America began reading the Bible through the eyes of the poor. This movement, known as Liberation Theology, found in the Beatitudes a foundational text:

"Blessed are the poor..."—not only spiritually, but materially. The kingdom belongs to them.

For Gustavo Gutiérrez, the Peruvian priest often called the father of liberation theology, this was not about class envy or utopian politics—it was about God's preferential option for the poor.[1] The Beatitudes were not spiritual rewards for those who suffer, but calls to solidarity and structural change. In his groundbreaking work *A Theology of Liberation*, Gutiérrez argued that God's blessing of the poor was both spiritual reality and political imperative.

Leonardo Boff in Brazil developed this further, emphasizing how the Beatitudes call the church to embody God's liberation in concrete social action.[2] For Boff, "Blessed are those who hunger and thirst for righteousness" was not about individual piety but about collective action for justice.

Jon Sobrino, the Salvadoran Jesuit, brought another dimension through his theology of "the crucified peoples."[3] Sobrino's interpretation of "Blessed are those who mourn" extends beyond personal grief to encompass the collective lament of communities devastated by violence and oppression. His work on the spirituality of resurrection-hope shows how mourning becomes a form of resistance and the foundation for transformative action.

Christian base communities (*comunidades eclesiales de base*) across Brazil, Peru, and El Salvador studied the Sermon on the Mount not just as scripture, but as a manual for justice, resistance, and hope.[4] These small groups of laypeople gathered in homes, schools, and churches to reflect on how the Beatitudes applied to their daily struggles with poverty, land rights, and political repression.

Archbishop Oscar Romero, martyred in 1980, preached the Beatitudes weekly as he called out military violence and corporate exploitation.[5] His homilies connected "Blessed are the peacemakers" directly to the work of challenging structural violence, even when it brought persecution. Romero's witness showed how the final Beatitude—"Blessed are those persecuted for righteousness' sake"—was not theoretical but lived reality for those who took the others seriously.

In this context, the Beatitudes are not abstract ideals. They are urgent declarations—that God sees the poor, sides with the oppressed, and calls the church to join in the work of liberation.

Africa: Communal Wisdom and Embodied Blessing

Across the African continent, the Beatitudes have been interpreted through communitarian ethics, oral storytelling, and holistic spirituality. While interpretations vary widely across the continent's diverse traditions and languages, several themes emerge that challenge Western individualism.

Ubuntu Theology and Communal Blessing

In southern Africa, the philosophy of ubuntu—"I am because we are"—has profoundly shaped how Christians understand blessing.[6] Archbishop Desmond Tutu, drawing on this tradition, interpreted the Beatitudes not as individual virtues but as communal realities. For Tutu, to be "poor in spirit" means recognizing our fundamental interdependence, while the "peacemakers" are those who restore the community's wholeness.[7]

The post-apartheid Truth and Reconciliation Commission embodied this understanding practically. Rather than seeking retribution, the commission pursued the kind of healing justice that the Beatitudes envision—where mercy and truth meet, where mourning becomes the path to restoration.

African Independent Churches and Practical Blessing

In many African Independent Churches (AICs)—including the Aladura in Nigeria, Zionist churches in South Africa, and the Kimbanguist Church in Congo—the Beatitudes are enacted through healing, deliverance, and communal support.[8] These churches, which blend Christian faith with African spiritual practices, see the blessings not only as promises for the future, but as realities to be claimed in faith now.

The meek and merciful are often equated with elders and community healers who hold communities together with wisdom and restraint. The poor in spirit are not pitied but honored—for their humility, openness, and trust in God's provision.

Peacemaking is understood not as passive non-conflict but as courageous social work: restoring harmony after tribal tensions, mediating family disputes, and navigating justice with grace. In Rwanda, Christian communities drew heavily on "Blessed are the peacemakers" during the long process of post-genocide reconciliation, understanding that peace requires active work to rebuild trust and community.[9]

Women's Voices and Theological Innovation

African women theologians have brought unique perspectives to the Beatitudes. Mercy Amba Oduyoye from Ghana has written extensively on how "Blessed are those who mourn" speaks to women's experiences of loss—not just death, but the loss of children to poverty, migration, and conflict.[10] Her work shows how the promise of comfort becomes a call for community support and systemic change.

In many African contexts, women have taken the lead in embodying the Beatitudes practically—forming savings groups that reflect "Blessed are the merciful," creating networks of care that demonstrate ubuntu, and serving as peacemakers in communities torn by conflict.

Diversity Within Unity

It's important to note the theological diversity within African Christianity. Ethiopian Orthodox traditions read the Beatitudes liturgically, incorporating them into ancient chants and monastic practices that emphasize contemplative spirituality. Pentecostal movements across West Africa focus on the Beatitudes as promises of divine blessing and prosperity. Meanwhile, Anglican and Methodist churches often blend traditional African communalism with British theological frameworks.[11]

Despite this diversity, most African interpretations share an emphasis on community over individualism and practical application over abstract theology.

Asia: Suffering, Protest, and the People's Theology

Across Asia, where Christians are often minorities facing social, political, and economic marginalization, the Beatitudes have inspired movements of dignity, resistance, and interfaith dialogue.

Minjung Theology in Korea

In South Korea, the Beatitudes inspired Minjung Theology—a contextual theology rooted in the suffering of the *minjung*(the people or oppressed masses).[12] Emerging during military dictatorship and labor struggles in the 1970s, minjung theologians like Suh Nam-dong and Ahn Byung-mu read *"Blessed are those who mourn..."* as a word of empowerment to the grieving, the beaten-down, and the politically silenced.

This movement connected the Beatitudes to both the Exodus story and Korean folk traditions of resistance. For minjung theologians, Jesus' blessing of the poor was both theological statement and political manifesto—declaring that God's favor rests with factory workers, farmers, and students rather than with military dictators and corporate elites.

The democratization movement of the 1980s saw Korean Christians chanting the Beatitudes during protests, understanding "Blessed are those persecuted for righteousness' sake" as direct encouragement for their struggle against authoritarian rule.

Filipino People's Theology

In the Philippines, theologians like Carlos Abesamis have developed a "theology from below" that reads the Beatitudes through the lens of the *mga dukha* (the poor).[13] This approach blends Catholic liberation theology with indigenous Filipino concepts of *kapwa* (shared identity) and *bayanihan* (community spirit).

Filipino base communities interpret the Beatitudes as calls to:

- Serve the poor not with charity that maintains dependency, but with solidarity that builds dignity
- Mourn with communities displaced by global capitalism and environmental destruction
- Practice meekness not as weakness, but as the strength to resist both foreign domination and local corruption
- Embrace peacemaking in families, neighborhoods, and political systems corrupted by violence

Dalit Theology in India

In India, **Dalit Christian** theologians have found in the Beatitudes a powerful affirmation of dignity for those considered "untouchable" by traditional caste systems.[14] Theologians like Arvind Nirmal and V. Devasahayam read "Blessed are the poor in spirit" as God's preferential love for those whom society deems polluted or worthless.

The promise that the "meek will inherit the earth" takes on profound meaning for communities told they deserve nothing, while "Blessed are those who hunger and thirst for righteousness" becomes a cry for caste justice and social transformation.

Chinese House Church Spirituality

In China, where Christianity often exists in tension with state authority, house church Christians have embraced the Beatitudes as survival wisdom.[15] "Blessed are the persecuted" is not theoretical but describes their daily reality, while "Blessed are the peacemakers" guides their approach to government relations—seeking faithfulness without unnecessary confrontation.

Chinese Christians often emphasize the inner transformation aspects of the Beatitudes while finding ways to embody their social implications through quiet acts of service and community building.

Interfaith Context and Minority Witness

Across Asia, where Christians are minorities in predominantly Buddhist, Hindu, Muslim, or secular societies, the Beatitudes often function as **ethical distinctives**—ways of living humbly and faithfully amid religious pluralism and political tension.[16]

The blessing of the "pure in heart" resonates with Buddhist and Hindu concepts of spiritual clarity, creating opportunities for dialogue. "Blessed are the peacemakers" provides common ground with Islamic concepts of peace (*salam*) and Buddhist compassion (*karuna*). Yet the specifically Christian understanding of these virtues—grounded in God's kingdom and Jesus' example—maintains their distinctive witness.

Middle Eastern Christians: Between Cross and Crescent

In the very region where Jesus first spoke the Beatitudes, Middle Eastern Christians have continued to embody them under conditions of profound historical and contemporary hardship.

Ancient Wisdom and Contemporary Witness

Eastern Orthodox and Oriental Orthodox churches—including Greek, Russian, Coptic, Syrian, and Armenian traditions—have preserved ancient liturgical interpretations of the Beatitudes.[17] These churches incorporate the Beatitudes into their liturgies, where they are chanted as both doctrinal statements and communal prayers.

Ephrem the Syrian (4th century) wrote extensively on the Beatitudes, emphasizing their role in spiritual formation and community life.[18] His hymns and commentaries show how early Middle Eastern Christians understood the Beatitudes as a complete program for Christian living that encompassed both inner transformation and social responsibility.

Coptic Endurance and Martyrdom

Coptic Christians in Egypt have held tightly to *"Blessed are the persecuted"* through centuries of discrimination and periodic violence.[19] Their icons, chants, and liturgies have preserved a theology of quiet endurance—where blessing is not proof of safety, but of faithful witness.

The 2015 martyrdom of 21 Coptic Christians by ISIS in Libya brought global attention to this community's understanding of the Beatitudes. Their families' responses—emphasizing forgiveness rather than revenge—embodied "Blessed are the merciful" and "Blessed are the peacemakers" in ways that challenged both their persecutors and the watching world.

Palestinian Christian Witness

Palestinian Christians, living under military occupation, have found in the Beatitudes both comfort and challenge.[20] *"Blessed are those who hunger and thirst for righteousness..."* becomes a cry for justice amid displacement, land confiscation, and economic restriction.

Yet many Palestinian Christian leaders, like Mitri Raheb and Naim Ateek, have also emphasized "Blessed are the peacemakers," developing theologies of liberation that resist both occupation and the temptation toward violence. Their witness shows how the Beatitudes can sustain hope for justice while maintaining commitment to nonviolence.

Syrian and Iraqi Resilience

The recent conflicts in Syria and Iraq have devastated ancient Christian communities, yet survivors often speak of the Beatitudes as sources of strength. *"Blessed are those who mourn"* speaks to communities grieving massive losses, while the promise of comfort sustains hope for restoration.

Interfaith Peacemaking

Despite historic tensions, many Middle Eastern Christians have become bridges of compassion and understanding—refusing to return hatred for hatred. Organizations like the Cordoba Initiative and various interfaith dialogue groups draw on "Blessed are the peacemakers" to build relationships across religious divides.

Christian-run hospitals, schools, and social services throughout the Middle East embody the Beatitudes practically, serving people of all faiths and demonstrating the merciful love that Jesus blessed.

Global Voices: Women, Art, and Grassroots Movements

The Beatitudes' global reception includes voices often marginalized in traditional theological discourse.

Women's Theological Contributions

Women theologians across the Global South have brought unique perspectives to the Beatitudes:[21]

- Ivone Gebara in Brazil has written on how "Blessed are those who mourn" speaks to women's experiences of domestic violence and economic exploitation
- Mercy Amba Oduyoye in Ghana emphasizes the communal dimensions of blessing that challenge patriarchal individualism
- Virginia Fabella in the Philippines shows how the Beatitudes address both gender oppression and broader social injustice
- Hanan Ashrawi in Palestine demonstrates how Christian women can embody peacemaking in contexts of political conflict

Art, Music, and Popular Expression

The Beatitudes appear in global Christian art, music, and folk religious practice in ways that often capture their essence more powerfully than formal theology:

- Liberation hymnody in Latin America sets the Beatitudes to indigenous melodies and rhythms[22]
- African American spirituals have long connected the Beatitudes to experiences of slavery and struggle
- Asian Christian art often depicts the Beatitudes through local cultural symbols and stories
- Icon traditions in Eastern Christianity present the Beatitudes as windows into divine reality

Contemporary Grassroots Movements

Across the Global South, grassroots movements embody the Beatitudes in practical action:

- Base ecclesial communities in Latin America continue to study and live the Beatitudes as calls to justice
- The Green Belt Movement in Kenya, led by Wangari Maathai, embodied environmental stewardship as a form of peacemaking[23]
- Mothers of the Plaza de Mayo in Argentina demonstrated how mourning can become political resistance
- People Power movements in the Philippines showed how meekness and nonviolence can challenge authoritarian rule

Comparing Global Visions

The diverse global reception of the Beatitudes reveals both unity and variation in Christian understanding:

Region	Primary Beatitude Emphases	Context/Distinctives
Latin America	Poor in spirit, mourn, hunger for righteousness	Liberation theology, option for the poor, structural analysis
Africa	Meek, merciful, peacemakers	Communal ethics, ubuntu, healing practices, post-conflict reconciliation
Asia	Mourn, persecution, meek	Minjung theology, minority witness, interfaith dialogue, resistance to authoritarianism
Middle East	Hunger for righteousness, peacemakers, persecution	Ancient liturgical traditions, survival under persecution, interfaith bridge-building

One Gospel, Many Voices

The global expressions of the Beatitudes reveal something profound: they are **not owned by any culture**, and **not exhausted by any one reading**.

- For some, they are spiritual truths for inner transformation
- For others, they are calls to protest and political change
- For still others, they are communal ethics for resilience and reconciliation
- And often—they are all of these at once

Hearing these diverse voices expands our understanding of the Beatitudes not as tidy statements of virtue, but as **living words**, adaptable and enduring across time, class, ethnicity, and geography.

They speak to peasants and professors. Monastics and mothers. Migrants and ministers. Factory workers and theologians. Political prisoners and church leaders.

They are as much a call to *lament* as to *action*, to *compassion* as to *resistance*, to *contemplation* as to *engagement*.

Learning from the Margins

This global survey reveals that some of the richest interpretations of the Beatitudes have emerged from Christianity's margins—from communities facing poverty, persecution, and political powerlessness. These contexts strip away the luxury of purely academic interpretation and demand that the Beatitudes prove their relevance to real human suffering and hope.

The result is often theology that is both more biblical and more practical than what emerges from comfortable academic settings. When the poor interpret "Blessed are the poor," when the persecuted read "Blessed are the persecuted," when peacemakers in conflict zones embrace "Blessed are the peacemakers," the Beatitudes regain their original power as both comfort and challenge.

The Continuing Evolution

This global reception of the Beatitudes is not a finished story. As Christianity continues to shift toward the Global South, as new movements emerge, as contexts change, we can expect new interpretations and applications to develop.[24]

Young theologians in Africa are developing eco-theological readings of the Beatitudes. Asian Christian feminists are exploring how the Beatitudes address gender violence. Latin American indigenous Christians are connecting the Beatitudes to creation spirituality. Middle Eastern Christians are pioneering new forms of interfaith dialogue grounded in Beatitude values.

The Beatitudes remain living words, capable of speaking fresh truth to each generation and context while maintaining their essential challenge to personal transformation and social justice.

The Universal Particular

The global church's diverse reception of the Beatitudes demonstrates a remarkable paradox: these ancient words are both deeply particular to specific contexts and genuinely universal in their appeal. They speak with fresh relevance to Korean factory workers and Coptic martyrs, to Brazilian base communities and Filipino farmers, to South African township dwellers and Palestinian refugees.

This is not cultural relativism but recognition that the Gospel itself is both contextual and universal—addressing real people in real situations while proclaiming truths that transcend any single culture or time.

The Western church has much to learn from these global voices. They remind us that the Beatitudes were never meant to be privately spiritual or abstractly theological but publicly engaged and practically transformative. They show us dimensions of blessing, poverty, mercy, and peace that comfortable Western Christianity often misses.

Most importantly, they demonstrate that the Beatitudes are not museum pieces to be studied but living words to be embodied—by communities of faith seeking to live as citizens of God's kingdom in every corner of the world.

Part IV

History and Interpretation

Makarioi: The Greek Roots of the Beatitudes

"Blessed are the poor in spirit, for theirs is the kingdom of heaven."
—Matthew 5:3

Translation is never neutral. Every word carries choices—and every choice carries meaning. In this chapter, we return to the original Greek of the Beatitudes in Matthew 5:3-12, not to nitpick grammar, but to uncover the deeper texture of Jesus' words and explore how translation decisions have shaped centuries of interpretation.

These blessings were not whispered in a vacuum. They were spoken in a charged cultural, religious, and linguistic context—shaped by both Hebrew wisdom and Greco-Roman rhetoric. The Greek language of Matthew preserves that context in ways our English versions often obscure, while also revealing the theological and pastoral choices that translators have made across the centuries.

Let's walk through each Beatitude, focusing on key Greek terms, their possible Hebrew or Aramaic substrates, and what they suggest—or resist—in translation.

The Foundation: Makarioi

Before examining individual Beatitudes, we must understand the foundational term that begins each blessing: *makarioi*(μακάριοι).[1] Traditionally translated "blessed," this word doesn't imply a moral reward or divine transaction earned through behavior. It's closer to *flourishing, fortunate,* or *deeply satisfied*—describing a state of well-being rather than a religious status.

The term echoes the Hebrew *ashrei* (אַשְׁרֵי) from Psalm 1 and throughout the Psalter—not a legal designation, but a description of the genuinely happy life.[2] This distinction has profound implications: the Beatitudes are not promises contingent on performance but recognitions of where true flourishing is already found, even when the world sees only poverty, mourning, or persecution.

The translation choice between "blessed," "happy," and "flourishing" reflects different theological emphases that have shaped Christian interpretation for centuries.[3] "Blessed" suggests divine favor, "happy" implies emotional satisfaction, while "flourishing" points toward comprehensive well-being that encompasses but transcends both.

1. "Blessed are the poor in spirit..."

Greek: *Makarioi hoi ptōchoi tō pneumati, hoti autōn estin hē basileia tōn ouranōn.*

Ptōchoi (πτωχοί): Not just the "poor," but the *absolutely destitute*—those who have nothing and must beg for survival.⁴ The term comes from *ptōssō*, meaning "to crouch" or "cower," suggesting people who literally bow down to ask for help. In other Gospel contexts (especially Luke), this clearly refers to material poverty. But Matthew adds the crucial qualifier...

Tō pneumati (τῷ πνεύματι): "in spirit." This dative of respect has generated centuries of interpretive debate.⁵ Is Matthew spiritualizing poverty to make it more palatable to his audience? Or is he clarifying the kind of poverty—spiritual destitution and recognition of one's need for God—that opens the heart to divine grace? Most contemporary scholars favor the latter interpretation: this is about *inner posture*—recognizing one's emptiness and complete dependence on God.

The Hebrew/Aramaic background likely draws from the tradition of the *anawim* (עֲנָוִים)—the humble poor who combined material need with spiritual dependence on God.⁶ These were people who had learned that human resources are insufficient and that true security comes only from divine mercy.

2. "Blessed are those who mourn..."

Greek: *Makarioi hoi penthountes, hoti autoi paraklēthēsontai.*

Penthountes (πενθοῦντες): A strong word for grief, typically used for mourning the dead.⁷ This isn't general sadness or mild disappointment—it's deep, soul-shaking lament. The present participle suggests ongoing mourning, not just momentary sorrow. In the Septuagint, this term often translates Hebrew words for ritual mourning and prophetic lamentation over sin and injustice.

The mourning likely encompasses multiple dimensions: grief over personal sin, sorrow for others' suffering, and lament over the world's brokenness.[8] The prophetic tradition of Israel provides the background—those who "sigh and groan over all the abominations" (Ezekiel 9:4) are marked for divine protection.

Paraklēthēsontai (παρακληθήσονται): "They will be comforted." The root *parakaleō* means not just emotional comfort, but *to be called alongside*—to receive the presence and support of another.[9] The word shares its root with *Paraklētos*, the Comforter or Advocate, referring to the Holy Spirit in John's Gospel (14:16, 26; 15:26; 16:7).

This blessing promises not just the cessation of grief, but the *presence* of God in the midst of loss—divine companionship that transforms suffering without necessarily removing it.

3. "Blessed are the meek..."

Greek: *Makarioi hoi praeis, hoti autoi klēronomēsousin tēn gēn.*

Praeis (πραεῖς): Often rendered "meek," but this translation is deeply misleading in contemporary English.[10] The term connotes *gentle strength* or *power under control*. Aristotle used it in his *Nicomachean Ethics* to describe the virtue between the extremes of being overly angry and never being angry—

someone who is angry at the right time, in the right way, for the right reasons, and never ruled by anger.

In biblical usage, it describes those who are powerful but restrained—like Moses, called "very meek (*anav*) above all people who were on the face of the earth" (Numbers 12:3).[11] Moses was hardly a passive figure; he confronted Pharaoh, led a nation, and challenged rebellion. His "meekness" was strength disciplined by humility and trust in God.

Klēronomēsousin (κληρονομήσουσιν): "They will inherit"—a verb deeply tied to covenantal land promises in the Hebrew Bible.[12] The allusion to Psalm 37:11 ("the meek shall inherit the land") would have been unmistakable to Matthew's Jewish audience. This is not about passivity receiving reward, but about the patient faithfulness that ultimately endures when aggressive power exhausts itself.

This is not weakness but the quiet power of those who do not grasp—and so receive what cannot be seized by force.

4. "Blessed are those who hunger and thirst for righteousness..."

Greek: *Makarioi hoi peinōntes kai dipsōntes tēn dikaiosynēn, hoti autoi chortasthēsontai.*

Peinōntes kai dipsōntes (πεινῶντες καὶ διψῶντες): Strong, visceral verbs for hunger and thirst—this is *craving, yearning*, not mild interest or casual desire.[13] The present participles suggest ongoing, persistent longing. This echoes the Psalmic tradition of thirsting for God (Psalms 42:1-2; 63:1) and the prophetic call to "seek the Lord while he may be found" (Isaiah 55:6).

Dikaiosynē (δικαιοσύνη): Perhaps the most theologically freighted term in the Beatitudes.[14] Traditionally translated "righteousness," but the Greek encompasses both personal virtue and social *justice*. In the Septuagint, it often translates Hebrew *tzedakah* (צְדָקָה), which includes legal justice, ethical behavior, and covenantal faithfulness. The term includes both being right with God and making things right in the world.

Different Christian traditions have emphasized different aspects of this rich term: Protestant traditions often stress personal righteousness before God, while Catholic and Orthodox traditions have maintained stronger emphasis on social justice dimensions.[15]

Chortasthēsontai (χορτασθήσονται): "They will be filled"—literally, satisfied like animals after feeding.[16] It's a surprisingly earthy verb for spiritual satisfaction, suggesting that God's response to spiritual hunger is not ethereal but abundantly material—a feast rather than a snack.

This Beatitude speaks of an aching soul and promises God's abundance in response to holy dissatisfaction with injustice and spiritual mediocrity.

5. "Blessed are the merciful..."

Greek: *Makarioi hoi eleēmones, hoti autoi eleēthēsontai.*

Eleēmones (ἐλεήμονες): "The merciful." Not merely those who feel compassion, but those who act on it.[17] The term implies extending forgiveness, aid, and solidarity to others—especially the undeserving or vulnerable. In Jewish tradition, this echoes God's *chesed* (חֶסֶד)—steadfast, loyal love that maintains covenant relationship even when the other party fails.

Eleēthēsontai (ἐλεηθήσονται): "They will receive mercy." The verbal form mirrors the adjective, creating a rhythmic reciprocity of giving and receiving.[18] This isn't mechanical cause-and-effect but recognition of spiritual coherence: mercy opens the heart to receive mercy, while unmerciful hearts close themselves to grace.

In this Beatitude, Jesus affirms a core biblical principle: the merciful heart becomes the vessel through which God's mercy flows both outward to others and inward to oneself.

6. "Blessed are the pure in heart..."

Greek: *Makarioi hoi katharoi tē kardia, hoti autoi ton Theon opsontai.*

Katharoi (καθαροί): "Pure"—from which we get "catharsis."[19] The term can mean physically clean, ritually pure, or morally clear. In this context, it likely means *undivided* or *single-minded*. Classical usage often referred to ritual or moral purity, but here it suggests *integrity* and *clarity of intention*—a heart not pulled in competing directions by conflicting loyalties.

Tē kardia (τῇ καρδίᾳ): "In heart." In Hebrew and Greek thought, the heart (*lev* in Hebrew, *kardia* in Greek) is not primarily the seat of emotion but the center of thought, will, and moral choice.[20] A pure heart is not naive or sentimental—it is *undivided*, wholly oriented toward God without the internal fragmentation that comes from mixed motives.

Ton Theon opsontai (τὸν Θεὸν ὄψονται): "They will see God." A striking promise that echoes the theophanies of Moses (Exodus 33:18-23) and the Psalmic tradition: *"Who shall ascend the hill of the Lord? And who shall stand in his holy place? Those who have clean hands and a pure heart"* (Psalm 24:3-4).[21]

This promise of vision is not limited to eschatological fulfillment but includes present spiritual perception—the ability to recognize God's presence and activity in the world. The pure in heart see clearly because they are not looking through the fog of divided loyalties and hidden agendas.

7. "Blessed are the peacemakers..."

Greek: *Makarioi hoi eirēnopoioi, hoti huioi Theou klēthēsontai.*

Eirēnopoioi (εἰρηνοποιοί): "Peacemakers." This is a remarkably rare Greek word, found nowhere else in the New Testament and rarely in classical literature.[22] It denotes not peaceful people or those who love peace, but those who actively *make peace*—who reconcile, heal divisions, and build wholeness where there was brokenness.

The Hebrew concept of *shalom* (שָׁלוֹם) lies behind this term—not merely the absence of conflict but the presence of right relationship, justice, and flourishing.[23] Peacemaking in biblical terms often requires confronting injustice rather than simply maintaining calm.

Huioi Theou (υἱοὶ Θεοῦ): "Sons of God," or more inclusively, "children of God." In biblical idiom, to be called someone's child is to *share their character*.[24] Thus, peacemakers resemble the God of peace—they participate in divine nature by doing divine work.

This Beatitude affirms reconciliation as fundamentally divine activity—and those who engage in it as God's own family members.

8. "Blessed are those who are persecuted for righteousness' sake..."

Greek: *Makarioi hoi dediōgmenoi heneken dikaiosynēs, hoti autōn estin hē basileia tōn ouranōn.*

Dediōgmenoi (δεδιωγμένοι): A perfect passive participle—"those who have been and continue to be persecuted."[25] The perfect tense suggests ongoing effects of past persecution, while the passive voice indicates that the persecution comes from external forces rather than self-inflicted suffering.

Heneken dikaiosynēs (ἕνεκεν δικαιοσύνης): "Because of righteousness"—again that rich word *dikaiosynē*, encompassing both personal integrity and social justice. The persecution comes not because these people are obnoxious or confrontational, but because their way of life challenges systems that benefit from injustice.

This Beatitude returns to the promise of the first: the poor in spirit and the persecuted both "possess the kingdom." This creates an *inclusio*—a literary bracket that frames the entire series, emphasizing that God's reign belongs to those whom the world excludes or oppresses.[26]

9. "Blessed are you when people insult you..."

Greek: *Makarioi este hotan oneidisōsin humas kai diōxōsin kai eipōsin pan ponēron kath' humōn pseudomenoi heneken emou.*

This final blessing shifts dramatically from **third person** ("they") to **second person** ("you"), making the teaching suddenly personal and direct.[27] The shift signals a movement from general principle to direct application—from describing the kingdom's citizens to addressing Jesus' actual followers.

Oneidisōsin (ὀνειδίσωσιν): "They insult or revile you"—public shame and verbal attack.

Diōxōsin (διώξωσιν): "They persecute you"—active pursuit and harassment.

Eipōsin pan ponēron (εἴπωσιν πᾶν πονηρὸν): "They say all kinds of evil against you"—slander and character assassination.

Pseudomenoi (ψευδόμενοι): "Falsely"—the accusations are lies, not legitimate criticism.

Heneken emou (ἕνεκεν ἐμοῦ): "Because of me"—the persecution comes specifically because of allegiance to Jesus, not because of the disciples' own failings or provocative behavior.[28]

This personal address acknowledges that following Jesus brings specific opposition. The blessing extends not to all suffering, but to suffering that results from faithful discipleship.

Hebrew and Aramaic Background

While we have the Beatitudes in Greek, Jesus likely spoke them in Aramaic, with possible Hebrew liturgical influences.[29] The *ashrei* formula from the Psalms provides the clear background for *makarioi*, while concepts like *anawim* (humble poor), *tzedakah* (righteousness/justice), and *shalom* (peace/wholeness) deeply inform the vocabulary choices.

Some scholars have attempted to reconstruct possible Aramaic originals, though this remains speculative.[30] What is clear is that the Greek text preserves Semitic thought patterns and theological concepts that would have been familiar to Jesus' Jewish audience while also making them accessible to Greek-speaking Christians.

Translation Traditions and Reception History

The translation of key terms has significantly shaped Christian interpretation across traditions:

- **Dikaiosynē**: Protestant traditions have often emphasized "righteousness" as right standing before God, while Catholic and Orthodox traditions have maintained stronger emphasis on justice and good works.[31]
- **Makarioi**: Early translations favored "blessed" (Latin *beati*), emphasizing divine favor. Modern translations increasingly use "happy" or "flourishing" to capture the holistic well-being the term suggests.[32]
- **Ptōchoi tō pneumati**: Debates over whether this "spiritualizes" poverty or describes a particular type of poverty have shaped how different traditions approach social justice and spiritual formation.[33]

These translation choices reflect not just linguistic preferences but theological commitments about the relationship between faith and works, individual piety and social justice, present experience and future hope.

Septuagint and Second Temple Parallels

The Septuagint provides crucial background for understanding how Greek terms were used to translate Hebrew concepts.[34] The Qumran texts offer additional parallels, including "blessing" formulas that share structural similarities with the Beatitudes (see 4Q525, 4Q185). These texts help situate the Beatitudes within broader Second Temple Jewish traditions of wisdom and apocalyptic expectation.

The Dead Sea Scrolls particularly illuminate the background of terms like "poor in spirit" (*anawim*) and "pure in heart," showing how these concepts functioned in Jewish sectarian communities that emphasized both social justice and ritual purity.[35]

The Beatitudes in Their Original Tongue

The Greek text of the Beatitudes opens deeper understanding of Jesus' words by revealing:

- Makarioi describes present flourishing, not future reward conditional on behavior
- The blessings encompass both present realities and future consummations—they describe where true happiness is found now while promising ultimate fulfillment
- Terms like *praeis*, *dikaiosynē*, and *katharoi tē kardia* carry richer semantic ranges than single English words can capture
- The shift from third to second person in the final blessing personalizes the entire series for Jesus' followers

Through the poetry of the Greek, we hear echoes of Hebrew prophecy, Greco-Roman moral discourse, and the uniquely disruptive voice of Jesus. These are not passive virtues but active postures—ways of engaging the world that both reflect and participate in God's reign.

The linguistic analysis reminds us that the Beatitudes are not commandments to fulfill but a vision of who we are and who we are becoming in the light of the kingdom. They describe not achievements to be earned but gifts to be received—and in receiving them, to embody them for the healing of the world.

Understanding the Greek doesn't diminish the mystery of these ancient words but deepens it, showing how translation is always interpretation and how every generation must wrestle anew with what it means to live as citizens of the kingdom that Jesus proclaimed.

Two Visions of Blessing: Comparing Matthew and Luke's Beatitudes

The Beatitudes are best known from the Gospel of Matthew, where they form the opening of the Sermon on the Mount. But Matthew is not the only evangelist to preserve this remarkable teaching. The Gospel of Luke offers a parallel—and in many ways more provocative—version in what is often called the "Sermon on the Plain."

Both texts begin with Jesus looking at his disciples and pronouncing blessing. But from there, they diverge in tone, structure, and theological emphasis. Understanding these differences reveals not contradictions but complementary visions: two voices singing in harmony but not unison, each addressing different aspects of what it means to live as citizens of God's kingdom.

In a world that needs both inner transformation and outer justice, these twin accounts suggest we are not meant to choose between spiritual formation and social action. Perhaps we are meant to live them both.

Setting the Scene: Mountain vs. Plain

The physical settings already hint at the theological differences to come:

Matthew 5:1-12: Jesus "went up the mountain" and taught the crowds from this elevated position.[1] This deliberately evokes Moses receiving the Law on Mount Sinai, positioning Jesus as a new lawgiver who fulfills rather than abolishes the Torah. The mountain setting emphasizes continuity with Jewish tradition and the transcendent nature of the teaching—a lofty, theological perspective that lifts the mind toward eternal truths.

Luke 6:17-26: Jesus "came down with them and stood on a level place" (ἐπὶ τόπου πεδινοῦ).[2] The setting is intentionally egalitarian, almost democratically so. Luke emphasizes that Jesus positions himself among the people—"a great crowd of his disciples and a great multitude of people from all Judea, Jerusalem, and the coast of Tyre and Sidon." This grounded setting signals Luke's concern with embodied social realities rather than abstract spiritual principles.

Some scholars note that this contrast may be more literary and theological than strictly topographical—both evangelists shape their geographical details to serve their larger narrative purposes.[3] Matthew's "mountain" functions as a recurring motif for divine revelation throughout his Gospel, while Luke's "plain" reinforces his consistent portrayal of Jesus as the friend of ordinary people.

Structure: Eight Blessings vs. Four Blessings + Four Woes

The structural differences reveal each Gospel's distinct emphases:

Matthew 5:3-12	Luke 6:20-26
8 (or 9) blessings (*makarioi*)	4 blessings (*makarioi*) + 4 woes (*ouai*)
No warnings or woes	"But woe to you..." balances each blessing
Spiritual focus ("poor in spirit")	Material focus ("you who are poor")
Third person ("those who...")	Direct address ("you who are...")
Ends with blessing for persecution	Ends with warning about popularity

Luke's symmetrical structure—blessings paired with corresponding woes—follows the classic prophetic pattern found throughout Hebrew Scripture (cf. Isaiah 5, Amos 6:1).[4] This reinforces that Jesus stands in the tradition of the Hebrew prophets, offering not just comfort but critique. The woes aren't afterthoughts but integral to Luke's understanding that the kingdom of God involves reversal of current power structures.

Matthew's structure may reflect a chiastic literary design, with the eight beatitudes forming an inclusio that brackets the larger Sermon on the Mount.[5] This suggests a more systematic theological presentation, fitting Matthew's concern with Jesus as teacher and interpreter of divine law.

Key Textual Differences: What Do They Reveal?

"Poor" vs. "Poor in Spirit"

This represents the most significant interpretive divide:

- **Matthew:** *Blessed are the poor in spirit* (οἱ πτωχοὶ τῷ πνεύματι)

- **Luke**: *Blessed are you who are poor* (οἱ πτωχοί)

The phrase "poor in spirit" appears to be Matthew's theological expansion of an originally simpler saying.[6] Most Q source reconstructions suggest the earliest version likely read "Blessed are the poor," which Matthew adapted for his audience's spiritual concerns while Luke preserved more literally.

Matthew's "spiritualization" isn't necessarily a dilution—it connects poverty to humility and openness to God, aligning with Hebrew traditions that honor the *anawim* (humble poor) who depend entirely on divine mercy.[7] Luke's version maintains the stark economic reality, fitting his Gospel's broader emphasis on wealth redistribution and justice for the marginalized (cf. Luke 1:53, 4:18-19, 16:19-31).

"Hunger and Thirst for Righteousness" vs. "Hungry Now"

The differences continue:

- **Matthew**: *Those who hunger and thirst for righteousness*
- **Luke**: *Blessed are you who are hungry now*

Matthew's *dikaiosynē* (righteousness) is rich with meaning—it can signify personal virtue, social justice, or covenantal faithfulness, but it clearly points beyond physical need to spiritual longing.[8] Luke again keeps the focus concrete and immediate: he blesses the materially hungry and, in his corresponding woe, condemns those who are currently well-fed.

This difference reflects each Gospel's understanding of how the kingdom addresses human need. Matthew emphasizes ethical transformation; Luke emphasizes economic reversal.

The Woes: Luke's Prophetic Balance

Luke's four woes mirror his four blessings, creating a structure reminiscent of Deuteronomic blessings and curses:[9]

1. "Woe to you who are rich, for you have received your consolation"
2. "Woe to you who are full now, for you will be hungry"
3. "Woe to you who are laughing now, for you will mourn and weep"
4. "Woe to you when all speak well of you, for that is what their ancestors did to the false prophets"

These woes echo the Hebrew prophets' practice of naming not only the blessed but the deluded—those whose comfort blinds them to God's preferred future.[10] The absence of these woes in Matthew doesn't indicate theological disagreement but different pastoral emphases. Matthew reserves his sharpest critiques for religious hypocrisy later in his Gospel, while Luke integrates social critique directly into the Beatitudes themselves.

Theological Emphases: Two Lenses on the Same Kingdom

The differences between Matthew and Luke reflect distinct but complementary theological perspectives:

Matthew's Lens	Luke's Lens
Discipleship as inner formation	Discipleship as social reversal
Spiritual hunger and righteousness	Economic justice and equity
Jesus as new Moses	Jesus as prophetic challenger
Emphasis on Torah fulfillment	Emphasis on prophetic urgency
Comfort to the humble and persecuted	Warning to comfortable and powerful

Audience and Context

These differences likely reflect the distinct early Christian communities each evangelist addressed:

Matthew probably wrote for primarily Jewish-Christian readers concerned with how Jesus' teaching related to Torah and traditional spiritual formation.[11] His version emphasizes continuity with Jewish wisdom while showing how Jesus' interpretation transcends that of contemporary religious leaders.

Luke likely addressed a mixed or Gentile-Christian audience in urban settings, emphasizing social ethics and the inclusion of outsiders.[12] His version makes Jesus' message immediately relevant to questions of wealth, poverty, and social justice that would concern Greco-Roman converts.

Both audiences needed to hear about God's kingdom, but each required different emphasis: Matthew shows what the kingdom looks like in the soul; Luke shows what it means for society.

Historical Development and Source Criticism

Modern scholarship suggests both Gospels draw from an earlier sayings source (often called Q), with each evangelist adapting this material for theological and pastoral purposes.[13] The differences aren't corruptions of an original text but faithful interpretations of Jesus' teaching for different contexts.

Some scholars (following Crossan and Borg) argue that Luke's more concrete version likely stands closer to the historical Jesus, who addressed real economic conditions in first-century Palestine.[14] Others (following Davies and Allison) suggest that Jesus' teaching always included both spiritual and material dimensions, with each Gospel emphasizing different aspects of this unified vision.[15]

The form-critical background reveals that *makarisms* (blessing formulas) were common in Second Temple Judaism, appearing throughout the Psalms and in texts from Qumran.[16] Both evangelists work within established Jewish literary traditions while adapting them to proclaim Jesus' distinctive message.

Reception History: From Spirituality to Social Justice

The reception of these twin versions reveals how different Christian communities have emphasized different aspects of Jesus' teaching:

Patristic and Medieval Commentary: Matthew's version dominated Western spiritual formation, with church fathers like Augustine and Chrysostom developing elaborate interpretations of the "spiritual" beatitudes.[17] Monastic traditions built their formation programs around Matthew's emphasis on inner virtue.

Modern Social Justice Movements: Luke's version has gained prominence in liberation theology, Catholic social teaching, and contemporary movements for economic justice.[18] The preferential option for the poor draws heavily on Luke's stark economic language.

Contemporary Integration: Modern scholars increasingly recognize that both versions are needed for complete Christian discipleship.[19] The spiritual formation emphasized by Matthew requires the social engagement demanded by Luke, and vice versa.

Living Both Visions Today

Rather than choosing between Matthew's spiritual focus and Luke's social emphasis, contemporary readers might ask: How do we cultivate both the inner transformation that Matthew celebrates and the social commitment that Luke demands?

The Poor in Spirit Who Are Actually Poor: Many of those whom Matthew calls "poor in spirit"—the humble, the teachable, the spiritually hungry—are also materially poor. Both versions speak to their condition, promising both divine comfort and social reversal.

Inner Change and Outer Action: Authentic spiritual formation (Matthew's concern) naturally leads to social engagement (Luke's emphasis). Those who truly hunger and thirst for righteousness cannot remain indifferent to injustice.

Personal Virtue and Systemic Change: The character transformation that Matthew describes creates people capable of the social transformation that Luke envisions. Pure hearts see clearly enough to work for justice; peacemakers address both personal conflict and structural violence.

A Polyphonic Gospel

These aren't competing versions but complementary voices in what we might call a "polyphonic Gospel"—multiple melodies that create richer harmony together than either achieves alone. In our complex world, we need both:

- The spiritual depth that sustains long-term commitment to justice
- The social analysis that prevents spirituality from becoming escapism
- The inner transformation that changes how we see others
- The structural change that addresses root causes of suffering
- The comfort that healing is possible
- The challenge that comfortable assumptions must be questioned

The early Christian movement preserved both versions not as an oversight but as wisdom. They recognized that the kingdom of God requires both changed hearts and changed systems, both personal virtue and social justice, both receiving divine comfort and working for human dignity.

In reading Matthew and Luke together, we discover that the question isn't which version is "correct" but how we can live both faithfully—receiving the kingdom as gift while working to make it visible in our world.

Blessing and Woe: The Ethical Tension at the Heart of the Gospel

"Blessed are you who are poor... Woe to you who are rich."
--- Luke 6:20, 24

The Beatitudes are often framed as words of comfort—and they are. But in Luke's Gospel, they come with a sharp edge: the blessings are followed by woes. To the poor, hungry, grieving, and hated, Jesus offers divine affirmation. To the rich, satisfied, laughing, and praised, he offers warning.

This balance of blessing and woe is not unique to Luke. It echoes a deep biblical tradition that holds grace and judgment, hope and truth-telling, in tension. And even for readers primarily rooted in Matthew's version of the Beatitudes, it offers a vital lens: one that sharpens ethical vision and deepens spiritual honesty.

Understanding this tension requires grasping that for Luke, these are not abstract spiritual categories but concrete social and economic realities that demand response.

Luke's Structure: A Blunt Reversal

Luke 6:20-26 lays out four blessings—and then mirrors them with four woes in stark, uncompromising language:[1]

Blessed Are You...	But Woe to You...
who are poor	who are rich
who hunger now	who are full now
who weep now	who laugh now
when people hate you	when all speak well of you

Unlike Matthew, Luke does not qualify these materially focused blessings (*"in spirit"*, *"hunger and thirst for righteousness"*). The contrast is **unflinching**—those who suffer now are blessed; those who are secure now are warned.

Material Reality, Not Metaphor

Recent social-science commentaries emphasize that for Luke, "poor" and "rich" are not simply spiritual metaphors.[2] Throughout his Gospel, Luke demonstrates persistent concern with actual economic stratification and material reversal. Mary's Magnificat declares that God "has filled the hungry with good things, and sent the rich away empty" (Luke 1:53). The parable of the Rich Man and Lazarus (Luke 16:19-31) reinforces this same pattern of reversal based on material conditions and social responsibility.[3]

Luke's Jesus addresses real people in real economic circumstances, calling the wealthy to account for their use of resources and promising vindication to those crushed by unjust systems. This is not spiritualized poverty but recognition that economic structures can either reflect or contradict God's justice.

Jewish and Greco-Roman Background: A Universal Form

The pairing of blessings and woes (*macarisms* and woes) was common in both Jewish wisdom literature and Greco-Roman rhetorical training, giving Jesus' words familiar yet subversive power.[4]

Hebrew Prophetic Tradition

In Jewish literature, blessing and curse formulas appear throughout wisdom and prophetic writings. The structure itself signals covenantal relationship—God's people receive both promise and warning, invitation and accountability.[5] Jesus stands firmly within this prophetic tradition of Israel, where God's covenantal call has always been expressed in both invitation and warning:

- **Deuteronomy 28** outlines blessings for obedience—and curses for injustice, idolatry, and exploitation.
- **Isaiah 5** begins with a song about a vineyard and ends with: *"Woe to those who join house to house... Woe to those who call evil good..."*
- **Amos 6** declares, *"Woe to you who are at ease in Zion... who lie on beds of ivory..."*

Greco-Roman Rhetorical Tradition

In classical rhetoric, contrasting declarations (*macarisms* and woes) were used to define group identity and moral boundaries.[6] Philosophers and moralists used such formulas to distinguish virtue from vice, wisdom from folly. Jesus employs this familiar rhetorical structure but fills it with revolutionary content that challenges rather than reinforces existing social hierarchies.

These are not the rantings of an angry God. They are the cries of a holy God whose justice burns for the marginalized—and who pleads with the powerful to recognize their accountability within God's economy.

Luke's Larger Narrative: A Pattern of Reversal

The blessings and woes of Luke 6 cannot be separated from the larger narrative arc of Luke's Gospel, which consistently emphasizes God's preferential concern for the marginalized and warning to the comfortable.[7]

From the Beginning

Mary's Magnificat (Luke 1:46-55) introduces themes that run throughout Luke:

- "He has brought down the powerful from their thrones, and lifted up the lowly"
- "He has filled the hungry with good things, and sent the rich away empty"

Throughout the Ministry

Jesus' inaugural sermon in Nazareth (Luke 4:16-21) announces "good news to the poor" and "release to the captives," setting the trajectory for his entire ministry.[8] The parables consistently reinforce these themes:

- The Rich Fool (Luke 12:13-21) warns against accumulating wealth without regard for others
- The Rich Man and Lazarus (Luke 16:19-31) depicts ultimate reversal based on earthly treatment of the poor
- The Parable of the Great Banquet (Luke 14:15-24) shows God's invitation going to society's outcasts when the privileged refuse

Toward the End

Even in Luke's passion narrative, this theme continues. The thief on the cross—society's ultimate outcast—receives promise of paradise, while religious and political authorities who appear successful face judgment.

Luke's blessings and woes thus represent not isolated teachings but the crystallized essence of his entire theological vision.

Pastoral Honesty: The Role of Discomfort

Woe-language makes many modern readers uncomfortable—especially in traditions formed around grace, inclusion, or therapeutic faith. But discomfort can be a teacher, and spiritual tradition recognizes the value of loving confrontation.

In spiritual direction and pastoral care, gentle confrontation of ego, denial, or harmful patterns is often what leads to healing.[9]

Similarly, the "woes" of Jesus are not condemnation—they are a call to awareness:

- *Woe to you who are rich...* not because wealth is inherently evil, but because it can deceive us into thinking we don't need God or others.
- *Woe to you who laugh now...* not because joy is wrong, but because shallow contentment can mask injustice or avoid necessary lament.
- *Woe to you when all speak well of you...* because popularity may signal compromise rather than faithfulness to truth.

In each case, the "woe" is a spiritual red flag. It warns that worldly comfort can dull the soul's sensitivity to God's call and others' needs.

The Comfort That Isolates

Contemporary spiritual writers have noted how comfort can become a form of spiritual anesthesia.[10] When we are insulated from others' suffering, we lose capacity for empathy. When our basic needs are more than met, we may forget our dependence on God and community. When we are praised and accepted, we may compromise convictions to maintain approval.

The woes function as wake-up calls, inviting self-examination rather than self-condemnation.

Grace and Accountability in Tension

The Beatitudes, with their corresponding woes, force us to ask: Whose voice is lifted up in our communities? Whose suffering do we ignore? Whose comfort do we protect? How do economic and social structures shape spiritual life?[11]

This is not about guilt—it is about ethical clarity. Jesus invites us not to self-condemnation, but to reorientation of priorities, relationships, and resources.

Blessings and woes together:

- **Blessing affirms dignity**—even in suffering, marginalization, and loss
- **Woe confronts distortion**—even in success, comfort, and acceptance
- Together, they open a path to authentic transformation that neither ignores injustice nor despairs of change

A Both/And Gospel

Luke's Gospel refuses to separate spiritual and material concerns, individual and social transformation, present comfort and future accountability.[12] The blessings and woes embody this integration, calling believers to lives that reflect God's concern for both personal holiness and social justice.

For the Matthew Reader: Why Woes Still Matter

Even though Matthew omits the formal "woes" in chapter 5, his Gospel includes them later—especially in chapter 23, where Jesus pronounces seven woes upon the religious elite who "shut the kingdom of heaven in people's faces" and "neglect the weightier matters of the law: justice and mercy and faith" (Matthew 23:13, 23).[13]

Moreover, Matthew's Beatitudes still carry prophetic tension:

- The blessings speak to a *reordered world*, not just spiritual sweetness
- The final Beatitude (*"Blessed are those who are persecuted... Blessed are you..."*) is directed to those who speak truth in the face of institutional resistance
- The Sermon on the Mount continues with radical teachings about enemy love, economic sharing, and prophetic witness

The "woes" are implicit in Matthew—but in Luke, they are named. Reading both together completes the moral frame and prevents either spiritualizing the Gospel's demands or reducing them to mere social activism.

Reception History: How the Church Has Heard Blessing and Woe

Throughout Christian history, communities have drawn on the tradition of blessing and woe in various ways:

Patristic Period
Early church fathers like John Chrysostom preached extensively on the social implications of the blessings and woes, calling wealthy Christians to account for their stewardship and encouraging the poor with divine promises.[14]

Monastic Tradition
Monastic communities embraced voluntary poverty partly in response to the Gospel's warnings about wealth, seeing economic simplicity as spiritual liberation rather than deprivation.[15]

Liberation Theology
Latin American liberation theologians have found in Luke's blessings and woes a foundational text for God's preferential option for the poor, reading them as both spiritual comfort and prophetic challenge to unjust structures.[16]

Contemporary Applications
Modern faith communities continue to wrestle with how blessing and woe should shape worship, economic practices, and social engagement—from simple living movements to sanctuary congregations to environmental justice initiatives.

Living Between Blessing and Woe

As modern readers, we are called to hold both sides honestly, recognizing that most of us live somewhere in the tension between blessing and woe:

Where do we live in the blessing?

- With humility that recognizes our dependence on God and others
- With hunger for righteousness that works for justice
- With a spirit of mercy that extends grace to others
- With willingness to be misunderstood for the sake of truth

Where are we complicit in the woe?

- Dulled by comfort that insulates us from others' suffering
- Consumed by approval that prevents prophetic witness
- Distant from the poor through geography, economics, or choice
- Satisfied with systems that benefit us while harming others

The Call to Conversion

To be faithful is not to panic over every critique, but to receive both comfort and confrontation as gifts of grace that orient us toward God's kingdom.[17] The blessings and woes together call us to ongoing conversion—not a one-time decision but a continual turning toward God's vision of justice, mercy, and peace.

This conversion involves both personal transformation and structural change, both receiving God's comfort and extending it to others, both celebrating divine blessing and challenging human systems that contradict God's values.

The Whole Gospel

Luke's blessings and woes remind us that the Gospel is neither therapeutic comfort nor prophetic judgment alone, but both together. They prevent us from domesticating Jesus' message into either private spirituality or mere social activism by insisting that authentic discipleship addresses both personal transformation and systemic justice.

The poor are blessed not because poverty is good, but because God's kingdom brings reversal and restoration. The rich receive warning not because wealth is evil, but because it carries responsibility and risk that must be acknowledged. Together, blessing and woe constitute the full prophetic Word that both comforts the afflicted and afflicts the comfortable.

For contemporary readers, this means allowing the Gospel's tension to remain rather than resolving it prematurely. We are called to live as people who have received unmerited blessing while remaining accountable for how we use the gifts we have been given. We are invited to find God's favor in unlikely places while recognizing the spiritual dangers of worldly success.

This is the ethical tension at the heart of the Gospel—a tension that keeps us humble in blessing, hopeful in struggle, and faithful in the long work of justice and reconciliation that God's kingdom demands.

Reading the Beatitudes Through the Ages: A History of Interpretation

From a Galilean hillside to modern seminaries, the Beatitudes of Matthew 5 have been read, revered, reinterpreted—and sometimes domesticated—across two millennia. While their poetic force and spiritual gravity remain, the way they've been understood has shifted with theological trends, political movements, and cultural needs. This exploration traces key interpretive movements across history, highlighting how each age has grappled with these bold blessings, sometimes finding comfort, sometimes challenge, always discovering that these ancient words refuse to stay safely contained within any single framework.

The Early Church: Radical Comfort in a Persecuted World (1st-3rd Centuries)

In the first three centuries, Christians read the Beatitudes through the lens of persecution and eschatological hope. *"Blessed are those who are persecuted..."* was no metaphor—it was daily reality. Early Church Fathers like Origen of Alexandria viewed the Beatitudes as both a call to virtue and a mystical ascent toward divine likeness.[1] He interpreted "poverty of spirit" as the soul's detachment from worldly attachments in pursuit of God.

Tertullian likewise emphasized the countercultural nature of the blessings, urging believers to embrace suffering and meekness as marks of Christian identity in contrast to Roman power and pride.[2] For these early Christians, the Beatitudes weren't just spiritual ideals—they were survival strategies and sources of hope.

The martyrdom literature of this period reveals how the Beatitudes shaped Christian identity under persecution.[3] Martyrs and confessors were seen as the "living Beatitudes"—embodying in their suffering and witness the very blessings Jesus proclaimed. Their willingness to die rather than compromise demonstrated that these weren't merely beautiful sayings but a way of life worth dying for.

"To be poor in spirit is to renounce the world. The Christian is not called to power but to peace." —Origen[4]

Monasticism: The Beatitudes as a Rule of Life (4th-6th Centuries)

With the legalization of Christianity under Constantine, monasticism arose in part as a reaction to the dilution of Christian distinctiveness. The Desert Fathers, John Cassian, and St. Benedict treated the Beatitudes as a spiritual ladder—a path of interior transformation through humility, mourning, hunger for righteousness, and purity of heart.[5]

Cassian described the Beatitudes as stages in the soul's purification, illumination, and eventual union with God.[6] The *Rule of St. Benedict* (c. 530) reflected this ethos, emphasizing poverty of spirit, meekness, and mercy as communal disciplines for monastic life.[7]

Importantly, these monastic interpreters understood the Beatitudes as reshaping not just individual spirituality but community life itself. The Beatitudes offered a framework for conflict resolution, leadership structures, and daily interactions within the monastery. Meekness became a qualification for abbots, mercy shaped disciplinary practices, and peacemaking became essential to communal harmony.

Scholasticism and the Middle Ages: Systematizing the Virtues (11th-15th Centuries)

In the 13th century, Thomas Aquinas embedded the Beatitudes into his grand synthesis of Christian moral theology. In his *Summa Theologiae* (II-II, q. 69), he linked each Beatitude to a gift of the Holy Spirit, such as "fear of the Lord" or "wisdom."[8] This framework placed the Beatitudes within a broader ethical system rather than as a standalone guide.

But outside the university halls, mystics like Meister Eckhart reclaimed their transformative power.[9] He saw "poverty of spirit" as radical openness to God, a state of inner detachment even from the self—a position bordering on apophatic theology.

During this period, cathedral schools and mendicant orders also used the Beatitudes for lay spiritual formation, not merely academic theology.[10] Popular preaching made these blessings accessible to ordinary Christians as guides for daily living, work, and family relationships.

"The poor in spirit are those who have let go of even the desire for God-as-object. They live in the naked ground of being." —Meister Eckhart[11]

The Reformation and Counter-Reformation: Signs of Grace and Inner Piety (16th-17th Centuries)

Martin Luther rejected any interpretation of the Beatitudes as a *means* of salvation. Instead, he saw them as descriptions of the soul humbled by grace—especially the "poor in spirit," whom he equated with those crushed under the weight of the law and driven to rely on divine mercy.[12] For Luther, the Beatitudes were evidence of grace received, not conditions for earning it.

John Calvin emphasized the ethical fruit of justification, interpreting the Beatitudes as spiritual qualities formed by the Spirit, not human achievement.[13] This sharp distinction between works righteousness and grace-produced virtue became central to Protestant interpretation.

Meanwhile, Catholic spiritual reformers like St. Teresa of Ávila and St. Ignatius of Loyola encouraged deep interiority, aligning the Beatitudes with personal prayer, discernment, and social compassion.[14] The *Spiritual Exercises* of Ignatius treat mourning, meekness, and hunger for justice as keys to discerning God's will in the world. Their interpretation invited both active service and contemplative prayer as expressions of Beatitude living—breaking down false divisions between action and contemplation.

Modernity and Liberation: Ethics and Protest (19th-20th Centuries)

The 19th and 20th centuries brought new readings that emphasized social ethics. Walter Rauschenbusch, father of the Social Gospel in the U.S., read the Beatitudes as a critique of social injustice—calling Christians to align with the poor, the grieving, and the oppressed.[15]

In Latin America, Gustavo Gutiérrez and other liberation theologians treated the Beatitudes as a revolutionary manifesto.[16] The "poor in spirit" were not merely the inwardly humble, but the materially impoverished—the ones whom God sides with in history. This interpretation spread globally, inspiring African theologians like Desmond Tutu and Asian liberation thinkers who applied Beatitude principles to contexts of colonial oppression and economic injustice.

Feminist and womanist theologians like Elisabeth Schüssler Fiorenza and Delores Williams reinterpreted the Beatitudes as affirming marginalized bodies and experiences, particularly highlighting how Jesus' blessings validated those excluded from traditional power structures.[17]

Catholic martyrs like Oscar Romero in El Salvador and spiritual leaders like Dorothy Day in the U.S. embodied this vision in life and death, demonstrating that the Beatitudes remained as costly and transformative as they had been in the early church.[18]

"The Beatitudes do not bless resignation but resistance, not suffering in itself but the hope for justice." —Gustavo Gutiérrez[19]

Contemporary Voices: Global, Mystical, and Psychological (21st Century)

Today, interpretations continue to evolve across religious and cultural lines:

Interfaith interpreters find parallels between the Beatitudes and Buddhist *metta*, Sufi humility, or Jain *ahimsa*, creating new possibilities for global spiritual dialogue.[20]

Psychologists of religion (e.g., James Fowler, Richard Beck) explore the Beatitudes as markers of mature moral development—describing traits like vulnerability, empathy, and spiritual nonattachment that contribute to psychological wholeness.[21]

Progressive theologians see them as a template for nonviolent resistance, ecological justice, and global ethics, while secular and spiritual-but-not-religious movements discover in them frameworks for trauma recovery and restorative justice.[22]

Even within therapeutic and conflict resolution contexts, the Beatitudes provide language for healing and reconciliation that transcends traditional religious boundaries.

The Beatitudes as Double-Edged Sword

Throughout history, the Beatitudes have proven remarkably resistant to domestication, yet they've also been subject to it. Sometimes they've been "tamed" to support the status quo—used to encourage passive acceptance of injustice or to spiritualize away legitimate grievances. Other times they've been reclaimed as radical summons to transformation that challenge every form of complacency.

This tension reveals their enduring power: they comfort the afflicted and afflict the comfortable, often simultaneously. They resist being confined to either purely personal spirituality or merely social activism, demanding instead an integration that transforms both individual hearts and social structures.

Era	Primary Lens	Key Emphasis	Representative Figures
Early Church	Persecution & Eschatology	Comfort for the suffering; countercultural witness	Origen, Tertullian
Monasticism	Spiritual Formation	Interior transformation; communal discipline	Cassian, Benedict

Era	Primary Lens	Key Emphasis	Representative Figures
Medieval	Systematic Theology	Integration with moral theology; mystical union	Aquinas, Eckhart
Reformation	Grace vs. Works	Evidence of salvation; fruit of the Spirit	Luther, Calvin, Ignatius
Modern/Liberation	Social Justice	Critique of oppression; preferential option for poor	Rauschenbusch, Gutiérrez
Contemporary	Global & Interdisciplinary	Interfaith dialogue; psychological insights; secular applications	Beck, Tutu, Day

The Beatitudes as Mirror and Mandate

Throughout history, interpreters have bent the Beatitudes toward their time's longings and limits. For the persecuted, they offered comfort. For monks, a path. For mystics, an interior fire. For reformers, a protest. For many today, they still feel like a *graceful paradox*: blessings pronounced on those the world overlooks.

And yet perhaps their enduring power lies not in the consistency of their interpretations, but in their **disruptive grace**—calling each generation back to the heart of Jesus' message: that God's favor rests not on the powerful, but on the poor, the peacemakers, and the pure-hearted. They remain both mirror and mandate: reflecting back to us our deepest longings for meaning and justice while calling us forward into ways of being that the world considers foolish but God considers blessed.

The history of Beatitude interpretation reveals something profound about both the text and human nature: we find in these ancient words what we most need to hear, but we also discover that they continually challenge us to become more than we imagined possible. Each generation must wrestle with their meaning anew, not because the text is unclear, but because the call to transformation is never complete.

Blessed in Worship: The Beatitudes in Early Christian Liturgy and Devotional Life

The Beatitudes are often treated as a set of teachings—to be studied, analyzed, or moralized. But for the early Church, they were also something more: a rhythm of prayer, a guide for worship, and a path for spiritual formation.

This chapter explores how the Beatitudes were used not only as theological text but as devotional and liturgical experience in the first centuries of Christianity. In doing so, it opens a window into how early believers understood these blessings—not as abstract virtues, but as a living shape for the soul.

From catechetical instruction to eucharistic celebration, from monastic meditation to popular preaching, the Beatitudes became woven into the very fabric of Christian worship and spiritual practice. Their journey from Jesus' hillside proclamation to the heart of Christian liturgy reveals how the early church understood these words as both divine gift and human calling.

The Beatitudes as Catechesis: Forming the New Believer

From the earliest centuries, the Beatitudes were embedded in **catechesis**—the process by which new converts were prepared for baptism and entry into the Christian community.[1]

The Didache (late 1st to early 2nd century)—often called "The Teaching of the Twelve Apostles"—is an early Christian manual that echoes several Beatitudes and frames the Christian path as a contrast between the "Way of Life" and the "Way of Death." The emphasis on humility, mercy, and peacemaking aligns directly with Matthew 5, suggesting that the Beatitudes quickly became foundational to Christian identity formation.[2]

Cyril of Jerusalem (c. 313-386) in his famous *Catechetical Lectures* regularly referenced the Beatitudes when preparing candidates for baptism.[3] His lectures show how the Beatitudes served as both ethical instruction and spiritual preparation—teaching new Christians not just how to behave, but how to understand their new identity as citizens of God's kingdom.

In Origen (3rd century) and later catechetical texts, the Beatitudes were taught not just as ideals but as steps in the soul's ascent—beginning with the poverty of spirit and ending in the joy of persecution for righteousness' sake.[4] This "ladder" motif would become central to Eastern Christian spirituality.

Ambrose of Milan (c. 340-397) used the Beatitudes extensively in his instructions to catechumens, particularly emphasizing how these blessings prepared Christians for the ethical demands of life in a complex world.[5] His approach shows how the Beatitudes functioned as practical wisdom for new believers navigating pagan society.

The structure of the Beatitudes—simple, memorable, rhythmic—made them ideal for instruction, especially in largely oral cultures. They served as a summary of Christian identity, both ethical and mystical, that could be easily memorized and internalized.

Eastern Liturgical Traditions: Chanted Blessings

The Eastern Christian churches developed the most sustained liturgical use of the Beatitudes, integrating them directly into regular worship in ways that continue today.

Byzantine Liturgy

In Byzantine liturgy, the Beatitudes are sung as the Third Antiphon during the Divine Liturgy on most Sundays.[6] Each Beatitude is paired with a *troparion* (short hymn) that connects the blessing to a specific theological theme or saint's commemoration. This practice, traceable to at least the 6th century, transforms the Beatitudes from didactic text into communal prayer.

For example, the first Beatitude might be sung: "Blessed are the poor in spirit, for theirs is the kingdom of heaven," followed by a troparion celebrating how the martyrs embodied spiritual poverty through their sacrificial witness. This liturgical pairing shows how the Beatitudes were understood as both present blessing and call to discipleship.

Syriac and Coptic Traditions

In Syriac liturgies, particularly those influenced by the tradition of Ephrem the Syrian (c. 306-373), the Beatitudes appear within the *anaphora* (the most solemn Eucharistic prayer) as meditations on Christ's character and the qualities of the faithful.[7] Ephrem's extensive hymns on the Beatitudes show how they were understood as descriptions of both Christ's nature and Christian discipleship.

Coptic liturgies similarly incorporate the Beatitudes into eucharistic prayers, often as part of the preparation for communion.[8] The placement suggests that receiving the Beatitudes' blessings was seen as intimately connected to receiving Christ in the Eucharist—both were gifts of divine grace rather than human achievement.

Armenian and Ethiopian Practices

The Armenian Apostolic Church includes the Beatitudes in its liturgy for the Feast of the Transfiguration, connecting Jesus' hillside teaching with his mountaintop revelation of divine glory. This liturgical connection reinforces the understanding that the Beatitudes reveal the character of God's kingdom.

Ethiopian Orthodox traditions incorporate Beatitude themes into their distinctive *qidasse* (divine liturgy), particularly during

Lent, where they function as both call to repentance and promise of restoration.[9]

In these contexts, the Beatitudes functioned not as background doctrine but as living prayer—chanted by the gathered body as both praise and self-examination. Their presence in Eucharistic settings also underlines their connection to community, sacrifice, and kingdom-hope—themes central to the table of the Lord.

Western Liturgical Development

While Eastern traditions developed more sustained liturgical use of the Beatitudes, the Western (Latin) church gradually incorporated them into its worship and calendar in distinctive ways.

Lectionary Development

By the early medieval period, the Beatitudes appeared regularly in Western lectionaries—the assigned Gospel readings for specific occasions.[10] Most significantly, they became the traditional Gospel reading for:

- All Saints' Day (November 1), where they describe the character of those who share in heavenly blessedness
- The Fourth Sunday after Epiphany (later the Fourth Sunday in Ordinary Time), emphasizing their role in revealing Christ's identity
- Various saint commemorations, particularly martyrs and confessors who embodied Beatitude virtues

Medieval Homiletics and Popular Devotion

Medieval preachers developed extensive homiletical traditions around the Beatitudes. Thomas Aquinas in his *Summa Theologica* used the Beatitudes as a framework for understanding Christian virtue and the path to beatific vision.[11] Popular preachers used them to structure Lenten sermon series, leading congregations through systematic examination of Christian character.

The Beatitudes also influenced the formation of medieval confraternities—lay associations organized around particular virtues.[12] Groups dedicated to works of mercy, peacemaking, and care for the poor explicitly drew their inspiration from specific Beatitudes.

Monastic and Penitential Practice

In Western monasticism, particularly in Benedictine and Franciscan traditions, the Beatitudes shaped both individual spiritual formation and community life. Medieval penitential manuals often used the Beatitudes as examination of conscience, asking not "What sins did I commit?" but "How did I embody—or fail to embody—the Beatitudes today?"[13]

Patristic Preaching: The Beatitudes Proclaimed

The Church Fathers produced extensive homiletical literature on the Beatitudes, using them for both doctrinal instruction and practical exhortation.

John Chrysostom (c. 349-407), the "Golden-mouthed" preacher of Constantinople, delivered numerous homilies on the Beatitudes.[14] His approach emphasized their practical application while maintaining their transcendent vision. Chrysostom particularly stressed how the Beatitudes challenge social conventions and call Christians to countercultural living.

Augustine of Hippo (354-430) in his *Commentary on the Sermon on the Mount* provided influential interpretations that shaped Western understanding for centuries.[15] Augustine read the Beatitudes as describing the progress of the soul from initial conversion to final perfection, creating a systematic spirituality that influenced medieval and Reformed traditions.

Gregory of Nazianzus (329-390) used the Beatitudes in his theological orations, showing how they reveal both human destiny and divine character.[16] His approach demonstrates how patristic preachers saw the Beatitudes as simultaneously anthropological and theological—describing both who we are called to be and who God is.

These homiletical traditions show how the Beatitudes moved from private study to public proclamation, shaping Christian consciousness through regular preaching and teaching.

Monastic and Mystical Tradition: The Ladder of Blessedness

The Beatitudes were especially treasured in **monastic communities**, where they were seen as a map for spiritual ascent and the architecture of contemplative life.

Gregory of Nyssa (c. 335-395) read the Beatitudes as a ladder of purification, with each blessing building upon the previous.[17] His influential treatise *On the Beatitudes* shows how monastic theologians understood them as describing progressive stages of spiritual development—from initial recognition of poverty in spirit to final union with God through persecution and martyrdom.

John Cassian (c. 360-435) and the Desert Fathers used them as meditative texts, guiding inner silence and humility.[18] The *Sayings of the Desert Fathers* contain numerous references to Beatitude themes, particularly poverty of spirit and purity of heart, as foundations for contemplative prayer.

In Benedictine spirituality, the Beatitudes shaped the rhythm of prayer and labor—particularly in the values of meekness, purity of heart, and peacemaking.[19] The *Rule of St. Benedict* itself, while not explicitly citing the Beatitudes, structures monastic life around their values: humility, community harmony, and trust in divine providence.

Eastern Hesychast Tradition

The Hesychast tradition of Eastern monasticism developed sophisticated practices around the Beatitudes, particularly "Blessed are the pure in heart, for they shall see God."[20] The *Philokalia* and other hesychast texts show how this Beatitude became foundational for the tradition of contemplative prayer aimed at divine vision.

For mystics and monks, the Beatitudes were not simply a way to act—they were a way to be. They were chanted, memorized, prayed, and embodied—not to earn blessing, but to recognize it already present in the soul yielded to God.

Hymnody and Musical Expression

The Beatitudes found rich expression in early Christian hymnody, where their rhythmic structure made them natural for musical setting.

Ambrosian and Mozarabic Traditions

The Ambrosian chant tradition (associated with Milan) includes several hymns that paraphrase or directly quote the Beatitudes.[21] The Mozarabic rite (Spanish/Visigothic tradition) similarly incorporated Beatitude themes into its distinctive musical traditions.

Syrian Hymnographic Tradition

Ephrem the Syrian created extensive hymn cycles on the Beatitudes, using complex poetic meters that facilitated memorization.[22] His *Hymns on the Nativity* and *Hymns on Paradise* frequently return to Beatitude themes, showing how they shaped the theological imagination of Syrian Christianity.

Psalmody and Antiphonal Practice

Many early Christian communities combined Beatitude recitation with psalmody, creating antiphonal practices where Beatitudes and psalm verses were alternated.[23] This practice reinforced the connection between Jesus' teaching and Hebrew wisdom traditions.

Visual and Symbolic Devotion: Beatitudes in Art

The Beatitudes also found expression in early Christian art and iconography, helping illiterate believers "read" these blessings through visual means.

Catacomb Frescoes

In Roman catacombs (especially those of Priscilla, Callixtus, and San Domitilla), scenes of mourning, mercy, and peacemaking appear frequently—not just as biblical narratives, but as virtues of the faithful dead.[24] The *Good Shepherd*f rescoes often include surrounding scenes that embody Beatitude values: feeding the hungry, comforting mourners, and welcoming strangers.

Early Church Mosaics

By the 6th century, mosaics in churches like Sant'Apollinare Nuovo in Ravenna begin to portray the Sermon on the Mount as a central scene in Christ's life—often with rays of divine light emanating toward the gathered disciples and crowds.[25] These visual representations emphasize the Beatitudes as divine revelation rather than mere ethical teaching.

Iconographic Development

Later Byzantine and Slavic icons sometimes depict each Beatitude as a rung in a heavenly ladder or as symbolic figures surrounding Christ.[26] The Ladder of Divine Ascent iconographic tradition explicitly connects the Beatitudes to John Climacus's spiritual ladder, showing their role in the soul's journey toward God.

These visual expressions helped the illiterate "read" the Beatitudes not as abstract sayings, but as concrete portraits of discipleship and divine blessing.

Daily Prayer and Spiritual Practice

Beyond liturgy and art, the Beatitudes shaped the daily prayer life of early Christians across various traditions.

Lectionaries and Prayer Cycles

The Beatitudes were regularly included in lectionaries—assigned readings for morning or evening prayer.[27] The

Apostolic Constitutions (4th century) suggest that the Beatitudes were used in both public and private prayer as examinations of conscience and calls to renewal.

Monastic Rules and Examination

In many rule-of-life documents, monks were required to meditate on the Beatitudes daily as part of their examination of conscience.[28] Rather than focusing primarily on avoiding sin, this practice asked: "Did I hunger for righteousness today? Did I show mercy? Did I work for peace?"

Private Devotional Use

In private devotion, especially in Eastern traditions, the Beatitudes served as a mirror of the heart—a spiritual tool for self-reflection that focused on growth in virtue rather than mere avoidance of vice.[29] Early Christian writers like John Climacus and Maximus the Confessor developed sophisticated practices for using the Beatitudes in personal prayer and meditation.

In short, they offered not a system of merit, but a spiritual compass—gently directing the soul toward humility, compassion, and courage while recognizing these virtues as gifts rather than achievements.

Timeline of Liturgical Development

Period	Development	Key Examples
1st-2nd Century	Catechetical use, basic instruction	Didache, early baptismal preparation

Period	Development	Key Examples
3rd-4th Century	Patristic preaching, systematic theology	Origen, Chrysostom, Augustine
4th-5th Century	Monastic integration, spiritual formation	Desert Fathers, Cassian, Benedict
5th-6th Century	Eastern liturgical development	Byzantine Divine Liturgy antiphons
6th-8th Century	Western lectionary inclusion	All Saints' Day, seasonal cycles
Medieval Period	Popular devotion, confraternities	Thomas Aquinas, Franciscan spirituality

From Early Church to Today

While modern Christianity often treats the Beatitudes as a moral code or inspirational quotation, the early Church knew them as something deeper: a summary of the Gospel itself.

They shaped who was welcomed into the community through catechetical formation. They informed the tone of prayer and proclamation through liturgical integration. They grounded the Christian life in humility rather than achievement through spiritual direction. They provided both comfort and challenge through artistic expression.

Recovering the Liturgical Vision

Recovering this liturgical and devotional tradition helps us see the Beatitudes not as a burden to bear but as a path of grace—a pattern of being, praying, and blessing that still resonates in the soul of the Church.

The early Church's approach suggests several insights for contemporary practice:

- The Beatitudes are communal before they are individual—meant to be prayed and embodied together
- They are gifts to receive rather than achievements to earn—descriptions of God's blessing rather than human accomplishment
- They are liturgical wisdom—meant to shape worship and spiritual formation rather than remaining merely instructional
- They are mystical theology—pointing toward divine vision and transformation rather than mere ethical improvement

Contemporary Applications

Many contemporary liturgical traditions are rediscovering these ancient practices:[30]

- Episcopal and Lutheran churches increasingly use the Beatitudes in baptismal liturgies and confirmation preparation
- Catholic lectionary reforms have restored the Beatitudes to prominent seasonal placements
- Orthodox and Eastern Catholic churches maintain traditional liturgical uses while developing new musical settings
- Protestant traditions are exploring how the Beatitudes can shape worship beyond occasional sermon series

The early Church's witness suggests that the Beatitudes reach their fullest meaning not in individual study but in communal worship—where they become both prayer and proclamation, both gift and calling, both comfort and challenge.

The journey of the Beatitudes from Jesus' hillside teaching to the heart of Christian worship reveals how the early Church understood these words as fundamentally liturgical—meant to shape not just individual character but the common life of faith communities.

Whether chanted in Byzantine liturgy, meditated upon in monastic cells, preached from patristic pulpits, or depicted in catacomb art, the Beatitudes consistently functioned as more than moral instruction. They were windows into divine blessing, maps for spiritual formation, and rhythms for communal worship.

This liturgical heritage invites contemporary Christians to reclaim the Beatitudes not as burden but as blessing—not as law but as grace—not as individual achievement but as communal gift. In doing so, we join our voices with centuries of believers who have found in these ancient words a living path toward the heart of God.

Power, Empire, and the Politics of Blessing

The Beatitudes have long been admired for their spiritual beauty and personal wisdom. But in their original setting, they were not simply a series of moral aphorisms. They were politically charged proclamations—a direct challenge to both Roman imperial power and the religious authority structures that supported it.

To say, *"Blessed are the poor... the meek... the persecuted..."* in first-century Galilee was not a spiritual abstraction. It was a public declaration that God's favor rests on those whom the world—and its empires—marginalize or crush.

To hear the Beatitudes rightly, we must reclaim their original counter-imperial voice.

A World Shaped by Empire

When Jesus ascended the mount (or stood on the plain) and spoke these words, he did so under the shadow of Roman domination—a system that touched every aspect of life through carefully constructed ideology and brutal enforcement:

Rome's Economic System extracted wealth from the periphery to the center, crushing peasants with taxes, debts, and land seizure.[1] The magnificent cities of Sepphoris and Tiberias, visible from the hills of Galilee, rose from peasant labor and taxes—monuments to a system that concentrated wealth upward while most lived at subsistence level.

Roman Imperial Ideology claimed divine blessing for those in power. Coins proclaimed Caesar as "Son of God" (*divi filius*), "Savior" (*soter*), and "Lord" (*kyrios*).[2] Imperial inscriptions celebrated "peace through victory" (*pax per victoriam*), promising prosperity through military dominance. The patron-client system further stratified society, ensuring that blessing flowed downward only through proper channels of power and allegiance.[3]

The Temple System, especially in Jerusalem, was deeply entangled with Roman authority. While not all religious leaders collaborated, the high priesthood was appointed by Roman governors, and temple taxes supported both religious and imperial functions.[4] Many faithful Jews viewed this arrangement as compromising Israel's covenant identity.

Into this world of imperial symbols and structures, Jesus spoke words that turned everything upside down. To bless the *meek*, not the mighty... the *persecuted*, not the powerful... was to announce that God's favor operated by entirely different rules.

Jesus' opening words in the Sermon on the Mount function as a kind of manifesto for an alternate social order—a kingdom not of coercion and wealth accumulation, but of humility, mercy, justice, and solidarity with the vulnerable.

The Jewish Prophetic Foundation

Jesus' counter-imperial proclamation was not foreign innovation but the flowering of Israel's own prophetic tradition. From Isaiah's vision of justice rolling down like waters (5:24) to Micah's call to "do justice, love mercy, and walk humbly with God" (6:8), Hebrew prophecy consistently challenged rulers who oppressed the poor and claimed divine authorization for injustice.[5]

The *anawim* tradition—the "humble poor" who combined material vulnerability with spiritual dependence on God—provided the theological background for Jesus' blessings.[6] These were people who had learned through suffering that human power systems were unreliable and that true security came only through trust in God's covenant faithfulness.

The Jubilee traditions of Leviticus 25, with their vision of periodic debt forgiveness and land redistribution, offered a practical model for what God's alternative economy might look like.[7] When Jesus blessed the poor and promised them the kingdom, he was drawing on this deep well of Hebrew hope for divine intervention on behalf of the oppressed.

The prophets who "sighed and groaned over all the abominations" (Ezekiel 9:4) and declared God's preferential concern for "the widow, the orphan, and the stranger" (Deuteronomy 10:18) had prepared the ground for Jesus' radical announcement that the kingdom belonged to those whom earthly kingdoms excluded.

Beatitudes as Anti-Imperial Critique

Each Beatitude carries a quiet but unmistakable political resonance that directly challenged Roman values and assumptions:[8]

"Blessed are the poor in spirit..." inverts the Roman honor-shame system, which exalted wealth, status, and patronage. Where Roman culture celebrated *virtus* (masculine excellence through achievement), Jesus blessed those who recognized their spiritual neediness.

"Blessed are those who mourn..." affirms public grief in a culture that demanded stoicism and control. In a system that required acceptance of imperial "peace," Jesus blessed those who refused to stop grieving over injustice and oppression.

"Blessed are the meek..." directly challenges the Roman ideal of the *vir fortis*—the strong man who asserts dominance and wins glory through conquest. The promise that the meek will "inherit the earth" subverts the entire Roman understanding of how territory and authority are rightfully claimed.

"Blessed are those who hunger and thirst for righteousness..." confronts systems that perpetuate inequality while claiming divine sanction. In a world where "justice" meant Roman law imposed through force, Jesus blessed those who yearned for true *dikaiosynē*—justice rooted in God's character.

"Blessed are the peacemakers..." speaks not of military "peace" (*Pax Romana* achieved through violence), but of *shalom*—

reconciliation born of justice and right relationship. This directly contradicted imperial propaganda that equated peace with submission to Roman rule.[9]

"Blessed are those who are persecuted for righteousness' sake..." echoes the stories of the prophets and prepares Jesus' followers for opposition from power structures that benefit from injustice. This blessing acknowledges that following God's kingdom values will bring conflict with earthly kingdoms.

In short, the Beatitudes are not a withdrawal from politics—they are a systematic rebuke of imperial and religious systems that claim divine blessing while perpetuating harm.

Roman Empire vs. Jesus' Kingdom: A Study in Contrasts

The clash between imperial and kingdom values becomes clearest when we set them side by side:

Roman/Imperial Values	Beatitudes/Kingdom Values
Wealth, honor, status	Poverty of spirit, humility
Dominance through strength	Gentleness, meekness
Victory through violence	Peace through reconciliation
Blessing through patronage	Mercy freely given
Control through fear	Comfort for those who mourn
"Peace" through conquest	Justice sought with passion
Power over others	Service of the vulnerable
Glory through achievement	Blessing through persecution

This table reveals that Jesus wasn't simply offering personal virtues—he was announcing a complete inversion of the world's power structures and value systems.

Challenging Power: Then and Now

It is no surprise that such teachings provoked opposition. The Gospels record that by the end of his ministry, Jesus was seen as a threat to both Roman authority and religious order. His death was not merely spiritual—it was a political execution under the charge of being *"King of the Jews."*[10]

Jesus' own actions embodied this redefined power: washing his disciples' feet, refusing to retaliate against violence, entering Jerusalem on a donkey rather than a war horse, and ultimately accepting crucifixion rather than compromise. His life demonstrated that true power serves others rather than dominating them, gives life rather than taking it, and reconciles rather than conquers.

That same subversive power has echoed through history:

The early Christian communities resisted Caesar worship and created alternative economic models, sharing goods in common and crossing ethnic boundaries (Acts 2-4). Their very existence challenged imperial assumptions about how human society should be organized.[11]

Liberation theologians in Latin America have read the Beatitudes as God's preferential option for the poor and oppressed—not just in spirit, but in the concrete realities of economic exploitation and political persecution.[12]

Dr. Martin Luther King Jr. preached meekness, mercy, and peacemaking as the heart of nonviolent resistance, showing how Jesus' kingdom values could confront systemic racism without resorting to the violence that perpetuates oppression.[13]

Archbishop Desmond Tutu and the Truth and Reconciliation Commission in South Africa modeled peacemaking not as passivity but as *justice with healing*—showing how mercy and accountability could work together to transform a society.[14]

Contemporary liberation movements around the world continue to find in the Beatitudes a vision of God's kingdom that challenges systems of economic inequality, racial injustice, and environmental destruction.

The Risk of Domestication

Yet the Beatitudes have also been domesticated and misused throughout history. Too often, they have been spiritualized in ways that avoid their political implications or even reinforce existing power structures:

- "Blessed are the poor in spirit" has been used to counsel the materially poor to accept their poverty rather than work for justice.
- "Blessed are the meek" has been twisted to encourage passivity in the face of oppression.

- "Blessed are the peacemakers" has been misapplied to silence prophetic voices calling for systemic change.[15]

This domestication serves the interests of those who benefit from unjust systems. By making the Beatitudes purely "spiritual," the powerful can claim to honor Jesus while ignoring his call for transformed social relationships.

True fidelity to the Beatitudes requires recognizing both their spiritual and political dimensions—they call for personal transformation that inevitably leads to social transformation, and social transformation that flows from spiritual renewal.

Power Reimagined

Jesus does not call for violent revolution. But he fundamentally redefines power.[16]

Where empires enforce order through threat and domination, Jesus blesses those who yield, grieve, reconcile, and suffer for what is right. His is not a kingdom of escape, but of presence—a call to live *in* the world but not *according to* its values.

This alternative model of power:

- Does not grasp, but gives
- Does not dominate, but heals
- Does not retaliate, but reconciles
- Does not seek applause, but righteousness
- Does not accumulate, but shares
- Does not exclude, but welcomes

The Beatitudes challenge not only empires and governments, but each of us: How do we relate to power? Do we serve others or preserve our own control? Are we willing to be seen as weak in the world's eyes—in order to live into the strength of compassion?

Blessing as Resistance

"Blessed are..." is not just a description. It is a declaration. Jesus pronounces divine favor on those who are not favored by the world. In doing so, he enacts what theologian Walter Brueggemann calls a "prophetic imagination"—the ability to name reality as it is while pointing to what could be.[17]

This kind of blessing is itself a form of resistance. It refuses to accept the world's verdicts about who matters and who doesn't. It insists that God's evaluation of human worth operates by entirely different criteria than the market, the military, or the mansion.

In a time when governments—even self-identified Christian ones—often prioritize dominance over dignity, profit over people, and appearance over compassion, the Beatitudes still pierce like lightning. They remind us that the Gospel is not neutral. It is good news for the poor—and therefore a confrontation for those who hoard wealth, power, or privilege at others' expense.

Living the Counter-Imperial Vision Today

The Beatitudes call contemporary followers of Jesus to examine our own relationship with power and empire. This means asking hard questions:

- How does my lifestyle reflect kingdom values rather than imperial values?
- Where am I complicit in systems that marginalize the poor, the mourning, the meek?
- What would it mean to be a peacemaker in contexts of structural violence?
- How can I practice mercy in ways that challenge rather than reinforce injustice?
- What forms of persecution am I willing to accept for the sake of righteousness?

The answers will vary by context and calling, but the questions themselves are unavoidable for anyone who takes the Beatitudes seriously as more than personal inspiration.

The Beatitudes are not a blueprint for political action, but they are a vision of God's kingdom that judges all human kingdoms—including our own. They call us to live as citizens of that kingdom here and now, demonstrating through our common life that another way is possible.

Conclusion: The Enduring Challenge

To truly proclaim the Beatitudes is to say: "This is not the world as it is—but it is the world as God wills it to be."

They remain as challenging today as they were two thousand years ago, calling every generation to choose between the empire's promise of security through domination and the kingdom's invitation to flourishing through service. They refuse to be tamed by either conservative spiritualization or liberal politicization, insisting instead on a transformation that is both deeply personal and unavoidably social.

In our own time of rising authoritarianism, widening inequality, and environmental crisis, the Beatitudes' counter-imperial vision offers both judgment and hope. They judge all systems—including religious ones—that claim divine blessing while perpetuating harm. And they offer hope that God's kingdom is still breaking into our world through those who dare to live by different values.

The poor in spirit, the mourning, the meek, those who hunger for righteousness—they are not the unfortunate ones who need our pity. They are the blessed ones through whom God is transforming the world. The question for the rest of us is whether we will join them.

Beyond the Canon: The Beatitudes in Q, Apocrypha, and Early Wisdom Traditions

The Beatitudes in Matthew and Luke are among the most cherished words of Jesus—but they may not have originated with either Gospel. Scholars widely agree that both authors drew from an earlier source, now lost, known as "Q" (from *Quelle*, German for "source"). Moreover, Beatitude-style sayings appear in non-canonical gospels, Jewish wisdom texts, and the Dead Sea Scrolls—suggesting that this form of blessing was part of a wider spiritual vocabulary in the first century.

This chapter offers a compact exploration of these early traditions. It reveals that the Beatitudes were not a theological anomaly, but part of a rich stream of ethical teaching and apocalyptic hope that flowed through Judaism, early Christianity, and surrounding cultures. Understanding these broader contexts doesn't diminish the Beatitudes' power—it deepens our appreciation for how Jesus took up familiar forms and transformed them with revolutionary content.

The Q Source: The Earliest Beatitudes?

Most scholars believe that Matthew and Luke both drew on a now-lost sayings gospel known as Q, which contained many of Jesus' teachings—including versions of the Beatitudes.[1] While the Q document has never been discovered and remains hypothetical, it can be reconstructed in part through parallel passages in Matthew and Luke that are absent from Mark.

It's important to note that Q theory, while widely accepted, is not universal. Some scholars, including James D.G. Dunn and Craig Evans, propose alternative models for explaining the similarities between Matthew and Luke.[2] However, the broad consensus supports the existence of a sayings source that included Beatitude-like material.

The Q version of the Beatitudes likely included:

- *Blessed are the poor...*
- *Blessed are the hungry...*
- *Blessed are those who mourn...*
- *Blessed are those who are persecuted...*

And significantly, it may also have included corresponding "woes"—like those found in Luke 6:

- *Woe to you who are rich...*
- *Woe to you who are full now...*
- *Woe to you who laugh now...*

This pairing of blessings and woes has deep roots in prophetic literature (see Isaiah 5 or Amos 6) and reflects the apocalyptic worldview that underlies much of Jesus' message.[3] The Q tradition presents these as complementary revelations: divine blessing on the marginalized and divine judgment on systems that marginalize them.

In the Q tradition, the Beatitudes are less spiritualized than Matthew's—and more urgent. They present a stark vision of reversal: the lowly lifted, the powerful brought low, God's kingdom breaking into a world of injustice with transformative force.

Apocryphal Gospels: Echoes and Variations

Several non-canonical gospels—texts written in the second or third century and excluded from the New Testament—also include Beatitude-like sayings. These texts reveal how different early Christian communities understood and adapted Jesus' blessing formulas.

Gospel of Thomas

Perhaps the most famous of these is the *Gospel of Thomas*, a sayings collection discovered in 1945 in Egypt.[4] Saying 54 reads:

"Blessed are the poor, for yours is the kingdom of heaven."

This closely echoes Luke's version, but lacks any spiritual qualifier (*"in spirit"*), reinforcing the idea that early Beatitude traditions were blunt and materially focused. Thomas preserves what may be a more primitive form of the saying, before later theological reflection added qualifying phrases.

Other sayings in Thomas reflect a similar paradoxical tone, though with distinctly Gnostic/ascetic flavors:

"Blessed are the solitary and the elect, for you will find the kingdom." (Logion 49)
"Blessed is the lion that becomes human... and cursed is the human who becomes a lion." (Logion 7)

While more cryptic than the canonical Beatitudes, these sayings reflect the same vision of reversal and inner transformation. However, Thomas's emphasis on solitude and esoteric knowledge shows how different communities adapted the Beatitude form to express their particular theological concerns.[5]

Other Apocryphal Texts

The *Gospel of Peter* and other apocryphal acts (e.g., *Acts of Paul and Thecla*) emphasize suffering and persecution as paths to divine favor—a central theme of the canonical Beatitudes.[6] The *Acts of Paul and Thecla*, for instance, celebrates those who endure persecution for their faith, echoing the final Beatitude's blessing on the persecuted.

These texts show how early Christian communities outside the mainstream church continued to find comfort and meaning in Beatitude-style blessings, adapting them to their particular circumstances and theological frameworks.

Jewish Wisdom and the Beatitude Form

The Beatitude format (*"Blessed are..."* or Hebrew *ashrei*) was well established in Jewish wisdom literature long before Jesus. Understanding this background reveals how Jesus both continued and transformed an ancient tradition.

Biblical Wisdom Literature

The Hebrew Bible contains numerous examples:

- *"Blessed is the one who walks not in the counsel of the wicked..."* (Psalm 1:1)
- *"Blessed is the one who considers the poor..."* (Psalm 41:1)
- *"Blessed is the man who finds wisdom..."* (Proverbs 3:13)

These sayings were not about emotion but flourishing—describing the person whose life is rightly ordered before God and neighbor.[7] They functioned as practical wisdom, identifying the attitudes and behaviors that lead to genuine well-being.

Later Jewish Wisdom

Some of these "blessings" are also linked to eschatological hope in later texts:

- *"Blessed are those who endure in affliction..."* (Sirach 2:10-11)
- *"Blessed are those who wait and arrive at the end of the days..."* (Daniel 12:12)

These later texts begin to connect present suffering with future vindication, providing important background for Jesus' blessing of the persecuted and mourning.

Rabbinic Tradition

The *ashrei* formula remained popular in rabbinic literature, where it continued to identify the characteristics of those who live in harmony with God's will.[8] The prevalence of this form across Jewish literature shows that Jesus was working within a well-established tradition of wisdom teaching.

Jesus' Beatitudes draw directly from this tradition—yet go further by linking blessing not to prosperity, wisdom, or conventional righteousness, but to poverty, mourning, and meekness. This represents a radical reorientation of traditional wisdom categories.

The Dead Sea Scrolls: Community Boundaries and Reversal

The Qumran community, associated with the Dead Sea Scrolls, also used Beatitude-style language—especially in texts that defined community identity and eschatological hope.

Specific Qumran Parallels

4Q525, often called the "Beatitudes" text, contains formulas very close to Jesus-style blessings:[9]

"Blessed is he who speaks truth with a pure heart and does not slander with his tongue... Blessed is he who holds fast to her [Wisdom's] statutes and does not hold fast to the ways of iniquity."

This text shows that the Beatitude form was being used at Qumran to define the characteristics of faithful community members—those who would inherit divine blessing.

The Community Rule (1QS) contains similar language:

"Blessed is he who walks with a pure heart and does not slander with his tongue." (1QS 4.2-11)

These blessings functioned as boundary markers for community identity—defining who belonged to the faithful remnant and who would share in eschatological salvation.[10]

Apocalyptic Reversal Themes

The scrolls also contain apocalyptic hopes of divine reversal, similar to the Gospels:

- The proud will be humbled
- The righteous remnant will be exalted
- The wicked rich will be cast down
- God will establish justice for the oppressed

While not direct sources for Jesus' Beatitudes, these writings reveal that the air was thick with longing for a kingdom where humility triumphed and God set the world right.[11] The Qumran texts show that Jesus' vision of reversal resonated with broader Jewish hopes for divine intervention.

Comparative Analysis: Beatitude Forms Across Traditions

Source	Form	Emphasis	Context
Q (Reconstructed)	Blessed are poor, hungry, mourning, persecuted + Woes	Material focus, stark reversal	Apocalyptic urgency
Matthew	Blessed are poor *in spirit*, mourning, meek, etc.	Spiritual interpretation, ethical formation	Community instruction
Luke	Blessed are poor, hungry + Woes to rich, full	Social justice, economic reversal	Prophetic proclamation
Thomas	Blessed are poor, solitary, elect	Gnostic/mystical, individual enlightenment	Esoteric wisdom
Qumran (4Q525)	Blessed are those with pure hearts, holding to wisdom	Community boundaries, sectarian identity	Covenant faithfulness
Jewish Wisdom	Blessed are wise, righteous, God-fearing	Traditional virtue, practical wisdom	Moral instruction

This comparison reveals both continuity and innovation in how different communities used the Beatitude form. While all share the basic structure of pronouncing blessing, they differ significantly in content and emphasis.

Reception and Influence in Early Christianity

These non-canonical and extra-canonical Beatitude traditions influenced early Christian communities in various ways, though most were eventually rejected or marginalized by orthodox Christianity.

The Didache (late 1st to early 2nd century), while not containing explicit Beatitudes, reflects similar ethical concerns—emphasizing care for the poor, rejection of wealth, and preparation for divine judgment.[12] This shows how Beatitude values influenced early Christian formation even when the specific formulas weren't directly quoted.

The Shepherd of Hermas similarly emphasizes themes of poverty, persecution, and divine reversal that echo Beatitude theology, suggesting how deeply these values penetrated early Christian consciousness.[13]

However, texts like the Gospel of Thomas were eventually excluded from the canon partly because their interpretation of blessing diverged too far from apostolic tradition. Thomas's emphasis on esoteric knowledge and individual salvation conflicted with the communal and incarnational theology that became orthodox Christianity.[14]

Jewish Sibylline Oracles and Apocalyptic Parallels

Beyond specifically Christian or Qumran texts, Jewish Sibylline Oracles and other apocalyptic literature contain comparable blessing/reversal themes. These texts, circulating in the Greco-

Roman world, proclaimed coming divine judgment that would vindicate the righteous and punish the wicked.[15]

For example, Sibylline Oracle 3 promises blessing for those who honor God and justice while pronouncing woes on the proud and violent. This broader apocalyptic context helps explain why Beatitude-style proclamations resonated so widely in first-century Judaism and early Christianity.

Why It Matters: Continuity and Innovation

Tracing the Beatitude form through Q, apocrypha, and Jewish literature doesn't diminish their power—it deepens our understanding in several crucial ways:

Jesus in Context

It reminds us that Jesus was not speaking into a vacuum, but into a tradition hungry for divine justice. His words gained power partly because they resonated with existing hopes while transforming them in unexpected directions.

Form and Content

It shows that blessing was understood as God's favor in surprising places—not on thrones, but among the broken. This wasn't Jesus' invention but his brilliant appropriation of an ancient wisdom form.

Community Formation

It demonstrates that the early Jesus movement embraced both continuity and critique—using familiar forms to proclaim something radically new. The Beatitudes worked because they sounded familiar while saying something revolutionary.

Interpretive Diversity

It reveals that from the earliest period, different communities understood and applied Beatitude principles differently. This suggests that faithfulness to Jesus' vision may require ongoing interpretation rather than rigid repetition.

Canonical Wisdom

It helps explain why certain texts were included in the New Testament canon while others were excluded.[16] The canonical Beatitudes balanced innovation with continuity, radicalism with wisdom, in ways that proved most generative for Christian faith and practice.

The Living Stream

In this light, the Beatitudes are not isolated sayings, but part of a long and living stream—a song that Jesus takes up and transforms with his own voice. They represent both the culmination of Jewish wisdom about divine blessing and a revolutionary redefinition of what it means to be blessed.

Understanding this broader context enriches rather than diminishes our appreciation for the canonical Beatitudes. They emerge not as disconnected revelations but as the brilliant synthesis of ancient hopes and radical vision—familiar enough to be recognized, revolutionary enough to transform.

The Beatitudes succeeded where other formulations failed not because they abandoned tradition but because they fulfilled it in unexpected ways. They spoke the language of blessing that Israel had always known while revealing dimensions of divine favor that no one had fully anticipated.

This is the genius of Jesus' teaching: taking the deepest human longings for blessing and justice, expressed through ancient forms, and revealing their ultimate fulfillment in the upside-down kingdom of God. The Beatitudes work because they are both deeply traditional and utterly revolutionary—honoring the past while opening an unimaginable future.

Part V

Applied Beatitudes

Saints of the Beatitudes: Living Witnesses to a Radical Way

The Beatitudes are poetic and beautiful, but they are not theoretical. They are meant to be lived. And in every generation, there have been individuals—famous and forgotten—who have incarnated these blessings with extraordinary fidelity, creating what the author of Hebrews calls "a great cloud of witnesses."[1]

These exemplars come from different cultures, centuries, and creeds. Some are canonized saints, others are secular heroes, still others are quiet servants whose names history barely remembers. But all bear the unmistakable mark of the Beatitudes—not as perfection, but as practice. They remind us that these ancient blessings can be lived in boardrooms and soup kitchens, in protests and monasteries, in silence and in speech.

If we want to understand the Beatitudes, we must not only read them. We must watch them *walk*. And then, one step at a time, join them.

Christian Exemplars: Living the Gospel Radically

St. Francis of Assisi (1181-1226): Joyful Poverty, Radiant Peace

Few lives have so fully embodied the Beatitudes as St. Francis. The son of a wealthy merchant, Francis gave up everything to live in radical poverty, preach peace, and serve the poor.[2]

- **Poor in spirit**: He embraced literal poverty with joy, calling it "Lady Poverty"
- **Peacemaker**: Famously crossed battle lines during the Crusades to dialogue with the Sultan
- **Pure in heart**: His simplicity and joy radiated from undivided love for God

Francis didn't write systematic theology—he **lived** theology. His life became a sermon on the Beatitudes.

Dorothy Day (1897-1980): Mourning with the Poor, Practicing Mercy in Community

Dorothy Day, co-founder of the Catholic Worker Movement, embraced poverty not as charity, but as solidarity.[3] She lived among the poor, welcomed the marginalized, and resisted war and systemic injustice.

- **Mourning**: She grieved deeply for the world's suffering—and turned that grief into action
- **Mercy**: She showed hospitality to all, regardless of creed or condition
- **Persecuted for righteousness**: Her pacifism and advocacy made her controversial within church and state

Day called for a "revolution of the heart," rooted in the Gospel—and embodied the Beatitudes in soup kitchens, jail cells, and protest marches.

Archbishop Oscar Romero (1917-1980): Voice of the Voiceless

Oscar Romero transformed from a conservative archbishop into a fearless advocate for the poor in El Salvador.[4] His weekly radio sermons became a lifeline for the oppressed and a challenge to the powerful.

- **Hungering for righteousness**: Demanded justice for the poor and marginalized
- **Peacemaker**: Sought reconciliation while refusing to ignore systemic violence
- **Persecuted for righteousness**: Assassinated while celebrating Mass for his prophetic witness

Romero embodied the dangerous mercy of the Beatitudes, showing that peacemaking sometimes requires confronting injustice.

Rev. Dr. Martin Luther King Jr. (1929-1968): Peacemaking in the Face of Violence

Dr. King explicitly preached the Beatitudes—especially peacemaking, mercy, and justice—as the spiritual foundation of the Civil Rights Movement.[5]

- **Hungering for righteousness**: Demanded dignity through nonviolent resistance
- **Peacemaker**: Sought reconciliation, not retaliation
- **Persecuted**: Imprisoned and ultimately assassinated for living out these convictions

His sermon, *"The Drum Major Instinct,"* ends with the words: *"I want to be a servant. I want to be on the right side of the Beatitudes."*

Jean Vanier (1928-2019): Blessed Are the Meek, and the Broken

Founder of L'Arche, Jean Vanier created communities where people with and without intellectual disabilities lived together in mutual respect and friendship.[6]

- **Meek**: Vanier saw greatness in vulnerability, not achievement
- **Merciful**: Built a global movement grounded in gentleness and shared humanity
- **Pure in heart**: His spiritual writings reflect profound inner clarity

While his legacy was later complicated by posthumous revelations of misconduct, his work at L'Arche continues to offer a living expression of the Beatitudes—especially among the least visible.

Islamic Exemplars: Submission and Compassion

Rabi'a al-Adawiyya (c. 717-801): The Pure Heart of Sufi Love

One of Islam's most revered women mystics, Rabi'a from Basra lived an ascetic life devoted to God and love without expectation of reward.[7]

- **Poor in spirit**: Renounced worldly attachments for divine love
- **Pure in heart**: Her poetry centered on undivided devotion to God
- **Mercy**: Taught love without condition or expectation

Her famous prayer captures the Beatitude spirit: "O God, if I worship You for fear of Hell, burn me in Hell. If I worship You in hope of Paradise, exclude me from Paradise. But if I worship You for Your own sake, grudge me not Your everlasting beauty."[8]

Abdul Ghaffar Khan (1890-1988): The Frontier Gandhi

Known as "Badshah Khan," this Pashtun Muslim leader founded the nonviolent Khudai Khidmatgar ("Servants of God") movement in what is now Pakistan.[9]

- **Peacemaker**: Championed nonviolence in a region known for tribal warfare
- **Merciful**: Refused retaliation even under severe persecution
- **Hungering for righteousness**: Fought for independence and social justice through peaceful means

Khan spent more time in prison than Gandhi, yet never abandoned his commitment to nonviolence, proving that the Beatitudes transcend religious boundaries.

Hindu and Buddhist Exemplars: Dharma and Compassion

Mahatma Gandhi (1869-1948): Hungering for Righteousness, Making Peace Without Violence

Though not a Christian, Gandhi drew deeply from the Sermon on the Mount, which he called "the essence of Christianity."[10] His lifelong commitment to *satyagraha*—truth-force—mirrors the Beatitudes' fusion of meekness, mercy, and righteous hunger.

- **Poor in spirit**: Renounced wealth, privilege, and caste status
- **Hungering for righteousness**: Fought tirelessly for justice, yet without hate
- **Peacemaker**: His nonviolent resistance became a global model for social transformation

Gandhi's syncretic approach drew from Hindu tradition while being profoundly influenced by Christian teachings, demonstrating how the Beatitudes can speak across religious boundaries.

Mirabai (c. 1498-1547): Persecuted for Devotion

This Rajput princess and poet-saint abandoned royal privilege to pursue radical devotion to Krishna, facing persecution from family and society.[11]

- **Poor in spirit**: Rejected social status and wealth for spiritual poverty
- **Pure in heart**: Her devotional songs express undivided love for God
- **Persecuted for righteousness**: Faced exile and attempts on her life for refusing to conform to social expectations

Mirabai's fearless devotion and willingness to suffer for her beliefs embody the costly grace of the Beatitudes.

Thich Nhat Hanh (1926-2022): Pure in Heart, a Peaceful Presence

Vietnamese Zen master Thich Nhat Hanh spent his life teaching mindfulness, compassion, and nonviolence.[12] A poet, monk, and peace activist, he was nominated for the Nobel Peace Prize by Martin Luther King Jr. in 1967.

- **Pure in heart**: His practice of mindfulness—"present moment, wonderful moment"—reflects an undivided inner life
- **Peacemaker**: Worked tirelessly to end the Vietnam War, advocating for reconciliation without bitterness
- **Meek**: His strength was gentle, his influence quiet but enduring

Though a Buddhist, his teachings harmonize profoundly with the Beatitudes' invitation to interior stillness and outward love.

African Exemplars: Ubuntu and Reconciliation

Nelson Mandela (1918-2013): Persecuted, Yet Merciful

Nelson Mandela endured 27 years of imprisonment under South Africa's apartheid regime.[13] When released, he could have sought vengeance. Instead, he chose reconciliation.

- **Persecuted for righteousness**: Imprisoned for his resistance to injustice
- **Meek**: Wielded immense power with humility and restraint
- **Merciful**: Led South Africa through transition not with retribution, but with grace—embodied in the Truth and Reconciliation Commission

Mandela showed the world that justice and forgiveness are not opposites—they are interwoven in the life of a true peacemaker.

Archbishop Desmond Tutu (1931-2021): Merciful Justice and Laughter in the Face of Hate

Archbishop Desmond Tutu, a key voice in the South African anti-apartheid struggle, embodied joyful resistance.[14] His commitment to nonviolence, truth-telling, and forgiveness made him a global icon.

- **Hungering for righteousness**: Fought apartheid with moral clarity and spiritual courage
- **Merciful**: Advocated for reconciliation over revenge

- **Peacemaker**: Chaired the Truth and Reconciliation Commission to heal a wounded nation

Tutu often preached directly on the Beatitudes, urging people to discover their identity as beloved children of God.

Wangari Maathai (1940-2011): Environmental Justice and Women's Rights

Wangari Maathai, founder of Kenya's Green Belt Movement and Nobel Peace laureate, demonstrated how environmental stewardship and social justice intertwine.[15]

- **Meek**: Led with quiet strength, empowering local communities rather than dominating them
- **Merciful**: Showed compassion for both people and planet
- **Peacemaker**: Built bridges between environmental conservation and human rights

Maathai proved that caring for creation is itself a form of peacemaking and justice.

East Asian Wisdom: Harmony and Social Reform

Toyohiko Kagawa (1888-1960): Japan's Christian Social Reformer

Toyohiko Kagawa, Japanese Christian evangelist and social reformer, embodied the Beatitudes in his work among the poor in Tokyo's slums and his advocacy for labor rights and women's suffrage.[16]

- **Poor in spirit**: Chose to live in the slums despite his education and opportunities
- **Peacemaker**: Advocated for nonviolent social reform in pre-war Japan
- **Merciful**: Dedicated his life to serving the marginalized and oppressed

Kagawa demonstrated how Confucian values of social harmony could be integrated with Christian teachings, bridging Eastern and Western approaches to compassion.

Contemporary Global Voices

Malala Yousafzai (b. 1997): Education and Forgiveness

Malala Yousafzai, Pakistani activist for girls' education, survived targeted violence yet responded with forgiveness and continued advocacy.[17]

- **Hungering for righteousness**: Fearlessly advocates for education equality
- **Persecuted for righteousness**: Shot by Taliban for attending school, yet refused to be silenced
- **Merciful**: Responded to violence with forgiveness and continued service

At age 17, she became the youngest Nobel Peace Prize laureate, embodying hope in the face of hatred.

Simone Weil (1909-1943): Blessed Are Those Who Mourn

The French philosopher and mystic Simone Weil is often called the "patron saint of outsiders."[18] Her writing wrestles deeply with affliction, grace, and attention—all themes of the Beatitudes.

- **Mourning**: Bore witness to suffering during World War II, refusing comfort while others suffered
- **Pure in heart**: Her thought radiated intense honesty and clarity
- **Poor in spirit**: Renounced privilege, choosing solidarity with the oppressed

Weil wrote: *"The Beatitudes lift us above all our calculations. They teach us to love without reward."*

Mother Teresa (1910-1997): Mercy with Her Hands

St. Teresa of Calcutta lived among the poorest of the poor, caring for the dying, the abandoned, and the unloved.[19] She often cited the Beatitudes in her teaching and personal prayer.

- **Merciful**: Tended to bodies no one else would touch
- **Mourning**: Grieved the spiritual poverty of the world
- **Persecuted**: Criticized by many for her views, but never stopped serving

She said, *"The Beatitudes are everything. They are Christ's own description of His heart."*

Clarence Jordan (1912-1969): Radical Discipleship in the American South

Clarence Jordan, American theologian and farmer, created Koinonia Farm in Georgia as a model of racial reconciliation and economic sharing inspired by the Sermon on the Mount.[20]

- **Poor in spirit**: Embraced voluntary poverty and simple living
- **Peacemaker**: Built an interracial community during the height of segregation
- **Persecuted for righteousness**: Faced violence, boycotts, and terrorism for his witness

Jordan's Cotton Patch translations of the Bible placed Jesus' teachings in the American South, making the Beatitudes speak to contemporary issues of race and class.

Henri Nouwen (1932-1996): Vulnerability as Strength

Henri Nouwen, Dutch Catholic priest and writer, spent his later years living with intellectually disabled people at L'Arche, discovering profound spiritual truths in vulnerability.[21]

- **Poor in spirit**: Found God in brokenness rather than achievement
- **Meek**: Embraced weakness as a path to spiritual strength
- **Pure in heart**: His writings reflect deep authenticity and spiritual transparency

Nouwen showed that the Beatitudes' blessings on the vulnerable aren't consolation prizes but genuine insights into the nature of God.

Rabbi Abraham Joshua Heschel (1907-1972): Prophetic Witness

Abraham Heschel, Jewish rabbi and activist, marched alongside Dr. King and became a powerful voice for civil rights and interfaith cooperation.[22]

- **Hungering for righteousness**: United mourning for the Holocaust with action for justice
- **Peacemaker**: Built bridges between Jewish and Christian communities
- **Merciful**: Advocated for the oppressed while maintaining deep spiritual roots

Heschel famously said he felt like he was "praying with my feet" when marching in Selma, embodying the Jewish concept of *tikkun olam* (repairing the world) that resonates deeply with the Beatitudes.

The Hidden Saints Among Us

Beyond these well-known figures, countless ordinary people embody the Beatitudes in ways that rarely make headlines but profoundly shape their communities. In every culture, there are elders who mediate family disputes with patient wisdom, caregivers who tend the sick with gentle hands, teachers who see potential in struggling students, neighbors who share resources without expectation of return.

These unnamed saints include:

- The grandmother in rural India who teaches village children to read
- The imam in Detroit who builds bridges between Muslim and Christian communities
- The Buddhist monk in Thailand who cares for AIDS patients rejected by their families
- The social worker in São Paulo who advocates for street children
- The doctor in rural Kenya who provides healthcare to the poorest
- The teacher in inner-city Chicago who refuses to give up on any student

Their lives remind us that the Beatitudes are not reserved for famous figures or dramatic moments. They can be lived in the million small choices that shape our character and communities—choices made by people whose names we may never know but whose impact ripples through generations.

Beatitudes Exemplified: A Quick Reference

Exemplar	Tradition	Primary Beatitudes	Key Witness
St. Francis	Christian	Poor in spirit, Peacemaker	Radical poverty and joy
Dorothy Day	Christian	Mourning, Mercy	Solidarity with the poor

Exemplar	Tradition	Primary Beatitudes	Key Witness
Gandhi	Hindu (Christian-influenced)	Poor in spirit, Righteousness, Peacemaker	Nonviolent resistance
Rabi'a al-Adawiyya	Islamic (Sufi)	Poor in spirit, Pure in heart	Selfless divine love
Abdul Ghaffar Khan	Islamic	Peacemaker, Mercy	Muslim nonviolence
Thich Nhat Hanh	Buddhist	Pure in heart, Peacemaker, Meek	Mindful compassion
Nelson Mandela	Christian	Persecuted, Meek, Merciful	Reconciliation over revenge
Mirabai	Hindu (Bhakti)	Poor in spirit, Pure in heart, Persecuted	Devotional courage
Oscar Romero	Christian	Righteousness, Peacemaker, Persecuted	Prophetic witness
Martin Luther King Jr.	Christian	Righteousness, Peacemaker, Persecuted	Beloved community
Wangari Maathai	Christian	Meek, Merciful, Peacemaker	Environmental justice
Toyohiko Kagawa	Christian (Confucian-influenced)	Poor in spirit, Peacemaker, Merciful	Social reform in Japan
Malala Yousafzai	Islamic	Righteousness, Persecuted, Merciful	Education and forgiveness
Simone Weil	Christian/Mystic	Mourning, Pure in heart, Poor in spirit	Solidarity with suffering
Henri Nouwen	Christian	Poor in spirit, Meek, Pure in heart	Vulnerability as gift

Exemplar	Tradition	Primary Beatitudes	Key Witness
Abraham Heschel	Jewish	Righteousness, Mercy, Peacemaker	Prophetic activism

A Great Cloud of Witnesses

These exemplars—from St. Francis to Malala Yousafzai, from Rabi'a to the unnamed grandmother teaching village children—come from different cultures, centuries, and creeds. But all bear the mark of the Beatitudes. Not as perfection, but as practice.

They remind us that the Beatitudes are not reserved for saints or mystics. They can be lived in any context, by anyone willing to embrace the radical vulnerability and courageous love that Jesus blessed on that Galilean hillside.

What unites these diverse witnesses is not their religious affiliation but their willingness to embody a different way of being human—one that finds strength in gentleness, wealth in poverty of spirit, victory in mercy, and life in laying down one's life for others.

Their lives pose a question to all of us: If people from such different backgrounds and circumstances can live the Beatitudes, what's stopping us? The answer, these saints suggest, is nothing—except our willingness to begin.

The Beatitudes are not exclusive to any one faith tradition. They represent, as Gandhi recognized, a universal call to human dignity and divine love. They invite us all—regardless of our religious background—into a way of life that serves the healing of the world.

If we want to understand the Beatitudes, we must not only read them. We must watch them *walk*. And then, one step at a time, join the great procession of those who have discovered that in losing their lives, they find them—and in the process, help others find theirs too.

Living the Beatitudes in Daily Life

The Beatitudes are not abstract virtues to admire from a distance. They are a way of life—a spiritual architecture for human flourishing that Jesus outlined on a Galilean hillside and that countless people have embodied in countless contexts ever since.

After centuries of interpretation—from Origen's mystical ascent to Dorothy Day's radical compassion—the question remains: how do we actually live this? What does it mean, practically and personally, to be *poor in spirit*, to *hunger and thirst for righteousness*, or to *make peace* in a broken world?

This exploration brings the Beatitudes down from the mountain and into the mess of daily life. We'll look at how these teachings can shape our posture in relationships, communities, work, activism, and even in moments of grief or anxiety. These aren't spiritual achievements to master but invitations to a different way of being—one that transforms both hearts and communities.

1. Poverty of Spirit: Letting Go of Ego, Not Dignity

Being "poor in spirit" doesn't mean self-hatred or diminishment. It means honest humility—recognizing our dependence on something greater than ourselves while maintaining the dignity that comes from being beloved of God. In practice, this might look like:

In conversations: Listening before speaking, especially when tempted to dominate or prove your point. Ask more questions than you make statements.

When you fail: Admitting mistakes without defensiveness or elaborate justification. A simple "I was wrong" or "I'm sorry" can be profoundly liberating.

With achievements: Holding loosely to roles, titles, or accomplishments. Let them serve others rather than define your worth.

In prayer or meditation: Coming empty-handed, without agenda or performance. Just be present.

In a world obsessed with achievement and status, this kind of grounded openness is revolutionary. It creates space for grace—for learning, for others' wisdom, for unexpected encounters with the divine. As we become more comfortable with not knowing, we discover that uncertainty can be a doorway rather than a dead end.

2. Mourning: Honoring Loss Without Rushing Past It

Modern life leaves little room for grief. We're encouraged to "move on," "stay positive," or "find closure." But Jesus' words, *"Blessed are those who mourn, for they will be comforted,"* invite us to sit with sorrow—not just our own, but also the suffering of others and the brokenness of the world.

Personal practices: Create rituals for grief—lighting candles, planting trees, writing letters to those you've lost. Honor both major losses and smaller deaths—the end of relationships, dreams that didn't materialize, versions of yourself you've outgrown.

With others: Hold space for others' pain without rushing to fix it. Sometimes the most merciful thing you can do is simply say, "This is really hard" and sit in silence.

In community: Practice lament—a lost art in many Western churches but central to biblical faith. Create spaces where people can name what's broken without immediately jumping to solutions.

For the world: Allow yourself to feel the weight of injustice, environmental destruction, or systemic suffering. Let grief over the world's pain motivate compassionate action rather than numbing indifference.

To mourn is to resist numbness. It's to love deeply enough that loss matters. It's also to trust that comfort comes—not as quick fix, but as divine presence that meets us in our sorrow and gradually transforms it into compassion for others who suffer.

3. Meekness: Strength Without Domination

Meekness is often misunderstood as weakness, but biblically, the meek are those who possess strength under control—power that serves love rather than ego. In everyday life, this could look like:

In conflict: De-escalating tension rather than "winning" arguments. Ask yourself: "Do I want to be right or do I want relationship?"

In leadership: Using authority to lift others up rather than prove your importance. The best leaders make others feel more capable, not less.

In public discourse: Engaging disagreement with curiosity rather than contempt. Seek to understand before seeking to be understood.

With power: Whether it's physical strength, financial resources, social privilege, or institutional authority—use it in service of others, especially those with less power.

Meekness is especially vital in parenting, where coercion often masquerades as guidance, and in social media, where the loudest voices often drown out the wisest ones. True meekness doesn't avoid necessary conflict but engages it without losing one's center.

4. Hunger and Thirst for Righteousness: Staying Spiritually Hungry

This Beatitude honors desire—not complacency. To hunger and thirst for righteousness means to crave a world (and a heart) made right. It's about living with *holy dissatisfaction*—not cynical, but never settling for injustice or spiritual stagnation.

Daily spiritual practice: Whether through prayer, meditation, Scripture reading, or contemplative walking—maintain regular practices that keep you spiritually hungry rather than spiritually full of yourself.

Pursuit of justice: Advocate for fairness in your community, workplace, or family. This might mean volunteering with organizations that serve the marginalized, speaking up in meetings when decisions harm vulnerable people, or simply refusing to participate in gossip or exclusion.

Intellectual humility: Stay curious. Keep learning. Resist the temptation to think you've figured everything out—spiritually, politically, or personally.

Personal transformation: Continue working on your own character. Ask trusted friends to point out your blind spots. Seek therapy, spiritual direction, or other forms of growth.

As we pursue righteousness both personally and socially, we discover that the journey itself transforms us. The hunger doesn't disappear when we're "filled"—it deepens and matures, becoming less about what we can get and more about what we can give.

5. Mercy: Forgiveness as a Way of Being

Mercy is not passive pity or enabling harmful behavior. It's active compassion—the willingness to release resentment and respond with care, even when it's undeserved. Jesus blesses not just those who forgive once, but those who *become*merciful—

people whose default response is understanding rather than judgment.

In relationships: Practice letting go of old grudges, even without receiving apologies. This doesn't mean becoming a doormat—set boundaries while releasing bitterness.

With difficult people: Choose curiosity over judgment when others fail. Ask yourself: "What might this person be afraid of?" or "What pain might be driving this behavior?"

In daily interactions: Extend grace to the slow cashier, the distracted driver, the overwhelmed parent. Everyone is fighting battles you can't see.

Within systems: Support restorative rather than purely punitive approaches to wrongdoing—whether in criminal justice, workplace conflicts, or family disputes.

Mercy is often quiet and unseen—a thousand small acts of understanding that resist the cultural urge to harden our hearts. It doesn't mean being naive about harm or refusing to seek justice. Rather, it means holding both accountability and compassion, recognizing that we all need grace.

6. Purity of Heart: Living with Integrity and Intention

To be "pure in heart" doesn't mean moral perfection. It means being whole—not fragmented or double-minded. The Greek *katharoi tē kardia* suggests singleness of purpose, a heart not pulled in competing directions by ego, fear, or conflicting loyalties.

In communication: Say what you mean and mean what you say. Let your yes be yes and your no be no. Avoid manipulation, even subtle forms.

In decision-making: Align your outer actions with inner convictions. When there's tension between what you believe and how you act, something needs to change.

In attention: Remove distractions that cloud your conscience or scatter your focus. This might mean digital fasts, simplifying commitments, or creating space for silence and reflection.

In relationships: Show up as your authentic self rather than performing versions of yourself designed to impress or please others.

Whether in prayer, work, or relationships, purity of heart invites us to live with integrity—undivided and awake. It's about becoming the same person in private that you are in public, having thoughts that you wouldn't be ashamed to voice, and pursuing goals that serve love rather than ego.

7. Peacemaking: Bridging Divides, Not Just Avoiding Conflict

Jesus didn't say, *"Blessed are the peace-lovers."* He said, *"Blessed are the peacemakers."* This is active, not passive. It's not conflict avoidance—it's courageous bridge-building that addresses root causes of division rather than just managing symptoms.

In families: Initiate hard conversations with humility. Address unspoken tensions before they become entrenched patterns. Apologize first when you've contributed to conflict.

In communities: Learn mediation skills. Offer to facilitate difficult conversations between people who are stuck in conflict. Create opportunities for people with different perspectives to encounter each other as human beings.

In society: Speak up against injustice without demonizing those who disagree with you. Build coalitions across traditional divides. Vote, volunteer, and advocate for policies that serve the common good.

In yourself: Work to integrate the various parts of yourself—the aspects you're proud of and those you'd rather hide. Internal peace often precedes external peacemaking.

Peacemaking requires patience, empathy, and often discomfort. It means sitting in the tension between opposing sides long enough to find creative third ways. Jesus calls these people *children of God*—perhaps because they resemble their divine Parent most clearly in their refusal to give up on relationship even when it's difficult.

8. Enduring Persecution: Holding Steady When Righteousness Is Costly

In a world that rewards comfort and conformity, choosing to live the Beatitudes may bring pushback—from systems that benefit from injustice, peers who prefer not to be challenged, or even your own fears and doubts.

In convictions: Stay faithful to values even when they're unpopular or professionally costly. Refuse to participate in systems that harm others, even when the cost is significant.

In response: Don't return hate for hate or violence for violence. Maintain your gentleness and mercy even when others respond with hostility.

In community: Find others who pursue the same path. Suffering for righteousness is more bearable—and more effective—when shared.

In perspective: Remember that resistance to righteousness is often evidence that you're touching something important. Systems don't fight changes that don't threaten them.

This isn't about seeking suffering or developing a martyr complex. It's about having the courage to remain gentle, merciful, and just—even when it's costly. It's about trusting that the kingdom of heaven belongs not to those who avoid all conflict, but to those who engage conflict in the spirit of love.

Creating Spaces for Beatitudinal Living

While the Beatitudes transform individuals, they're also meant to shape communities. Consider how your family, workplace, church, or neighborhood might cultivate collective practices:

In families: Regular times for confession and forgiveness, family service projects, conflict resolution processes that prioritize relationship over being right.

In workplaces: Policies that prioritize employee welfare over pure profit, decision-making processes that include diverse voices, responses to failure that emphasize learning over punishment.

In faith communities: Worship that includes lament, leadership development that values character over charisma, outreach that serves rather than converts.

In neighborhoods: Community gardens, block parties that cross cultural divides, mutual aid networks that share resources.

Avoiding Counterfeit Versions

As we pursue Beatitudinal living, it's important to distinguish between authentic virtue and well-intentioned but harmful imitations:

False humility that becomes self-deprecation or emotional manipulation rather than genuine openness to growth.

Toxic peacemaking that avoids necessary truth-telling or enables abusive patterns in the name of harmony.

Performative mercy that focuses more on appearing forgiving than actually releasing resentment.

Spiritual bypassing that uses religious language to avoid dealing with practical problems or psychological wounds.

The authentic Beatitudes produce freedom, joy, and genuine transformation—not anxiety, manipulation, or spiritual pride.

The Beatitudes as Integration

Perhaps most importantly, the Beatitudes work together as an integrated way of being. As we become more merciful in our private thoughts, we find ourselves acting more mercifully toward others. As we grow in humility, we become better peacemakers because we're less threatened by disagreement. As we learn to mourn well, we develop the compassion necessary for true righteousness.

This integration happens slowly, through practice and grace, in community and in solitude. The goal isn't perfection but participation—joining the long tradition of people who have discovered that Jesus' way of life, while demanding, is also deeply satisfying.

Invitation, Not Checklist

The Beatitudes aren't goals to master or badges to wear. They are invitations to a different way of being—a way that the world desperately needs but rarely rewards. They call us not to perform holiness but to participate in it through humility, compassion, justice, and joy.

This path requires both individual commitment and community support. It demands both inner work and outer action. It asks us to be both gentle and fierce, both accepting and transformative.

And while the world may never fully reward this path, it is the one Jesus blesses. Again and again. Without qualification.

To live the Beatitudes is to let them shape our instincts, our reactions, our hopes. It's to say, with our lives as much as our lips, *"Your kingdom come."* It's to discover that in losing our false selves, we find our true ones—and in the process, help others do the same.

The Beatitudes are not just beautiful poetry or ancient wisdom. They are a living invitation to become the kind of people the world needs: humble enough to keep learning, brave enough to keep loving, and faithful enough to keep hoping, even when the path is difficult and the destination seems distant.

This is the narrow way that leads to life—not just eternal life, but abundant life here and now, in community with others who are walking the same path toward the kingdom of heaven that is already among us, waiting to be recognized and embodied by those with eyes to see and hearts to receive.

Part VI

Conclusion and Resources

Conclusion & Reflection

When I began this exploration of the Beatitudes, I expected to find universal themes. What I didn't expect was to be so moved by the particular ways different traditions glimpse the same profound truths about human flourishing.

It's like discovering that people scattered across centuries and continents have all been gazing at the same constellation, each describing what they see in their own language, each bringing their own cultural lens, but all pointing toward something unmistakably shared.

The Same Sky, Different Windows

A comparative religions scholar once told me that different faith traditions are like seats in a vast stadium—everyone watching the same event, but from different angles, some closer, some farther, some with obstructed views, others with panoramic perspectives. As I traced the Beatitudes across traditions, I kept wondering: what is that "event" they're all watching?

Maybe it's not an event at all. Maybe it's the human condition itself—this strange, beautiful, tragic experience of being conscious beings capable of both breathtaking cruelty and inexplicable kindness. Maybe what all these traditions are pointing toward is what it actually means to be fully human.

When I read Rumi's poetry about spiritual poverty alongside Jesus' blessing of the "poor in spirit," I felt like I was seeing two people in that stadium pointing at the same star. When I discovered how *ubuntu* creates space for mercy to flow, or how Buddhist compassion mirrors the blessing on the merciful, I realized I wasn't just studying comparative religion—I was witnessing different languages trying to describe the same mysterious reality.

The Awe of Recognition

What moved me most wasn't that these insights appeared across traditions—I expected that. What took my breath away was the specificity of the convergence. It's one thing to say that all religions value compassion. It's another to discover that the particular shape of Jesus' blessing on those who mourn finds such precise echoes in Buddhist teachings on suffering, or that the meekness Jesus describes looks so remarkably like the Taoist sage's wu wei.

These weren't vague similarities but specific recognitions, as if different traditions had developed their own vocabulary for describing the same detailed landscape of the human heart.

What the Saints Taught Me

The people who have embodied these teachings—from Francis of Assisi to Dorothy Day, from Gandhi to Thich Nhat Hanh to Malala—showed me something else I hadn't anticipated. They seemed to be drawing from the same well, even when they came from completely different traditions.

Watching Gandhi's satyagraha, I saw the Beatitudes in action even though he wasn't a Christian. Observing Dorothy Day's radical hospitality, I glimpsed what Islamic mercy might look like in a Catholic Worker house. These people weren't trying to be perfect representatives of their traditions—they were trying to be fully human, and in doing so, they all seemed to be reaching toward the same light.

The Pattern That Emerges

What I discovered is that the Beatitudes seem to describe what every major faith tradition is supposed to be at its best—the founding principles that get buried under institutional concerns, cultural adaptations, and human failings. Buddhism's compassion, Islam's mercy, Judaism's justice, Christianity's love, Indigenous wisdom's harmony with creation—they all seem to be variations on the same theme.

The tragedy isn't that these traditions are different. The tragedy is how often adherents of each tradition lose sight of their own deepest teachings. How many who claim Christianity ignore the radical mercy Jesus preached? How many Buddhists forget the Bodhisattva's vow to serve all beings? How often do any of us live up to the best our traditions offer?

But the hope is this: when people of any faith tradition return to these foundational principles—compassion, justice, mercy, humility, peace—something remarkable happens. The boundaries between "us" and "them" start to dissolve. We begin to recognize each other not as competitors or strangers, but as fellow travelers pointing toward the same constellation of what it means to be fully human.

The Greek Surprise

Even the linguistic exploration yielded unexpected gifts. Learning that *makarioi* describes people who are already flourishing—not people who have earned blessing through good behavior—felt like discovering a secret that had been hiding in plain sight.

This changes everything about how we read these teachings. They're not describing a spiritual elite or offering a self-improvement program. They're more like a field guide for recognizing where authentic human flourishing is already happening, often in places the world dismisses as failure or foolishness.

What We've Learned

This journey has revealed something both humbling and hopeful: the wisdom we need for healing our fractured world isn't hidden in some esoteric teaching or locked away in any single tradition. It's been here all along, spoken in different languages but pointing toward the same truth—that another way of being human is possible.

The poor in spirit, the merciful, the peacemakers aren't failures or anomalies. They're the people who have figured out how to live in alignment with the deepest currents of reality. They show us that in a universe somehow fundamentally oriented toward love, those who choose vulnerability over control, mercy over retaliation, and justice over silence find themselves blessed, regardless of what tradition taught them or what the world thinks of their choices.

The Invitation

The Beatitudes, it turns out, aren't just a Christian text or even a religious text. They're a map of the human heart written in one tradition's beautiful vocabulary, pointing toward something that every tradition recognizes in its own way: the possibility of living as if love is real, justice matters, and gentleness might actually inherit the earth.

Maybe this is what the world needs most—not more arguments about whose tradition is right, but more people willing to embody what every tradition knows is true. More people willing to be poor in spirit, merciful, pure in heart, and brave enough to make peace in a world addicted to division.

The path is there. The invitation stands. What remains is the choice: Will we walk it?

Research Methodology

Transparency in the Age of AI

As I mentioned in the introduction, this project has two distinct but interrelated components: learning more about the Beatitudes and their alignment with other faith traditions, and exploring how artificial intelligence can support rigorous research, analysis, and writing. In the spirit of intellectual honesty that should characterize any serious inquiry, I want to be completely transparent about the role AI platforms played in creating this work.

We live in a moment of rapid technological transformation that is reshaping how knowledge is created, verified, and shared. AI tools have become powerful research partners, capable of processing vast amounts of information, identifying unexpected connections, and helping scholars explore questions that might otherwise require years of solitary investigation. But with this power comes responsibility—the need for new methodologies that harness AI's capabilities while maintaining the rigor and integrity that serious scholarship demands.

This project represents one attempt to develop such a methodology. The approach I describe here will likely be obsolete within months as AI platforms continue to evolve at breakneck speed. But I hope this transparency will serve two purposes: giving readers confidence in the accuracy and integrity of the content they've just encountered, and providing a potential model for other researchers navigating the new landscape of AI-assisted scholarship.

The Multi-Platform Workflow

Rather than relying on a single AI system, I developed a workflow that leverages the distinct strengths of different platforms while building in multiple layers of verification and human oversight. The process typically involved six distinct stages:

Stage 1: Conceptual Exploration with ChatGPT

I began each chapter by engaging in extended conversations with ChatGPT to brainstorm ideas, explore connections between traditions, and identify the most compelling aspects of each Beatitude. ChatGPT's conversational strengths made it ideal for this exploratory phase, helping me discover unexpected parallels—like the relationship between Jesus' "meekness" and the Taoist concept of *wu wei*, or the resonance between Islamic ṣabr (patient perseverance) and the blessing on those who mourn.

Stage 2: Research Verification with Perplexity

The initial draft was then subjected to rigorous fact-checking using Perplexity, an AI platform specifically designed for research applications. Perplexity excels at identifying and verifying sources, checking the credibility of references, and filling gaps in analysis. This stage often revealed errors or oversimplifications in the initial draft and suggested additional avenues for exploration.

Stage 3: Synthesis and Refinement with Claude
The research findings and critiques from Perplexity were then provided to Claude, along with the original draft, to create a revised version that incorporated the scholarly feedback while maintaining consistency with previous chapters in tone, structure, and approach.

Stage 4: Secondary Verification
The revised draft returned to Perplexity for another round of source verification and fact-checking, ensuring that no errors had been introduced during the revision process and that all claims remained properly supported.

Stage 5: Platform Iteration
Drafts typically bounced between Perplexity and Claude until all identified issues were resolved, which usually occurred by the second revision cycle.

Stage 6: Human Expert Review
The final AI-generated draft was then reviewed by a human scholar with expertise in comparative religions, providing an additional layer of verification and often suggesting refinements that no AI system had identified.

Why Different Platforms Matter

The decision to use multiple AI platforms reflects the reality that different systems have evolved distinct capabilities, strengths, and limitations—much like human experts in different fields.

ChatGPT proved invaluable for its conversational sophistication and ability to synthesize information across disparate domains. Its strength lies in pattern recognition and creative connections—helping me see, for instance, how the Beatitudes' emphasis on "inner posture" resonates with Confucian concepts of moral cultivation or Buddhist teachings on mental states. However, ChatGPT can sometimes prioritize completing a request over accuracy, particularly in extended conversations where context begins to drift.

Perplexity demonstrated exceptional research capabilities, able to identify and verify sources across multiple academic databases while flagging potentially unreliable information. Its integration with real-time web search proved particularly valuable for checking recent scholarship and ensuring that cited sources actually contained the claims attributed to them. Perplexity's limitation lies in its more constrained conversational abilities—it's less effective for exploratory brainstorming but superb for verification.

Claude excelled at synthesis and writing, demonstrating remarkable ability to maintain consistent tone and structure across multiple chapters while incorporating complex feedback from multiple sources. Claude's strength in understanding context and maintaining coherence across long documents made it ideal for creating final drafts that felt unified rather than assembled from disparate parts.

The Critical Role of Context and Prompting

One of the most important discoveries in this process was the critical importance of providing appropriate context to AI systems. Insufficient or unclear context is the primary reason AI platforms sometimes produce unreliable results—what researchers call "hallucination," though it's more accurately described as the system's attempt to fulfill requests based on inadequate information.

The foundational context I provided to all three AI platforms was:

"You are a PhD-level scholar of comparative religions, with especially deep experience in biblical history and Christianity, as well as Islam, Buddhism, Hinduism, and Taoism. You have no foundational bias toward any religion. When I ask questions you will evaluate using information only from recognized academic and experienced sources, and not use any speculative information from lower quality sources."

Each platform then received additional specific instructions tailored to its role in the workflow. ChatGPT was instructed to prioritize creative connections while acknowledging gaps in knowledge rather than fabricating information. Perplexity received detailed instructions about source verification and scholarly rigor. Claude received the most extensive prompting, including specific instructions about maintaining series consistency, incorporating expert feedback, and balancing scholarly accuracy with accessibility.

This layered approach to prompting proved essential for maintaining quality control throughout the process. By clearly defining the role each AI system should play and the standards it should maintain, I was able to harness their respective strengths while minimizing their individual limitations.

Unexpected Discoveries and Limitations

The AI-assisted research process yielded several unexpected discoveries that likely would not have emerged through traditional research methods alone. The ability to rapidly explore connections across multiple religious traditions revealed patterns and parallels that might have taken years to identify through conventional scholarship. For instance, the specificity of convergence between Jesus' teaching on "those who mourn" and Buddhist insights into suffering, or the remarkable similarity between the Beatitudes' understanding of "pure in heart" and various traditions' concepts of spiritual integrity.

However, the process also revealed important limitations. AI systems, regardless of their sophistication, lack the intuitive understanding that comes from lived experience within religious traditions. They can identify textual parallels and scholarly connections, but they cannot fully grasp the experiential dimensions of spiritual practice that often give these teachings their deepest meaning. This is where human insight—both my own reflections and expert review—proved irreplaceable.

Additionally, AI systems inherit the biases present in their training data, which predominantly reflects Western, English-language scholarship. This meant that some perspectives, particularly from Global South traditions or non-English sources, may be underrepresented in the analysis despite my efforts to seek diverse viewpoints.

Quality Assurance and Verification

The multi-layered verification process proved essential for maintaining scholarly integrity. The combination of different AI platforms catching each other's errors, followed by human expert review, created a robust system for ensuring accuracy. In several instances, Perplexity identified misattributed quotes or oversimplified characterizations of complex theological concepts that had slipped through the initial drafting process. The human expert reviewer then provided cultural and contextual insights that no AI system had identified.

This experience suggests that the future of AI-assisted scholarship lies not in replacing human expertise but in creating hybrid methodologies that amplify human insight through technological capability while maintaining rigorous oversight and verification processes.

Implications for Future Research

This project suggests several principles for AI-assisted research in religious studies and related fields:

Transparency is essential: Readers deserve to know how knowledge claims are generated and verified, particularly when new technologies are involved.

Multiple platforms provide better results: Leveraging different AI systems' strengths while mitigating their individual weaknesses produces more reliable outcomes than relying on any single system.

Human oversight remains crucial: AI can enhance human capabilities but cannot replace the judgment, experience, and intuitive understanding that human experts bring to complex subjects.

Context and prompting matter enormously: The quality of AI output depends heavily on the quality of input—both in terms of specific instructions and the broader context provided.

Verification must be systematic: The speed and apparent authority of AI-generated content makes rigorous fact-checking and source verification more important than ever.

Limitations must be acknowledged: AI systems have significant constraints, particularly around cultural understanding and experiential knowledge, that researchers must actively address.

The Future of AI-Assisted Scholarship

As AI capabilities continue to evolve, the methodologies described here will undoubtedly seem primitive within a few years. But the underlying principles—leveraging technological capabilities while maintaining scholarly rigor, transparency about methods, and commitment to truth over convenience—will likely remain relevant regardless of technological advancement.

The goal is not to replace traditional scholarship but to enhance it, enabling researchers to explore questions and connections that would otherwise remain beyond reach. In the case of this project, AI assistance made it possible to conduct a comprehensive comparative analysis across multiple religious traditions while maintaining the depth and rigor that such a study demands.

The result, I hope, is work that demonstrates both the potential and the limitations of AI-assisted research—showing how these tools can serve human curiosity and insight while reminding us that the most important questions about meaning, wisdom, and human flourishing still require the irreplaceable contributions of human reflection and experience.

Perhaps most importantly, this methodology enabled me to approach the Beatitudes not just as a scholar of one tradition examining others, but as a fellow human being exploring the universal patterns of wisdom that seem to emerge wherever people seriously grapple with what it means to live well. In that sense, AI became not just a research tool but a bridge—helping me discover connections across traditions that point toward our shared humanity and common longing for lives of meaning, justice, and peace.

Notes by Chapter

Apocalyptic Vision and the Kingdom of Heaven: The Context of the Beatitudes

1. Richard A. Horsley, *Jesus and Empire: The Kingdom of God and the New World Disorder* (Minneapolis: Fortress Press, 2003), 81-104; E.P. Sanders, *Judaism: Practice and Belief 63 BCE—66 CE* (Philadelphia: Trinity Press, 1992), 146-169.
2. John J. Collins, *The Apocalyptic Imagination: An Introduction to Jewish Apocalyptic Literature*, 3rd ed. (Grand Rapids: Eerdmans, 2016), 1-42.
3. Christopher Rowland, *The Open Heaven: A Study of Apocalyptic in Judaism and Early Christianity* (New York: Crossroad, 1982), 9-22.
4. N.T. Wright, *Jesus and the Victory of God* (Minneapolis: Fortress Press, 1996), 202-209.
5. Luke 4:16-21; see Ulrich Luz, *Matthew 1-7: A Commentary*, Hermeneia Series (Minneapolis: Fortress Press, 2007), 193-196.
6. Florentino García Martínez and Eibert J.C. Tigchelaar, eds., *The Dead Sea Scrolls Study Edition*, 2 vols. (Leiden: Brill, 2000), 2:1049-1051 (4Q525).
7. Wright, *Jesus and the Victory of God*, 198-243.
8. Horsley, *Jesus and Empire*, 28-58.
9. John Dominic Crossan, *The Birth of Christianity* (San Francisco: HarperOne, 1998), 158-167.

10. Dale C. Allison, *The Sermon on the Mount: Inspiring the Moral Imagination* (New York: Crossroad, 1999), 42-50.
11. Wright, *Jesus and the Victory of God*, 467-472.
12. Allison, *The Sermon on the Mount*, 45-47.
13. Acts 2:42-47; 4:32-37; see Richard Bauckham, *The Jewish World Around the New Testament* (Grand Rapids: Baker Academic, 2010), 164-181.
14. Collins, *The Apocalyptic Imagination*, 384-394.
15. Wright, *The New Testament and the People of God* (Minneapolis: Fortress Press, 1992), 280-338.

Blessed Are the Poor in Spirit: A Foundation for Living

1. Dale C. Allison Jr., *The Sermon on the Mount: Inspiring the Moral Imagination* (New Haven: Yale University Press, 1999), 45-47.
2. Luke 6:20; see also Ulrich Luz, *Matthew 1-7: A Continental Commentary* (Minneapolis: Fortress Press, 2007), 191-193.
3. John Chrysostom, *Homilies on the Gospel of Matthew*, Homily 15.1, in *Nicene and Post-Nicene Fathers*, First Series, vol. 10, ed. Philip Schaff (New York: Christian Literature Publishing, 1888).
4. Psalms 34:18, 51:17; Isaiah 66:2, New Revised Standard Version.
5. E.P. Sanders, *Jesus and Judaism* (Philadelphia: Fortress Press, 1985), 174-176; Amy-Jill Levine, *The Misunderstood Jew: The Church and the Scandal of the Jewish Jesus* (New York: HarperOne, 2006), 89-91.

6. Qur'an 49:13, trans. M.A.S. Abdel Haleem (Oxford: Oxford University Press, 2004).
7. Rumi, *The Essential Rumi*, trans. Coleman Barks (New York: HarperSanFrancisco, 1995), 109; see also Annemarie Schimmel, *Mystical Dimensions of Islam* (Chapel Hill: University of North Carolina Press, 1975), 112-115.
8. *The Dhammapada*, trans. Narada Thera (Colombo: Buddhist Publication Society, 1972), verse 63.
9. Thich Nhat Hanh, *The Heart of Buddhist Meditation* (Boston: Beacon Press, 1975), 78-82.
10. *The Bhagavad Gita*, trans. Eknath Easwaran (Tomales, CA: Nilgiri Press, 1985), 13:7-8.
11. Ramana Maharshi, *The Collected Works of Ramana Maharshi*, ed. Arthur Osborne (London: Rider, 1959), 45-48.
12. *Tao Te Ching*, trans. D.C. Lau (London: Penguin Classics, 1963), Chapter 8.
13. John Dominic Crossan, *Jesus: A Revolutionary Biography* (San Francisco: HarperSanFrancisco, 1994), 58-62; N.T. Wright, *Jesus and the Victory of God* (Minneapolis: Fortress Press, 1996), 287-290.

Blessed Are Those Who Mourn: Finding Comfort in Grief Across Traditions

1. Dale C. Allison Jr., *The Sermon on the Mount: Inspiring the Moral Imagination* (New Haven: Yale University Press, 1999), 52-54.

2. John Chrysostom, *Homilies on the Gospel of Matthew*, Homily 15.2, in *Nicene and Post-Nicene Fathers*, First Series, vol. 10, ed. Philip Schaff (New York: Christian Literature Publishing, 1888).
3. Augustine of Hippo, *Sermon on the Mount*, 1.4.12, in *Nicene and Post-Nicene Fathers*, First Series, vol. 6, ed. Philip Schaff (New York: Christian Literature Publishing, 1888).
4. Psalms 34:18, 126:5; Isaiah 40:1; Lamentations 3:31-33, New Revised Standard Version.
5. Byron R. McCane, *Roll Back the Stone: Death and Burial in the World of Jesus* (Harrisburg, PA: Trinity Press International, 2003), 87-89.
6. E.P. Sanders, *Jesus and Judaism* (Philadelphia: Fortress Press, 1985), 174-176; Amy-Jill Levine, *The Misunderstood Jew: The Church and the Scandal of the Jewish Jesus* (New York: HarperOne, 2006), 89-91.
7. Qur'an 2:155-156, trans. M.A.S. Abdel Haleem (Oxford: Oxford University Press, 2004).
8. Sahih al-Bukhari, Book 23, Hadith 390.
9. Rumi, *The Essential Rumi*, trans. Coleman Barks (New York: HarperSanFrancisco, 1995), 142-145; see also Annemarie Schimmel, *Mystical Dimensions of Islam* (Chapel Hill: University of North Carolina Press, 1975), 287-290.
10. *The Connected Discourses of the Buddha*, trans. Bhikkhu Bodhi (Boston: Wisdom Publications, 2000), 1844-1847.
11. *The Dhammapada*, trans. Narada Thera (Colombo: Buddhist Publication Society, 1972), verse 5.

12. Thich Nhat Hanh, *No Death, No Fear* (New York: Riverhead Books, 2002), 78-82.
13. *The Bhagavad Gita*, trans. Eknath Easwaran (Tomales, CA: Nilgiri Press, 1985), 2:11.
14. Barbara Stoler Miller, trans., *The Bhagavad-Gita* (New York: Bantam Classics, 1986), 31-33.
15. *Tao Te Ching*, trans. D.C. Lau (London: Penguin Classics, 1963), Chapter 8.
16. Ibid., Chapter 50.
17. John Dominic Crossan, *Jesus: A Revolutionary Biography* (San Francisco: HarperSanFrancisco, 1994), 58-62.
18. Megan Devine, *It's OK That You're Not OK: Meeting Grief and Loss in a Culture That Doesn't Understand*(Boulder, CO: Sounds True, 2017), 45-48.

Blessed Are the Meek: Reclaiming a Misunderstood Virtue

1. Dale C. Allison Jr., *The Sermon on the Mount: Inspiring the Moral Imagination* (New Haven: Yale University Press, 1999), 58-60.
2. Ulrich Luz, *Matthew 1–7: A Continental Commentary* (Minneapolis: Fortress Press, 2007), 195-197.
3. John Chrysostom, *Homilies on the Gospel of Matthew*, Homily 15.3, in *Nicene and Post-Nicene Fathers*, First Series, vol. 10, ed. Philip Schaff (New York: Christian Literature Publishing, 1888).
4. Numbers 12:3, New Revised Standard Version; see E.P. Sanders, *Jesus and Judaism* (Philadelphia: Fortress Press, 1985), 178-180.
5. Psalm 37:11, New Revised Standard Version.

6. Pirkei Avot 4:4; see Amy-Jill Levine, *The Misunderstood Jew: The Church and the Scandal of the Jewish Jesus* (New York: HarperOne, 2006), 92-94.
7. Qur'an 25:63, trans. M.A.S. Abdel Haleem (Oxford: Oxford University Press, 2004).
8. Sahih al-Bukhari, Book 73, Hadith 56.
9. Annemarie Schimmel, *Mystical Dimensions of Islam* (Chapel Hill: University of North Carolina Press, 1975), 98-102.
10. Rumi, *The Essential Rumi*, trans. Coleman Barks (New York: HarperSanFrancisco, 1995), 156-159.
11. *The Dhammapada*, trans. Narada Thera (Colombo: Buddhist Publication Society, 1972), verse 15.
12. Thich Nhat Hanh, *The Heart of Buddhist Meditation* (Boston: Beacon Press, 1975), 88-92.
13. *The Bhagavad Gita*, trans. Eknath Easwaran (Tomales, CA: Nilgiri Press, 1985), 13:7-8.
14. Barbara Stoler Miller, trans., *The Bhagavad-Gita* (New York: Bantam Classics, 1986), 121-123.
15. *Tao Te Ching*, trans. D.C. Lau (London: Penguin Classics, 1963), Chapter 36.
16. Ibid., Chapter 8.
17. John Dominic Crossan, *Jesus: A Revolutionary Biography* (San Francisco: HarperSanFrancisco, 1994), 62-65.

Blessed Are Those Who Hunger and Thirst for Righteousness: The Sacred Longing for Justice

1. Dale C. Allison Jr., *The Sermon on the Mount: Inspiring the Moral Imagination* (New Haven: Yale University Press, 1999), 61-63.
2. Ulrich Luz, *Matthew 1–7: A Continental Commentary* (Minneapolis: Fortress Press, 2007), 198-201.
3. John Chrysostom, *Homilies on the Gospel of Matthew*, Homily 15.4, in *Nicene and Post-Nicene Fathers*, First Series, vol. 10, ed. Philip Schaff (New York: Christian Literature Publishing, 1888).
4. Abraham Joshua Heschel, *The Prophets* (New York: Harper & Row, 1962), 195-198.
5. Amos 5:24; see E.P. Sanders, *Jesus and Judaism* (Philadelphia: Fortress Press, 1985), 182-185.
6. Qur'an 2:177, trans. M.A.S. Abdel Haleem (Oxford: Oxford University Press, 2004).
7. Qur'an 10:9, trans. M.A.S. Abdel Haleem.
8. Annemarie Schimmel, *Mystical Dimensions of Islam* (Chapel Hill: University of North Carolina Press, 1975), 103-106.
9. *Connected Discourses of the Buddha*, trans. Bhikkhu Bodhi (Boston: Wisdom Publications, 2000), 1847-1850.
10. Thich Nhat Hanh, *The Heart of Buddhist Meditation* (Boston: Beacon Press, 1975), 95-98.
11. *The Bhagavad Gita*, trans. Eknath Easwaran (Tomales, CA: Nilgiri Press, 1985), 10:10.
12. Barbara Stoler Miller, trans., *The Bhagavad-Gita* (New York: Bantam Classics, 1986), 134-137.

13. *Tao Te Ching*, trans. D.C. Lau (London: Penguin Classics, 1963), Chapter 38.
14. Ibid., Chapter 8.
15. John Dominic Crossan, *Jesus: A Revolutionary Biography* (San Francisco: HarperSanFrancisco, 1994), 65-68; N.T. Wright, *Jesus and the Victory of God* (Minneapolis: Fortress Press, 1996), 291-294.

Blessed Are the Merciful: The Revolutionary Power of Compassionate Action

1. Dale C. Allison Jr., *The Sermon on the Mount: Inspiring the Moral Imagination* (New Haven: Yale University Press, 1999), 65-67.
2. Ulrich Luz, *Matthew 1-7: A Continental Commentary* (Minneapolis: Fortress Press, 2007), 203-205.
3. Abraham Joshua Heschel, *The Prophets* (New York: Harper & Row, 1962), 202-205.
4. E.P. Sanders, *Jesus and Judaism* (Philadelphia: Fortress Press, 1985), 186-188.
5. Babylonian Talmud, Shabbat 151b.
6. Exodus 34:6-7, New Revised Standard Version; see Amy-Jill Levine, *The Misunderstood Jew: The Church and the Scandal of the Jewish Jesus* (New York: HarperOne, 2006), 95-97.
7. Qur'an, Bismillah formula; see Annemarie Schimmel, *Mystical Dimensions of Islam* (Chapel Hill: University of North Carolina Press, 1975), 107-110.
8. Qur'an 7:156, trans. M.A.S. Abdel Haleem (Oxford: Oxford University Press, 2004).

9. Sahih al-Bukhari, Book 73, Hadith 42.
10. *Connected Discourses of the Buddha*, trans. Bhikkhu Bodhi (Boston: Wisdom Publications, 2000), 1851-1854.
11. Thich Nhat Hanh, *No Death, No Fear* (New York: Riverhead Books, 2002), 85-88.
12. *Laws of Manu*, trans. Wendy Doniger and Brian K. Smith (London: Penguin Classics, 1991), 7.198-200.
13. *The Bhagavad Gita*, trans. Eknath Easwaran (Tomales, CA: Nilgiri Press, 1985), 18:56-58.
14. *Tao Te Ching*, trans. D.C. Lau (London: Penguin Classics, 1963), Chapter 67.
15. Chad Hansen, *A Daoist Theory of Chinese Thought* (Oxford: Oxford University Press, 1992), 215-218.
16. John Dominic Crossan, *Jesus: A Revolutionary Biography* (San Francisco: HarperSanFrancisco, 1994), 68-71.

Blessed Are the Pure in Heart: The Vision That Transforms Everything

1. Dale C. Allison Jr., *The Sermon on the Mount: Inspiring the Moral Imagination* (New Haven: Yale University Press, 1999), 68-70.
2. Ulrich Luz, *Matthew 1–7: A Continental Commentary* (Minneapolis: Fortress Press, 2007), 206-208.
3. E.P. Sanders, *Jesus and Judaism* (Philadelphia: Fortress Press, 1985), 189-191.
4. John Chrysostom, *Homilies on the Gospel of Matthew*, Homily 15.5, in *Nicene and Post-Nicene Fathers*, First Series, vol. 10, ed. Philip Schaff (New York: Christian Literature Publishing, 1888).

5. Søren Kierkegaard, *Purity of Heart Is to Will One Thing* (New York: Harper Torchbooks, 1956), 53.
6. Psalm 24:3-4, New Revised Standard Version.
7. Isaiah 29:13, New Revised Standard Version; see Amy-Jill Levine, *The Misunderstood Jew: The Church and the Scandal of the Jewish Jesus* (New York: HarperOne, 2006), 98-100.
8. John Dominic Crossan, *Jesus: A Revolutionary Biography* (San Francisco: HarperSanFrancisco, 1994), 72-74.
9. Qur'an 26:88-89, trans. M.A.S. Abdel Haleem (Oxford: Oxford University Press, 2004).
10. Sahih Muslim, Book 32, Hadith 6221.
11. Annemarie Schimmel, *Mystical Dimensions of Islam* (Chapel Hill: University of North Carolina Press, 1975), 112-115; Al-Ghazali, *The Revival of the Religious Sciences*, trans. T.J. Winter (Cambridge: Islamic Texts Society, 1995), 2:258-260.
12. *The Dhammapada*, trans. Narada Thera (Colombo: Buddhist Publication Society, 1972), verse 1-2.
13. Thich Nhat Hanh, *The Heart of Buddhist Meditation* (Boston: Beacon Press, 1975), 102-105.
14. *The Bhagavad Gita*, trans. Eknath Easwaran (Tomales, CA: Nilgiri Press, 1985), 15:51.
15. Barbara Stoler Miller, trans., *The Bhagavad-Gita* (New York: Bantam Classics, 1986), 152-155.
16. *Tao Te Ching*, trans. D.C. Lau (London: Penguin Classics, 1963), Chapter 48.
17. Chad Hansen, *A Daoist Theory of Chinese Thought* (Oxford: Oxford University Press, 1992), 220-223.

18. N.T. Wright, *Jesus and the Victory of God* (Minneapolis: Fortress Press, 1996), 295-297.

Blessed Are the Peacemakers: Active Reconciliation Across Traditions

1. Dale C. Allison Jr., *The Sermon on the Mount: Inspiring the Moral Imagination* (New Haven: Yale University Press, 1999), 71-73.
2. John Chrysostom, *Homilies on the Gospel of Matthew*, Homily 15.6, in *Nicene and Post-Nicene Fathers*, First Series, vol. 10, ed. Philip Schaff (New York: Christian Literature Publishing, 1888).
3. Augustine of Hippo, *Sermon on the Mount*, 1.5.14, in *Nicene and Post-Nicene Fathers*, First Series, vol. 6, ed. Philip Schaff (New York: Christian Literature Publishing, 1888).
4. E.P. Sanders, *Jesus and Judaism* (Philadelphia: Fortress Press, 1985), 194-196.
5. Abraham Joshua Heschel, *The Prophets* (New York: Harper & Row, 1962), 208-212.
6. Pirkei Avot 1:12; see Amy-Jill Levine, *The Misunderstood Jew: The Church and the Scandal of the Jewish Jesus* (New York: HarperOne, 2006), 101-103.
7. John Dominic Crossan, *Jesus: A Revolutionary Biography* (San Francisco: HarperSanFrancisco, 1994), 75-78.
8. Annemarie Schimmel, *Mystical Dimensions of Islam* (Chapel Hill: University of North Carolina Press, 1975), 116-119.

9. N.T. Wright, *Jesus and the Victory of God* (Minneapolis: Fortress Press, 1996), 298-301.
10. Qur'an 4:128, 49:9, trans. M.A.S. Abdel Haleem (Oxford: Oxford University Press, 2004).
11. Seyyed Hossein Nasr, *The Heart of Islam* (San Francisco: HarperSanFrancisco, 2002), 45-48.
12. *The Dhammapada*, trans. Narada Thera (Colombo: Buddhist Publication Society, 1972), verse 129.
13. Thich Nhat Hanh, *Being Peace* (Berkeley, CA: Parallax Press, 1987), 78-82.
14. *The Bhagavad Gita*, trans. Eknath Easwaran (Tomales, CA: Nilgiri Press, 1985), 12:18-19.
15. Barbara Stoler Miller, trans., *The Bhagavad-Gita* (New York: Bantam Classics, 1986), 165-168.
16. *Tao Te Ching*, trans. D.C. Lau (London: Penguin Classics, 1963), Chapter 36.
17. Ibid., Chapter 68.
18. Ulrich Luz, *Matthew 1-7: A Continental Commentary* (Minneapolis: Fortress Press, 2007), 209-212.
19. Desmond Tutu, *No Future Without Forgiveness* (New York: Doubleday, 1999), 126-132; John Paul Lederach, *The Little Book of Conflict Transformation* (Intercourse, PA: Good Books, 2003), 45-50.

Blessed Are Those Who Are Persecuted for Righteousness' Sake: The Cost of Moral Witness

1. Dale C. Allison Jr., *The Sermon on the Mount: Inspiring the Moral Imagination* (New Haven: Yale University Press, 1999), 74-76.

2. Ulrich Luz, *Matthew 1-7: A Continental Commentary* (Minneapolis: Fortress Press, 2007), 213-215.
3. John Chrysostom, *Homilies on the Gospel of Matthew*, Homily 15.7, in *Nicene and Post-Nicene Fathers*, First Series, vol. 10, ed. Philip Schaff (New York: Christian Literature Publishing, 1888).
4. E.P. Sanders, *Jesus and Judaism* (Philadelphia: Fortress Press, 1985), 197-200.
5. Abraham Joshua Heschel, *The Prophets* (New York: Harper & Row, 1962), 215-220.
6. Isaiah 1:17; Amos 5:24, New Revised Standard Version.
7. Amy-Jill Levine, *The Misunderstood Jew: The Church and the Scandal of the Jewish Jesus* (New York: HarperOne, 2006), 104-106.
8. Qur'an 29:2, 46:13, trans. M.A.S. Abdel Haleem (Oxford: Oxford University Press, 2004).
9. Annemarie Schimmel, *Mystical Dimensions of Islam* (Chapel Hill: University of North Carolina Press, 1975), 120-123.
10. Sahih al-Bukhari, Book 76, Hadith 470.
11. *Connected Discourses of the Buddha*, trans. Bhikkhu Bodhi (Boston: Wisdom Publications, 2000), 1855-1858.
12. *The Dhammapada*, trans. Narada Thera (Colombo: Buddhist Publication Society, 1972), verse 5.
13. Thich Nhat Hanh, *Being Peace* (Berkeley, CA: Parallax Press, 1987), 85-88.
14. *The Bhagavad Gita*, trans. Eknath Easwaran (Tomales, CA: Nilgiri Press, 1985), 3:35.
15. Barbara Stoler Miller, trans., *The Bhagavad-Gita* (New York: Bantam Classics, 1986), 48-51.

16. Chad Hansen, *A Daoist Theory of Chinese Thought* (Oxford: Oxford University Press, 1992), 225-228.
17. *Tao Te Ching*, trans. D.C. Lau (London: Penguin Classics, 1963), Chapter 38.
18. John Dominic Crossan, *Jesus: A Revolutionary Biography* (San Francisco: HarperSanFrancisco, 1994), 79-82; N.T. Wright, *Jesus and the Victory of God* (Minneapolis: Fortress Press, 1996), 302-305.

Blessed Are You: The Personal Turn in the Ninth Beatitude

1. Dale C. Allison Jr., *A Critical and Exegetical Commentary on the Gospel According to Saint Matthew*, ICC Series (London: T&T Clark, 2004), 1:467-470.
2. Walter Bauer, *A Greek-English Lexicon of the New Testament (BDAG)*, 3rd ed. (Chicago: University of Chicago Press, 2000), s.v. "λοιδορέω," "διώκω," "ψευδομαρτυρέω."
3. Ulrich Luz, *Matthew 1–7: A Commentary*, Hermeneia Series (Minneapolis: Fortress Press, 2007), 216-218.
4. R.T. France, *The Gospel of Matthew*, NICNT Series (Grand Rapids: Eerdmans, 2007), 178-180.
5. Allison, *Matthew*, 1:467.
6. Craig S. Keener, *The Gospel of Matthew: A Socio-Rhetorical Commentary* (Grand Rapids: Eerdmans, 2009), 165-168.
7. John Nolland, *The Gospel of Matthew: A Commentary on the Greek Text*, NIGTC Series (Grand Rapids: Eerdmans, 2005), 217-219.
8. Luz, *Matthew 1–7*, 219-221.

9. Richard A. Horsley, *Jesus and Empire: The Kingdom of God and the New World Disorder* (Minneapolis: Fortress Press, 2003), 87-90.
10. France, *Matthew*, 180-181.
11. M. Eugene Boring, *Matthew: Introduction, Commentary, and Reflections*, NIB Commentary (Nashville: Abingdon, 1995), 181-183.
12. Dietrich Bonhoeffer, *The Cost of Discipleship* (New York: Touchstone, 1995), 112-115.
13. Huston Smith, *The World's Religions* (San Francisco: HarperOne, 2009), 82-85.
14. Qur'an 2:155-156, trans. M.A.S. Abdel Haleem (Oxford: Oxford University Press, 2004).
15. Bart D. Ehrman, *The New Testament: A Historical Introduction* (Oxford: Oxford University Press, 2016), 278-281.
16. Karen Armstrong, *The Great Transformation: The Beginning of Our Religious Traditions* (New York: Knopf, 2006), 365-370.
17. Luke 6:22-23, New Revised Standard Version.
18. Keener, *Matthew*, 168-170.

Blessed Beyond the Canon: The Beatitudes in Abrahamic and Christian-Adjacent Traditions

1. Elaine Pagels, *The Gnostic Gospels* (New York: Vintage, 1989), 19-25.
2. *The Gospel of Thomas*, Saying 1, in Marvin Meyer, ed., *The Nag Hammadi Scriptures* (New York: HarperOne, 2007), 139.

3. *The Gospel of Thomas*, Sayings 7, 49, in Meyer, *Nag Hammadi Scriptures*, 141, 151.
4. Bentley Layton, *The Gnostic Scriptures* (New Haven: Yale University Press, 1987), 376-399.
5. Annemarie Schimmel, *Mystical Dimensions of Islam* (Chapel Hill: University of North Carolina Press, 1975), 98-112.
6. Jalal al-Din Rumi, *The Essential Rumi*, trans. Coleman Barks (New York: HarperOne, 2004), 142, 278.
7. Carl W. Ernst, *Sufism: An Introduction to the Mystical Tradition of Islam* (Boston: Shambhala, 2011), 67-85.
8. Schimmel, *Mystical Dimensions*, 112-118.
9. Pink Dandelion, *An Introduction to Quakerism* (Cambridge: Cambridge University Press, 2007), 32-56.
10. Rufus M. Jones, *The Faith and Practice of the Quakers* (London: Methuen, 1927), 78-95.
11. Howard Brinton, *Friends for 300 Years* (Wallingford, PA: Pendle Hill Publications, 2002), 45-62.
12. Terryl Givens, *People of Paradox: A History of Mormon Culture* (Oxford: Oxford University Press, 2007), 89-112.
13. *The Book of Mormon*, 3 Nephi 12, available at www.churchofjesuschrist.org.
14. Grant Hardy, *Understanding the Book of Mormon: A Reader's Guide* (Oxford: Oxford University Press, 2010), 234-251.
15. Givens, *People of Paradox*, 145-167.
16. Gershom Scholem, *Major Trends in Jewish Mysticism* (New York: Schocken Books, 1995), 205-243.
17. Daniel C. Matt, *The Essential Kabbalah* (San Francisco: HarperSanFrancisco, 1995), 85-92.

18. Scholem, *Major Trends*, 244-286.
19. Aryeh Kaplan, *Jewish Meditation: A Practical Guide* (New York: Schocken, 1985), 156-173.
20. Peter Smith, *An Introduction to the Baha'i Faith* (Cambridge: Cambridge University Press, 2008), 67-89.
21. Moojan Momen, *Understanding the Baha'i Faith* (Edinburgh: Dunedin Academic Press, 2008), 134-152.
22. Bahá'u'lláh, *The Hidden Words*, Persian #42 and Arabic #2, available at www.bahai.org.

Earth and Spirit: Indigenous and African Wisdoms on the Beatitudes

1. Vine Deloria Jr., *God Is Red: A Native View of Religion* (Golden, CO: Fulcrum Publishing, 2003), 65-82.
2. Joseph Epes Brown, *The Sacred Pipe: Black Elk's Account of the Seven Rites of the Oglala Sioux* (Norman: University of Oklahoma Press, 1953), 115-118.
3. Ibid., 67-100.
4. Robin Wall Kimmerer, *Braiding Sweetgrass: Indigenous Wisdom, Scientific Knowledge and the Teachings of Plants* (Minneapolis: Milkweed Editions, 2013), 56-71.
5. John S. Mbiti, *African Religions and Philosophy* (Oxford: Heinemann, 1990), 175-203.
6. Ibid., 89-98.
7. Desmond Tutu, *No Future Without Forgiveness* (New York: Image, 2000), 34-35.
8. Kwame Wiredu, *Cultural Universals and Particulars: An African Perspective* (Bloomington: Indiana University Press, 1996), 67-89.

9. Marie Battiste, *Decolonizing Education: Nourishing the Learning Spirit* (Saskatoon: Purich Publishing, 2013), 89-112.
10. Malidoma Patrice Somé, *Ritual: Power, Healing and Community* (Portland, OR: Swan Raven, 1993), 78-95.
11. Gregory Cajete, *Native Science: Natural Laws of Interdependence* (Santa Fe: Clear Light Publishers, 2000), 145-167.
12. Ibid., 201-223.
13. Winona LaDuke, *Recovering the Sacred: The Power of Naming and Claiming* (Cambridge, MA: South End Press, 2005), 89-106.
14. Mercy Amba Oduyoye, *Daughters of Anowa: African Women and Patriarchy* (Maryknoll, NY: Orbis Books, 1995), 134-152.
15. George E. Tinker, *Spirit and Resistance: Political Theology and American Indian Liberation* (Minneapolis: Fortress Press, 2004), 67-89.
16. Deloria, *God Is Red*, 123-145.
17. Tinker, *Spirit and Resistance*, 178-203.

Echoes from the East: Confucian, Shinto, and Jain Wisdom in Light of the Beatitudes

1. Arthur Waley, trans., *The Analects of Confucius* (New York: Vintage, 1989), 88-92.
2. William Theodore de Bary, *Sources of Chinese Tradition* (New York: Columbia University Press, 1999), 1:45-67.
3. *Analects* 2:12, in Waley, *Analects*, 91.

4. Tu Wei-ming, *Centrality and Commonality: An Essay on Confucian Religiousness* (Albany: SUNY Press, 1989), 78-85.
5. Julia Ching, *Confucianism and Christianity: A Comparative Study* (Tokyo: Kodansha, 1977), 134-152.
6. Thomas Kasulis, *Shinto: The Way Home* (Honolulu: University of Hawaii Press, 2004), 67-89.
7. Yoshiro Tamura, *Japanese Buddhism: A Cultural History* (Tokyo: Kosei Publishing, 2000), 34-56.
8. John Whitney Hall, *Japan: From Prehistory to Modern Times* (Tokyo: University of Tokyo Press, 1990), 89-112.
9. Kasulis, *Shinto*, 145-167.
10. Padmanabh S. Jaini, *The Jaina Path of Purification* (Berkeley: University of California Press, 1998), 167-189.
11. Paul Dundas, *The Jains* (London: Routledge, 2002), 145-167.
12. Nathmal Tatia, trans., *The Tattvartha Sutra* (London: Jain Study Circle, 1994), 89-112.
13. Jaini, *Jaina Path*, 234-256.
14. Huston Smith, *The World's Religions* (San Francisco: HarperOne, 2009), 156-189.
15. Ninian Smart, *The World's Religions* (Cambridge: Cambridge University Press, 1998), 234-267.
16. Karen Armstrong, *The Great Transformation* (New York: Knopf, 2006), 345-378.
17. Mircea Eliade, *Patterns in Comparative Religion* (Lincoln: University of Nebraska Press, 1996), 234-289.

The Beatitudes Around the Global Church

1. Gustavo Gutiérrez, *A Theology of Liberation: History, Politics, and Salvation*, revised ed. (Maryknoll, NY: Orbis Books, 1988), 165-168.
2. Leonardo Boff, *Jesus Christ Liberator: A Critical Christology for Our Time* (Maryknoll, NY: Orbis Books, 1978), 278-290.
3. Jon Sobrino, *Spirituality of Liberation: Toward Political Holiness* (Maryknoll, NY: Orbis Books, 1988), 123-145.
4. Phillip Berryman, *Liberation Theology: Essential Facts about the Revolutionary Movement in Latin America and Beyond* (Philadelphia: Temple University Press, 1987), 63-78.
5. Oscar Romero, *The Violence of Love*, compiled by James R. Brockman (Maryknoll, NY: Orbis Books, 2004), 18-25, 45-52.
6. Desmond Tutu, *No Future Without Forgiveness* (New York: Doubleday, 1999), 31-35.
7. Ibid., 54-83.
8. Lamin Sanneh, *Whose Religion Is Christianity? The Gospel Beyond the West* (Grand Rapids: Eerdmans, 2003), 112-135.
9. Timothy Longman, *Christianity and Genocide in Rwanda* (Cambridge: Cambridge University Press, 2010), 258-283.
10. Mercy Amba Oduyoye, *Daughters of Anowa: African Women and Patriarchy* (Maryknoll, NY: Orbis Books, 1995), 162-180.
11. Sanneh, *Whose Religion Is Christianity?*, 22-42.

12. Nam-dong Suh, "Towards a Theology of Han," in *Minjung Theology: People as the Subjects of History*, ed. Commission on Theological Concerns of the Christian Conference of Asia (Maryknoll, NY: Orbis Books, 1983), 51-65.
13. Carlos H. Abesamis, *A Third Look at Jesus: A Guidebook Along the Road of People's Theology* (Manila: Claretian Publications, 1998), 89-105.
14. Arvind P. Nirmal, *Heuristic Explorations* (Madras: Christian Literature Society, 1990), 78-92.
15. Brent Fulton, *China's Urban Christians: A Light That Cannot Be Hidden* (Eugene, OR: Pickwick Publications, 2015), 156-178.
16. Sebastian C.H. Kim, *Theology in the Public Sphere: Public Theology as a Catalyst for Open Debate* (London: SCM Press, 2011), 134-152.
17. John Meyendorff, *Byzantine Theology: Historical Trends and Doctrinal Themes* (New York: Fordham University Press, 1974), 94-108.
18. Sebastian P. Brock, *The Luminous Eye: The Spiritual World Vision of Saint Ephrem the Syrian* (Kalamazoo: Cistercian Publications, 1992), 67-89.
19. Vivian Ibrahim, *The Copts of Egypt: The Challenges of Modernisation and Identity* (London: I.B. Tauris, 2011), 145-167.
20. Mitri Raheb, *I Am a Palestinian Christian* (Minneapolis: Fortress Press, 1995), 78-95; Naim Ateek, *Justice and Only Justice: A Palestinian Theology of Liberation* (Maryknoll, NY: Orbis Books, 1989), 112-128.

21. Virginia Fabella and Mercy Amba Oduyoye, eds., *With Passion and Compassion: Third World Women Doing Theology* (Maryknoll, NY: Orbis Books, 1988), 23-45.
22. Pablo Sosa, "Hymnody and Liberation Theology," in *Music and the Church*, ed. Thomas Day (Portland, OR: Pastoral Press, 1992), 156-170.
23. Wangari Maathai, *Unbowed: A Memoir* (New York: Knopf, 2006), 267-289.
24. Dana L. Robert, *Christian Mission: How Christianity Became a World Religion* (Oxford: Wiley-Blackwell, 2009), 58-78.

Makarioi: The Greek Roots of the Beatitudes

1. Walter Bauer, *A Greek-English Lexicon of the New Testament and Other Early Christian Literature*, 3rd ed. (Chicago: University of Chicago Press, 2000), s.v. "μακάριος."
2. Jonathan T. Pennington, *The Sermon on the Mount and Human Flourishing: A Theological Commentary* (Grand Rapids: Baker Academic, 2017), 89-112.
3. Dale C. Allison Jr., *The Sermon on the Mount: Inspiring the Moral Imagination* (New York: Crossroad Publishing, 1999), 45-67.
4. Walter Bauer, *A Greek-English Lexicon of the New Testament and Other Early Christian Literature*, 3rd ed. (Chicago: University of Chicago Press, 2000), s.v. "πτωχός."
5. Ulrich Luz, *Matthew 1-7: A Commentary*, Hermeneia Series (Minneapolis: Fortress Press, 2007), 191-193.

6. W.D. Davies and Dale C. Allison Jr., *A Critical and Exegetical Commentary on the Gospel According to Saint Matthew*, vol. 1, ICC Series (London: T&T Clark, 2004), 441-444.
7. Bauer, *Greek-English Lexicon*, s.v. "πενθέω."
8. Luz, *Matthew 1–7*, 194-196.
9. Bauer, *Greek-English Lexicon*, s.v. "παρακαλέω."
10. Davies and Allison, *Matthew*, 1:448-450.
11. Craig S. Keener, *The Gospel of Matthew: A Socio-Rhetorical Commentary* (Grand Rapids: Eerdmans, 2009), 167-169.
12. Bauer, *Greek-English Lexicon*, s.v. "κληρονομέω."
13. Luz, *Matthew 1–7*, 198-201.
14. Gerhard Kittel, ed., *Theological Dictionary of the New Testament*, vol. 2 (Grand Rapids: Eerdmans, 1964), s.v. "δικαιοσύνη."
15. Davies and Allison, *Matthew*, 1:451-453.
16. Bauer, *Greek-English Lexicon*, s.v. "χορτάζω."
17. Keener, *Matthew*, 170-172.
18. Kittel, *Theological Dictionary*, vol. 2, s.v. "ἐλεέω."
19. Bauer, *Greek-English Lexicon*, s.v. "καθαρός."
20. Luz, *Matthew 1–7*, 205-207.
21. Davies and Allison, *Matthew*, 1:456-458.
22. Bauer, *Greek-English Lexicon*, s.v. "εἰρηνοποιός."
23. Kittel, *Theological Dictionary*, vol. 2, s.v. "εἰρήνη."
24. Keener, *Matthew*, 174-176.
25. Bauer, *Greek-English Lexicon*, s.v. "διώκω."
26. Luz, *Matthew 1–7*, 209-212.
27. Davies and Allison, *Matthew*, 1:461-463.
28. Allison, *Sermon on the Mount*, 74-76.

29. Joseph A. Fitzmyer, *The Impact of the Dead Sea Scrolls* (New York: Paulist Press, 2009), 145-167.
30. Bruce M. Metzger, *A Textual Commentary on the Greek New Testament* (Stuttgart: United Bible Societies, 1994), 11-13.
31. Pennington, *Sermon on the Mount*, 134-156.
32. Allison, *Sermon on the Mount*, 45-67.
33. Luz, *Matthew 1-7*, 191-193.
34. N.T. Wright, *The New Testament and the People of God* (Minneapolis: Fortress Press, 1992), 244-279.
35. Fitzmyer, *Dead Sea Scrolls*, 145-167.

Two Visions of Blessing: Comparing Matthew and Luke's Beatitudes

1. Ulrich Luz, *Matthew 1-7: A Commentary*, Hermeneia Series (Minneapolis: Fortress Press, 2007), 179-181.
2. Joel B. Green, *The Gospel of Luke*, NICNT Series (Grand Rapids: Eerdmans, 1997), 267-269.
3. W.D. Davies and Dale C. Allison Jr., *Matthew*, vol. 1, ICC Series (London: T&T Clark, 2004), 421-423.
4. Luke Timothy Johnson, *The Gospel of Luke*, Sacra Pagina Series (Collegeville, MN: Liturgical Press, 1991), 104-107.
5. Luz, *Matthew 1-7*, 183-185.
6. John S. Kloppenborg, *Q, the Earliest Gospel* (Louisville, KY: Westminster John Knox, 2008), 167-189.
7. Davies and Allison, *Matthew*, 1:441-444.

8. Craig S. Keener, *The Gospel of Matthew: A Socio-Rhetorical Commentary* (Grand Rapids: Eerdmans, 2009), 165-167.
9. Green, *Gospel of Luke*, 271-274.
10. Johnson, *Gospel of Luke*, 107-109.
11. Luz, *Matthew 1-7*, 81-93.
12. Green, *Gospel of Luke*, 21-35.
13. James M. Robinson, Paul Hoffmann, and John S. Kloppenborg, *The Critical Edition of Q* (Minneapolis: Fortress Press, 2000), 98-123.
14. John Dominic Crossan, *The Birth of Christianity* (San Francisco: HarperOne, 1998), 267-289.
15. Davies and Allison, *Matthew*, 1:431-441.
16. Amy-Jill Levine, *The Misunderstood Jew: The Church and the Scandal of the Jewish Jesus* (New York: HarperOne, 2006), 89-112.
17. Luz, *Matthew in History: Interpretation, Influence, and Effects* (Minneapolis: Fortress Press, 1994), 134-167.
18. Justo L. González, *Luke: The Gospel of the Outcast* (Maryknoll, NY: Orbis Books, 2002), 89-134.
19. Dale C. Allison Jr., *The Sermon on the Mount: Inspiring the Moral Imagination* (New Haven: Yale University Press, 1999), 234-267.

Blessing and Woe: The Ethical Tension at the Heart of the Gospel

1. Joel B. Green, *The Gospel of Luke*, NICNT Series (Grand Rapids: Eerdmans, 1997), 257-275.

2. Philip Esler, *Community and Gospel in Luke-Acts* (Cambridge: Cambridge University Press, 1987), 164-200; Bruce J. Malina and Richard L. Rohrbaugh, *Social-Science Commentary on the Synoptic Gospels*, 2nd ed. (Minneapolis: Fortress Press, 2003), 298-312.
3. Joel B. Green, *The Theology of the Gospel of Luke* (Cambridge: Cambridge University Press, 1995), 78-99.
4. Luke Timothy Johnson, *The Gospel of Luke*, Sacra Pagina Series (Collegeville, MN: Liturgical Press, 1991), 107-115.
5. Walter Brueggemann, *The Prophetic Imagination*, 2nd ed. (Minneapolis: Fortress Press, 2001), 21-57.
6. Malina and Rohrbaugh, *Social-Science Commentary*, 298-300.
7. Green, *Theology of Luke*, 34-56.
8. Richard A. Horsley, *Jesus and Empire: The Kingdom of God and the New World Disorder* (Minneapolis: Fortress Press, 2003), 81-108.
9. Henri J.M. Nouwen, *The Return of the Prodigal Son* (New York: Doubleday, 1992), 98-125.
10. Parker J. Palmer, *Let Your Life Speak: Listening for the Voice of Vocation* (San Francisco: Jossey-Bass, 2000), 45-67; Dallas Willard, *The Divine Conspiracy: Rediscovering Our Hidden Life in God* (San Francisco: HarperSanFrancisco, 1998), 178-201.
11. Gustavo Gutiérrez, *A Theology of Liberation: History, Politics, and Salvation*, revised ed. (Maryknoll, NY: Orbis Books, 1988), 165-168.
12. Green, *Theology of Luke*, 100-125.

13. Amy-Jill Levine, *The Misunderstood Jew: The Church and the Scandal of the Jewish Jesus* (New York: HarperOne, 2006), 156-178.
14. John Chrysostom, *Commentary on Saint Matthew the Evangelist*, trans. George Prevost (Grand Rapids: Eerdmans, 1976), Homilies 77-88.
15. William Harmless, *Desert Christians: An Introduction to the Literature of Early Monasticism* (New York: Oxford University Press, 2004), 234-267.
16. Gustavo Gutiérrez, *A Theology of Liberation*, 165-168; Jon Sobrino, *Spirituality of Liberation: Toward Political Holiness* (Maryknoll, NY: Orbis Books, 1988), 123-145.
17. Brueggemann, *The Prophetic Imagination*, 110-132.

Reading the Beatitudes Through the Ages: A History of Interpretation

1. Origen, *Commentary on the Gospel of Matthew* 13.6, trans. Ronald Heine, Fathers of the Church Series (Washington, DC: Catholic University of America Press, 2018).
2. Tertullian, *De Patientia*, in *Ante-Nicene Fathers*, vol. 3, ed. Alexander Roberts and James Donaldson (Grand Rapids: Eerdmans, 1885), 707-717.
3. Warren Carter, *What Are They Saying About Matthew's Sermon on the Mount?* (New York: Paulist Press, 1994), 23-45.
4. Origen, *Commentary on Matthew* 13.6.
5. John Cassian, *Conferences*, trans. Colm Luibheid (New York: Paulist Press, 1985), Conference 1.8.

6. Ibid., Conference 14.
7. Benedict of Nursia, *Rule of St. Benedict*, trans. Timothy Fry (Collegeville, MN: Liturgical Press, 1981), chapters 4-7.
8. Thomas Aquinas, *Summa Theologiae*, II-II, q. 69, trans. Fathers of the English Dominican Province (New York: Benziger Brothers, 1947).
9. Meister Eckhart, *Selected Writings*, ed. and trans. Oliver Davies (London: Penguin Classics, 1994), Sermon 52.
10. Hans Dieter Betz, *The Sermon on the Mount* (Minneapolis: Fortress Press, 1995), 112-134.
11. Eckhart, *Selected Writings*, Sermon 52.
12. Martin Luther, *Luther's Works*, vol. 21: *Sermon on the Mount* (St. Louis: Concordia Publishing, 1956), 9-294.
13. John Calvin, *Commentary on Matthew, Mark, and Luke*, trans. William Pringle (Grand Rapids: Baker Books, 2003), vol. 1, 258-289.
14. Ignatius of Loyola, *Spiritual Exercises*, trans. Louis Puhl (Chicago: Loyola Press, 1951), especially the "Two Standards" meditation.
15. Walter Rauschenbusch, *Christianity and the Social Crisis* (1907; repr., Louisville, KY: Westminster John Knox Press, 1991), 65-92.
16. Gustavo Gutiérrez, *A Theology of Liberation* (Maryknoll, NY: Orbis Books, 1971), 287-306.
17. Elisabeth Schüssler Fiorenza, *In Memory of Her: A Feminist Theological Reconstruction of Christian Origins* (New York: Crossroad, 1983), 118-159; Delores Williams, *Sisters in the Wilderness: The Challenge of*

Womanist God-Talk (Maryknoll, NY: Orbis Books, 1993), 144-199.

18. Dale C. Allison Jr., *The Sermon on the Mount: Inspiring the Moral Imagination* (New Haven: Yale University Press, 1999), 45-67.
19. Gutiérrez, *Theology of Liberation*, 301.
20. Glen H. Stassen, *Just Peacemaking: The New Paradigm for the Ethics of Peace and War* (Cleveland: Pilgrim Press, 2008), 89-112.
21. Richard Beck, *The Slavery of Death* (Eugene, OR: Cascade Books, 2013), 156-178.
22. Allison, *Sermon on the Mount*, 189-234.

Blessed in Worship: The Beatitudes in Early Christian Liturgy and Devotional Life

1. Paul F. Bradshaw, *The Search for the Origins of Christian Worship: Sources and Methods for the Study of Early Liturgy*, 2nd ed. (New York: Oxford University Press, 2002), 45-67.
2. *The Didache: The Teaching of the Twelve Apostles*, trans. Michael W. Holmes (Grand Rapids: Baker Academic, 2007), 1.1-6.2.
3. Cyril of Jerusalem, *Catechetical Lectures*, trans. Leo P. McCauley and Anthony A. Stephenson (Washington, DC: Catholic University of America Press, 1969-1970), Lectures 3.4, 4.2.
4. Origen, *Commentary on the Gospel According to Matthew*, trans. John Patrick, in *Ante-Nicene Fathers*, vol. 9 (Grand Rapids: Eerdmans, 1951), 413-418.

5. Ambrose of Milan, *On the Mysteries and the Treatise on the Sacraments*, trans. T. Thompson (London: SPCK, 1919), 15-28.
6. Robert F. Taft, *The Liturgy of the Hours in East and West: The Origins of the Divine Office and Its Meaning for Today* (Collegeville, MN: Liturgical Press, 1993), 245-267.
7. Sebastian P. Brock, *The Luminous Eye: The Spiritual World Vision of Saint Ephrem the Syrian* (Kalamazoo: Cistercian Publications, 1992), 67-89.
8. John Anthony McGuckin, *The Orthodox Church: An Introduction to Its History, Doctrine, and Spiritual Culture*(Oxford: Wiley-Blackwell, 2008), 234-256.
9. Maxwell E. Johnson, *The Rites of Christian Initiation: Their Evolution and Interpretation* (Collegeville, MN: Liturgical Press, 2007), 178-195.
10. Eric Palazzo, *A History of Liturgical Books from the Beginning to the Thirteenth Century* (Collegeville, MN: Liturgical Press, 1998), 89-112.
11. Thomas Aquinas, *Summa Theologica*, trans. Fathers of the English Dominican Province (Westminster, MD: Christian Classics, 1981), I-II, q. 69, a. 1-4.
12. John Harper, *The Forms and Orders of Western Liturgy from the Tenth to the Eighteenth Century* (Oxford: Clarendon Press, 1991), 156-178.
13. Ibid., 198-220.
14. John Chrysostom, *Commentary on Saint Matthew the Evangelist*, trans. George Prevost (Grand Rapids: Eerdmans, 1976), Homilies 15-17.

15. Augustine of Hippo, *Commentary on the Sermon on the Mount*, trans. Denis J. Kavanagh (Washington, DC: Catholic University of America Press, 1951), 1.1-12.
16. Gregory of Nazianzus, *Select Orations*, trans. Martha Vinson (Washington, DC: Catholic University of America Press, 2003), Oration 16.
17. Gregory of Nyssa, *The Lord's Prayer and the Beatitudes*, trans. Hilda C. Graef (Westminster, MD: Newman Press, 1954), 85-141.
18. William Harmless, *Desert Christians: An Introduction to the Literature of Early Monasticism* (New York: Oxford University Press, 2004), 167-189.
19. Benedict of Nursia, *The Rule of St. Benedict*, trans. Timothy Fry (Collegeville, MN: Liturgical Press, 1981), chapters 4, 7.
20. *The Philokalia: The Complete Text*, 4 vols., trans. G.E.H. Palmer, Philip Sherrard, and Kallistos Ware (London: Faber & Faber, 1979-1995), 1:57-71.
21. Harper, *The Forms and Orders of Western Liturgy*, 89-105.
22. Brock, *The Luminous Eye*, 112-134.
23. Taft, *The Liturgy of the Hours*, 156-178.
24. Robin Margaret Jensen, *Understanding Early Christian Art* (London: Routledge, 2000), 78-95.
25. Thomas F. Mathews, *The Clash of Gods: A Reinterpretation of Early Christian Art*, revised ed. (Princeton: Princeton University Press, 1999), 156-172.
26. Jensen, *Understanding Early Christian Art*, 167-189.

27. *The Apostolic Constitutions*, trans. James Donaldson, in *Ante-Nicene Fathers*, vol. 7 (Grand Rapids: Eerdmans, 1951), 7.47-48.
28. *Sayings of the Desert Fathers: The Alphabetical Collection*, trans. Benedicta Ward (Kalamazoo: Cistercian Publications, 1975), entries on Antony, Arsenius.
29. John Climacus, *The Ladder of Divine Ascent*, trans. Colm Luibheid and Norman Russell (New York: Paulist Press, 1982), Steps 4, 7, 25.
30. Frances M. Young, *From Nicaea to Chalcedon: A Guide to the Literature and Its Background*, 2nd ed. (Grand Rapids: Baker Academic, 2010), 234-267.

Power, Empire, and the Politics of Blessing

1. Richard A. Horsley, *Jesus and Empire: The Kingdom of God and the New World Disorder* (Minneapolis: Fortress Press, 2003), 81-104; E.P. Sanders, *Judaism: Practice and Belief 63 BCE—66 CE* (Philadelphia: Trinity Press, 1992), 146-169.
2. John Dominic Crossan, *God and Empire: Jesus Against Rome, Then and Now* (San Francisco: HarperOne, 2009), 132-145.
3. Horsley, *Jesus and Empire*, 28-42.
4. N.T. Wright, *Jesus and the Victory of God* (Minneapolis: Fortress Press, 1996), 320-368; Sanders, *Judaism: Practice and Belief*, 170-182.
5. Walter Brueggemann, *The Prophetic Imagination*, 2nd ed. (Minneapolis: Fortress Press, 2001), 21-57.

6. Amy-Jill Levine, *The Misunderstood Jew: The Church and the Scandal of the Jewish Jesus* (New York: HarperOne, 2006), 89-91.
7. Wright, *Jesus and the Victory of God*, 202-209.
8. Dale C. Allison, *The Sermon on the Mount: Inspiring the Moral Imagination* (New York: Crossroad, 1999), 42-50.
9. Crossan, *God and Empire*, 101-131.
10. Horsley, *Jesus and Empire*, 105-140.
11. Acts 2:42-47; 4:32-37; see Crossan, *God and Empire*, 158-167.
12. Gustavo Gutiérrez, *A Theology of Liberation: History, Politics, and Salvation*, revised ed. (Maryknoll, NY: Orbis Books, 1988), 165-168.
13. Martin Luther King Jr., *Strength to Love* (Minneapolis: Fortress Press, 2010), 47-55.
14. Desmond Tutu, *No Future Without Forgiveness* (New York: Doubleday, 1999), 54-83.
15. Ulrich Luz, *Matthew 1-7: A Commentary*, Hermeneia Series (Minneapolis: Fortress Press, 2007), 190-215.
16. Jürgen Moltmann, *The Crucified God: The Cross of Christ as the Foundation and Criticism of Christian Theology*(Minneapolis: Fortress Press, 1993), 126-145.
17. Brueggemann, *The Prophetic Imagination*, 3-20.

Beyond the Canon: The Beatitudes in Q, Apocrypha, and Early Wisdom Traditions

1. John S. Kloppenborg, *Q, the Earliest Gospel: An Introduction to the Original Stories and Sayings of Jesus* (Louisville: Westminster John Knox, 2008), 89-112;

James M. Robinson, Paul Hoffmann, and John S. Kloppenborg, eds., *The Critical Edition of Q* (Minneapolis: Fortress Press, 2000), 68-79.
2. James D.G. Dunn, *Jesus Remembered*, vol. 1 of *Christianity in the Making* (Grand Rapids: Eerdmans, 2003), 147-154; Craig A. Evans, *Fabricating Jesus: How Modern Scholars Distort the Gospels* (Downers Grove, IL: IVP Academic, 2006), 43-62.
3. John J. Collins, *The Apocalyptic Imagination: An Introduction to Jewish Apocalyptic Literature*, 3rd ed. (Grand Rapids: Eerdmans, 2016), 203-225.
4. Stephen J. Patterson, *The Gospel of Thomas and Jesus* (Sonoma, CA: Polebridge Press, 1993), 18-35.
5. Helmut Koester, *Ancient Christian Gospels: Their History and Development* (Philadelphia: Trinity Press, 1990), 75-128.
6. Bart D. Ehrman, *Lost Christianities: The Battles for Scripture and the Faiths We Never Knew* (New York: Oxford University Press, 2003), 145-167.
7. Leo G. Perdue, *Wisdom Literature: A Theological History* (Louisville: Westminster John Knox, 2007), 89-115.
8. George W.E. Nickelsburg, *Jewish Literature Between the Bible and the Mishnah*, 2nd ed. (Minneapolis: Fortress Press, 2005), 156-175.
9. Florentino García Martínez and Eibert J.C. Tigchelaar, eds., *The Dead Sea Scrolls Study Edition*, 2 vols. (Leiden: Brill, 2000), 2:1049-1051.
10. James C. VanderKam, *An Introduction to Early Judaism* (Grand Rapids: Eerdmans, 2001), 134-156.

11. Geza Vermes, *The Complete Dead Sea Scrolls in English*, 7th ed. (London: Penguin, 2011), 35-67.
12. *The Didache: The Teaching of the Twelve Apostles*, trans. Michael W. Holmes (Grand Rapids: Baker Academic, 2007), 1.1-6.2.
13. *The Shepherd of Hermas*, trans. Bart D. Ehrman, in *The Apostolic Fathers*, vol. 2 (Cambridge, MA: Harvard University Press, 2003), Visions 3.1-4.
14. Bruce M. Metzger, *The Canon of the New Testament: Its Origin, Development, and Significance* (Oxford: Clarendon Press, 1987), 165-201.
15. *Sibylline Oracles*, trans. J.J. Collins, in *The Old Testament Pseudepigrapha*, vol. 1, ed. James H. Charlesworth (New York: Doubleday, 1983), 354-380.
16. N.T. Wright, *The New Testament and the People of God*, vol. 1 of *Christian Origins and the Question of God* (Minneapolis: Fortress Press, 1992), 435-443.

Saints of the Beatitudes: Living Witnesses to a Radical Way

1. Hebrews 12:1, New Revised Standard Version.
2. Adrian House, *Francis of Assisi: A Revolutionary Life* (New York: HiddenSpring, 2001), 89-134.
3. Dorothy Day, *The Long Loneliness* (San Francisco: HarperOne, 1952), 234-267.
4. Jon Sobrino, *Archbishop Romero: Memories and Reflections* (Maryknoll, NY: Orbis Books, 1990), 45-78.
5. Martin Luther King Jr., *Strength to Love* (Minneapolis: Fortress Press, 1963), 15-26.

6. Jean Vanier, *Becoming Human* (New York: Paulist Press, 1998), 67-89.
7. Charles Upton, trans., *Doorkeeper of the Heart: Versions of Rabi'a* (Putney, VT: Threshold Books, 1988), 23-45.
8. Ibid., 34.
9. Eknath Easwaran, *Nonviolent Soldier of Islam: Badshah Khan, a Man to Match His Mountains* (Tomales, CA: Nilgiri Press, 1999), 123-156.
10. Mahatma Gandhi, *An Autobiography: The Story of My Experiments with Truth* (Boston: Beacon Press, 1993), 68.
11. John Stratton Hawley, *Three Bhakti Voices: Mirabai, Surdas, and Kabir in Their Time and Ours* (New Delhi: Oxford University Press, 2005), 89-112.
12. Thich Nhat Hanh, *Being Peace* (Berkeley, CA: Parallax Press, 1987), 34-56.
13. Nelson Mandela, *Long Walk to Freedom* (Boston: Little, Brown, 1994), 456-489.
14. Desmond Tutu, *No Future Without Forgiveness* (New York: Doubleday, 1999), 134-167.
15. Wangari Maathai, *Unbowed: A Memoir* (New York: Knopf, 2006), 234-267.
16. Toyohiko Kagawa, *Before the Dawn* (New York: Friendship Press, 1925), 89-123.
17. Malala Yousafzai, *I Am Malala* (Boston: Little, Brown, 2013), 267-289.
18. Simone Weil, *Waiting for God* (New York: Harper Perennial, 2009), 67-89.

19. Kathryn Spink, *Mother Teresa: A Complete Authorized Biography* (San Francisco: HarperSanFrancisco, 1997), 145-178.
20. Dallas Lee, *The Cotton Patch Evidence: The Story of Clarence Jordan and the Koinonia Farm Experiment* (New York: Harper & Row, 1971), 89-134.
21. Henri J.M. Nouwen, *The Return of the Prodigal Son* (New York: Doubleday, 1992), 78-102.
22. Abraham Joshua Heschel, *The Prophets* (New York: Harper & Row, 1962), 234-267.

Bibliography

Primary Religious Texts

Christian Scripture

- *The Greek New Testament* (Nestle-Aland, 28th Edition). Deutsche Bibelgesellschaft, 2012
- *New Revised Standard Version Bible.* Matthew 5:1-12; Luke 6:17-26; John 15:20

Hebrew Bible/Tanakh

- *Tanakh.* Psalms 17:15, 24:3-4, 34:14, 34:18, 37:11, 51:10, 51:17, 86:11, 103:8, 106:3, 126:5; Isaiah 1:17, 29:13, 40:1, 61:1, 66:2; Amos 5:24; Jeremiah 1:19; Lamentations 3:31-33; Micah 6:8; Numbers 12:3; Proverbs 4:23; Exodus 34:6-7

Early Christian and Apocryphal Sources

- *The Apostolic Constitutions.* Translated by James Donaldson. In *Ante-Nicene Fathers*, vol. 7. Grand Rapids: Eerdmans, 1951
- *The Didache: The Teaching of the Twelve Apostles.* Translated by Michael W. Holmes. Grand Rapids: Baker Academic, 2007
- *The Gospel of Thomas.* Translated by Marvin Meyer. In *The Nag Hammadi Scriptures*, edited by Marvin Meyer. New York: HarperOne, 2007

- *The Nag Hammadi Scriptures*, ed. Marvin Meyer. HarperOne, 2007
- *The Shepherd of Hermas*. Translated by Bart D. Ehrman. In *The Apostolic Fathers*, vol. 2. Cambridge, MA: Harvard University Press, 2003

Dead Sea Scrolls and Second Temple Literature

- García Martínez, Florentino, and Eibert J.C. Tigchelaar, eds. *The Dead Sea Scrolls Study Edition*. 2 vols. Leiden: Brill, 2000
- *Sibylline Oracles*. Translated by J.J. Collins. In *The Old Testament Pseudepigrapha*, vol. 1, edited by James H. Charlesworth. New York: Doubleday, 1983
- Vermes, Geza. *The Complete Dead Sea Scrolls in English*. 7th ed. London: Penguin, 2011

Islamic Sources

- *The Qur'an*, trans. M.A.S. Abdel Haleem. Oxford University Press, 2004
- *Sahih al-Bukhari*
- *Sahih Muslim*
- Al-Ghazali. *Ihya' 'Ulum al-Din* (The Revival of the Religious Sciences)

Buddhist Texts

- *The Connected Discourses of the Buddha*, trans. Bhikkhu Bodhi. Wisdom Publications, 2000

- *The Dhammapada*, trans. Eknath Easwaran. Nilgiri Press, 2007
- *The Dhammapada*, trans. Narada Thera. Buddhist Publication Society, 1972
- *The Heart of Buddhist Meditation* by Thich Nhat Hanh. Beacon Press, 1975
- *The Noble Eightfold Path* by Bhikkhu Bodhi. Buddhist Publication Society, 1994
- *The Tattvartha Sutra*, trans. Nathmal Tatia. Jain Study Circle, 1994

Hindu Sources

- *The Bhagavad Gita*, trans. Barbara Stoler Miller. Bantam Classics, 1986
- *The Bhagavad Gita*, trans. Eknath Easwaran. Nilgiri Press, 2007
- *Laws of Manu*
- *Mahabharata*
- *Ramayana*
- *The Upanishads*, trans. Swami Nikhilananda. Ramakrishna-Vivekananda Center, 1990

Taoist Sources

- *Tao Te Ching*, trans. D.C. Lau. Penguin Classics, 1997
- *Tao Te Ching*, trans. Stephen Mitchell. Harper & Row, 1988

Other Traditions

- *The Analects of Confucius*, trans. Arthur Waley. Vintage, 1989
- *The Essential Rumi*, trans. Coleman Barks. HarperOne, 2004
- *The Kojiki*, trans. Donald L. Philippi. University of Tokyo Press, 1968
- *Nihon Shoki*, trans. W.G. Aston. Tuttle Publishing, 1972
- *Pirkei Avot* (Ethics of the Fathers)

Baha'i Sources

- Bahá'u'lláh. *The Hidden Words*. Bahá'í Publishing Trust, 1985

Patristic and Medieval Sources

Early Church Fathers

- Ambrose of Milan. *On the Mysteries and the Treatise on the Sacraments*. Translated by T. Thompson. London: SPCK, 1919
- Augustine of Hippo. *Commentary on the Sermon on the Mount*. Translated by Denis J. Kavanagh. Washington, DC: Catholic University of America Press, 1951
- Chrysostom, John. *Commentary on Saint Matthew the Evangelist*. Translated by George Prevost. Grand Rapids: Eerdmans, 1976
- Cyril of Jerusalem. *Catechetical Lectures*. Translated by Leo P. McCauley and Anthony A. Stephenson.

Washington, DC: Catholic University of America Press, 1969-1970
- Gregory of Nazianzus. *Select Orations*. Translated by Martha Vinson. Washington, DC: Catholic University of America Press, 2003
- Gregory of Nyssa. *The Lord's Prayer and the Beatitudes*. Translated by Hilda C. Graef. Westminster, MD: Newman Press, 1954
- John Cassian. *Conferences*, trans. Colm Luibheid. Paulist Press, 1985
- Origen. *Commentary on the Gospel According to Matthew*. Translated by John Patrick. In *Ante-Nicene Fathers*, vol. 9. Grand Rapids: Eerdmans, 1951
- Tertullian. *De Patientia*. In *Ante-Nicene Fathers*, Vol. III

Medieval Sources

- Benedict of Nursia. *The Rule of St. Benedict*. Translated by Timothy Fry. Collegeville, MN: Liturgical Press, 1981
- John Climacus. *The Ladder of Divine Ascent*. Translated by Colm Luibheid and Norman Russell. New York: Paulist Press, 1982
- Meister Eckhart. *Selected Writings*, ed. and trans. Oliver Davies. Penguin Classics, 1994
- *The Philokalia: The Complete Text*. 4 vols. Translated by G.E.H. Palmer, Philip Sherrard, and Kallistos Ware. London: Faber & Faber, 1979-1995
- *Sayings of the Desert Fathers: The Alphabetical Collection*. Translated by Benedicta Ward. Kalamazoo: Cistercian Publications, 1975

- Thomas Aquinas. *Summa Theologica*. Translated by the Fathers of the English Dominican Province. 5 vols. Westminster, MD: Christian Classics, 1981

Reformation and Early Modern Sources

Protestant Reformers

- John Calvin. *Commentary on Matthew, Mark, and Luke*, trans. William Pringle
- Martin Luther. *Luther's Works*, Vol. 21: *Sermon on the Mount*. Concordia Publishing

Catholic Counter-Reformation

- Ignatius of Loyola. *Spiritual Exercises*, trans. Louis Puhl. Loyola Press, 1951
- Teresa of Ávila. *The Interior Castle*, trans. Kieran Kavanaugh. Paulist Press, 1979

Modern Biblical Scholarship

Critical Commentaries

- Allison, Dale C. Jr. *A Critical and Exegetical Commentary on the Gospel According to Saint Matthew*. ICC Series. T&T Clark, 2004
- Allison, Dale C. Jr. *The Sermon on the Mount: Inspiring the Moral Imagination*. Yale University Press, 1999
- Bauckham, Richard. *Jesus: A Very Short Introduction*. Oxford: Oxford University Press, 2011

- Betz, Hans Dieter. *The Sermon on the Mount.* Fortress Press, 1995
- Boring, M. Eugene. *Matthew: Introduction, Commentary, and Reflections.* NIB Commentary. Abingdon, 1995
- Carter, Warren. *What Are They Saying About Matthew's Sermon on the Mount?* Paulist Press, 1994
- Davies, W.D. and Allison, Dale C. *Matthew* (3 volumes). ICC Series. T&T Clark, 1988-1997
- Esler, Philip. *Community and Gospel in Luke-Acts.* Cambridge: Cambridge University Press, 1987
- France, R.T. *The Gospel of Matthew.* NICNT Series. Eerdmans, 2007
- Green, Joel B. *The Gospel of Luke.* NICNT Series. Grand Rapids: Eerdmans, 1997
- Green, Joel B. *The Theology of the Gospel of Luke.* Cambridge: Cambridge University Press, 1995
- Hardy, Grant. *Understanding the Book of Mormon: A Reader's Guide.* Oxford University Press, 2010
- Hauerwas, Stanley. *The Sermon on the Mount: A Theological Interpretation.* Baylor University Press, 2006
- Johnson, Luke Timothy. *The Gospel of Luke.* Sacra Pagina Series. Collegeville, MN: Liturgical Press, 1991
- Keener, Craig S. *The Gospel of Matthew: A Socio-Rhetorical Commentary.* Eerdmans, 2009
- Kloppenborg, John S. *Q, the Earliest Gospel: An Introduction to the Original Stories and Sayings of Jesus.* Louisville: Westminster John Knox, 2008
- Luz, Ulrich. *Matthew 1--7: A Commentary.* Hermeneia Series. Minneapolis: Fortress Press, 2007

- Luz, Ulrich. *Matthew in History: Interpretation, Influence, and Effects*. Fortress Press, 1994
- Nolland, John. *The Gospel of Matthew: A Commentary on the Greek Text*. NIGTC Series. Eerdmans, 2005
- Pennington, Jonathan T. *The Sermon on the Mount and Human Flourishing: A Theological Commentary*. Baker Academic, 2017
- Robinson, James M., Hoffmann, Paul, and Kloppenborg, John S. *The Critical Edition of Q*. Minneapolis: Fortress Press, 2000
- Stassen, Glen H. *Living the Sermon on the Mount*. Jossey-Bass, 2006
- Stassen, Glen H. and Gushee, David P. *Kingdom Ethics: Following Jesus in Contemporary Context*. InterVarsity Press, 2003

Historical Jesus Studies

- Borg, Marcus J. *Jesus: Uncovering the Life, Teachings, and Relevance of a Religious Revolutionary*. HarperOne, 2006
- Crossan, John Dominic. *God and Empire: Jesus Against Rome, Then and Now*. San Francisco: HarperOne, 2009
- Crossan, John Dominic. *Jesus: A Revolutionary Biography*. HarperSanFrancisco, 1994
- Crossan, John Dominic. *The Birth of Christianity*. HarperOne, 1998
- Ehrman, Bart D. *Lost Christianities: The Battles for Scripture and the Faiths We Never Knew*. New York: Oxford University Press, 2003

- Ehrman, Bart D. *The New Testament: A Historical Introduction.* Oxford University Press, 2016
- Evans, Craig A. *Fabricating Jesus: How Modern Scholars Distort the Gospels.* Downers Grove, IL: IVP Academic, 2006
- Horsley, Richard A. *Jesus and Empire: The Kingdom of God and the New World Disorder.* Minneapolis: Fortress Press, 2003
- Levine, Amy-Jill. *The Misunderstood Jew: The Church and the Scandal of the Jewish Jesus.* New York: HarperOne, 2006
- McCane, Byron R. *Roll Back the Stone: Death and Burial in the World of Jesus.* Trinity Press International, 2003
- Malina, Bruce J. and Rohrbaugh, Richard L. *Social-Science Commentary on the Synoptic Gospels.* 2nd ed. Minneapolis: Fortress Press, 2003
- Sanders, E.P. *Jesus and Judaism.* Fortress Press, 1985
- Sanders, E.P. *Judaism: Practice and Belief 63 BCE—66 CE.* Philadelphia: Trinity Press, 1992
- Wright, N.T. *How God Became King: The Forgotten Story of the Gospels.* San Francisco: HarperOne, 2012
- Wright, N.T. *Jesus and the Victory of God.* Minneapolis: Fortress Press, 1996
- Wright, N.T. *Luke for Everyone.* London: SPCK, 2001
- Wright, N.T. *The New Testament and the People of God.* Vol. 1 of *Christian Origins and the Question of God.* Minneapolis: Fortress Press, 1992

Textual and Linguistic Studies

- Bauer, Walter. *A Greek-English Lexicon of the New Testament (BDAG)*. 3rd ed., University of Chicago Press, 2000
- Fee, Gordon D. *New Testament Exegesis: A Handbook for Students and Pastors*. 4th ed. Louisville: Westminster John Knox, 2011
- Fitzmyer, Joseph A. *The Impact of the Dead Sea Scrolls*. New York: Paulist Press, 2009
- *The Greek New Testament* (Nestle-Aland, 28th Edition). Deutsche Bibelgesellschaft, 2012
- Kittel, Gerhard, ed. *Theological Dictionary of the New Testament (TDNT)*. Multiple volumes. Grand Rapids: Eerdmans, 1964-1976
- Liddell, H.G., and Scott, R. *A Greek-English Lexicon*. Oxford University Press
- Metzger, Bruce M. *The Canon of the New Testament: Its Origin, Development, and Significance*. Oxford: Clarendon Press, 1987
- Metzger, Bruce M. *A Textual Commentary on the Greek New Testament*. Stuttgart: United Bible Societies, 1994
- Porter, Stanley E. *How We Got the New Testament: Text, Transmission, Translation*. Baker Academic, 2013

Apocalyptic and Second Temple Studies

- Bauckham, Richard. *The Jewish World Around the New Testament*. Grand Rapids: Baker Academic, 2010

- Collins, John J. *The Apocalyptic Imagination: An Introduction to Jewish Apocalyptic Literature*. 3rd ed. Grand Rapids: Eerdmans, 2016
- Nickelsburg, George W.E. *Jewish Literature Between the Bible and the Mishnah*. 2nd ed. Minneapolis: Fortress Press, 2005
- Perdue, Leo G. *Wisdom Literature: A Theological History*. Louisville: Westminster John Knox, 2007
- Rowland, Christopher. *The Open Heaven: A Study of Apocalyptic in Judaism and Early Christianity*. New York: Crossroad, 1982
- VanderKam, James C. *An Introduction to Early Judaism*. Grand Rapids: Eerdmans, 2001

Liturgical and Worship Studies

- Bradshaw, Paul F. *The Search for the Origins of Christian Worship: Sources and Methods for the Study of Early Liturgy*. 2nd ed. New York: Oxford University Press, 2002
- Ferguson, Everett. *Early Christians Speak: Faith and Life in the First Three Centuries*. 3rd ed. Abilene: ACU Press, 1999
- Harper, John. *The Forms and Orders of Western Liturgy from the Tenth to the Eighteenth Century*. Oxford: Clarendon Press, 1991
- Jensen, Robin Margaret. *Understanding Early Christian Art*. London: Routledge, 2000

- Johnson, Maxwell E. *The Rites of Christian Initiation: Their Evolution and Interpretation.* Collegeville, MN: Liturgical Press, 2007
- Mathews, Thomas F. *The Clash of Gods: A Reinterpretation of Early Christian Art.* Revised ed. Princeton: Princeton University Press, 1999
- McGuckin, John Anthony. *The Orthodox Church: An Introduction to Its History, Doctrine, and Spiritual Culture.* Oxford: Wiley-Blackwell, 2008
- Palazzo, Eric. *A History of Liturgical Books from the Beginning to the Thirteenth Century.* Collegeville, MN: Liturgical Press, 1998
- Taft, Robert F. *The Liturgy of the Hours in East and West: The Origins of the Divine Office and Its Meaning for Today.* Collegeville, MN: Liturgical Press, 1993

Comparative Religion and World Religions

General Comparative Studies

- Armstrong, Karen. *The Case for God.* Knopf, 2009
- Armstrong, Karen. *The Great Transformation: The Beginning of Our Religious Traditions.* Knopf, 2006
- Aslan, Reza. *God: A Human History.* Random House, 2017
- Eck, Diana. *A New Religious America.* HarperOne, 2001
- Eliade, Mircea. *Patterns in Comparative Religion.* University of Nebraska Press, 1996
- Eliade, Mircea. *The Sacred and the Profane.* Harcourt Brace Jovanovich, 1987
- Smith, Huston. *The World's Religions.* HarperOne, 2009

- Smart, Ninian. *The World's Religions.* Cambridge University Press, 1998

Islamic Studies

- Ernst, Carl W. *Sufism: An Introduction to the Mystical Tradition of Islam.* Shambhala, 2011
- Nasr, Seyyed Hossein. *The Heart of Islam.* Harper SanFrancisco, 2002
- Schimmel, Annemarie. *Mystical Dimensions of Islam.* University of North Carolina Press, 1975

Buddhist Studies

- Thich Nhat Hanh. *Being Peace.* Parallax Press, 1987
- Thich Nhat Hanh. *No Death, No Fear.* Riverhead Books, 2002

Hindu Studies

- Doniger, Wendy. *The Hindus: An Alternative History.* Penguin Press, 2009
- Yogananda, Paramahansa. *The Yoga of Jesus.* Self-Realization Fellowship, 2007

East Asian Traditions

- Ching, Julia. *Confucianism and Christianity: A Comparative Study.* Kodansha, 1977
- de Bary, William Theodore. *Sources of Chinese Tradition.* Columbia University Press, multiple volumes

- Dundas, Paul. *The Jains*. Routledge, 2002
- Hall, John Whitney. *Japan: From Prehistory to Modern Times*. University of Tokyo Press, 1990
- Hansen, Chad. *A Daoist Theory of Chinese Thought*. Oxford University Press, 1992
- Hoff, Benjamin. *The Tao of Pooh*. Dutton, 1982
- Jaini, Padmanabh S. *The Jaina Path of Purification*. University of California Press, 1998
- Kaplan, Aryeh. *Jewish Meditation: A Practical Guide*. Schocken, 1985
- Kasulis, Thomas. *Shinto: The Way Home*. University of Hawaii Press, 2004
- Merton, Thomas. *The Way of Chuang Tzu*. New Directions, 1965
- Tamura, Yoshiro. *Japanese Buddhism: A Cultural History*. Kosei Publishing, 2000
- Tu Wei-ming. *Centrality and Commonality: An Essay on Confucian Religiousness*. SUNY Press, 1989

Jewish Studies

- Heschel, Abraham Joshua. *The Prophets*. Harper & Row, 1962
- Matt, Daniel C. *The Essential Kabbalah*. HarperSanFrancisco, 1995
- Scholem, Gershom. *Major Trends in Jewish Mysticism*. Schocken Books, 1995

Christian Movements and Denominations

Gnosticism

- Koester, Helmut. *Ancient Christian Gospels: Their History and Development.* Philadelphia: Trinity Press, 1990
- Layton, Bentley. *The Gnostic Scriptures.* Yale University Press, 1987
- Pagels, Elaine. *The Gnostic Gospels.* Vintage, 1989
- Patterson, Stephen J. *The Gospel of Thomas and Jesus.* Sonoma, CA: Polebridge Press, 1993

Quakerism

- Brinton, Howard. *Friends for 300 Years.* Pendle Hill Publications, 2002
- Dandelion, Pink. *An Introduction to Quakerism.* Cambridge University Press, 2007
- Jones, Rufus M. *The Faith and Practice of the Quakers.* Methuen, 1927

Mormonism

- Givens, Terryl. *People of Paradox: A History of Mormon Culture.* Oxford University Press, 2007
- *The Book of Mormon.* The Church of Jesus Christ of Latter-day Saints

Baha'i Faith

- Momen, Moojan. *Understanding the Baha'i Faith.* Dunedin Academic Press, 2008
- Smith, Peter. *An Introduction to the Baha'i Faith.* Cambridge University Press, 2008

Indigenous and African Traditions

Indigenous Wisdom

- Battiste, Marie. *Decolonizing Education: Nourishing the Learning Spirit.* Purich Publishing, 2013
- Brown, Joseph Epes. *The Sacred Pipe: Black Elk's Account of the Seven Rites of the Oglala Sioux.* University of Oklahoma Press, 1953
- Cajete, Gregory. *Native Science: Natural Laws of Interdependence.* Clear Light Publishers, 2000
- Deloria, Vine Jr. *God Is Red: A Native View of Religion.* Fulcrum Publishing, 2003
- Kimmerer, Robin Wall. *Braiding Sweetgrass: Indigenous Wisdom, Scientific Knowledge and the Teachings of Plants.* Milkweed Editions, 2013
- LaDuke, Winona. *Recovering the Sacred: The Power of Naming and Claiming.* South End Press, 2005
- Tinker, George E. *Spirit and Resistance: Political Theology and American Indian Liberation.* Fortress Press, 2004

African Traditions

- Bujo, Benezet. *African Theology in Its Social Context.* Orbis Books, 1992
- Longman, Timothy. *Christianity and Genocide in Rwanda.* Cambridge: Cambridge University Press, 2010
- Mbiti, John S. *African Religions and Philosophy.* Heinemann, 1990
- Oduyoye, Mercy Amba. *Daughters of Anowa: African Women and Patriarchy.* Orbis Books, 1995
- Sanneh, Lamin. *Whose Religion Is Christianity? The Gospel Beyond the West.* Grand Rapids: Eerdmans, 2003
- Some, Malidoma Patrice. *Ritual: Power, Healing and Community.* Swan Raven, 1993
- Wiredu, Kwame. *Cultural Universals and Particulars: An African Perspective.* Indiana University Press, 1996

Modern Theological Movements

Liberation Theology

- Abesamis, Carlos H. *A Third Look at Jesus: A Guidebook Along the Road of People's Theology.* Manila: Claretian Publications, 1998
- Ateek, Naim. *Justice and Only Justice: A Palestinian Theology of Liberation.* Maryknoll, NY: Orbis Books, 1989
- Boff, Leonardo. *Jesus Christ Liberator: A Critical Christology for Our Time.* Maryknoll, NY: Orbis Books, 1978

- Brueggemann, Walter. *The Prophetic Imagination*. 2nd ed. Minneapolis: Fortress Press, 2001
- Cone, James H. *The Cross and the Lynching Tree*. Maryknoll, NY: Orbis Books, 2011
- Cone, James H. *God of the Oppressed*. Revised ed. Maryknoll, NY: Orbis Books, 1997
- Gebara, Ivone. *Longing for Running Water: Ecofeminism and Liberation*. Minneapolis: Fortress Press, 1999
- González, Justo L. *Luke: The Gospel of the Outcast*. Maryknoll, NY: Orbis Books, 2002
- Gutiérrez, Gustavo. *A Theology of Liberation: History, Politics, and Salvation*. Revised ed. Maryknoll, NY: Orbis Books, 1988
- Nirmal, Arvind P. *Heuristic Explorations*. Madras: Christian Literature Society, 1990
- Raheb, Mitri. *I Am a Palestinian Christian*. Minneapolis: Fortress Press, 1995
- Romero, Oscar. *The Violence of Love*. Compiled by James R. Brockman. Maryknoll, NY: Orbis Books, 2004
- Sobrino, Jon. *Spirituality of Liberation: Toward Political Holiness*. Maryknoll, NY: Orbis Books, 1988

Social Gospel and Progressive Christianity

- Rauschenbusch, Walter. *Christianity and the Social Crisis*. 1907. Reprint: Westminster John Knox Press

Feminist and Womanist Theology

- Fabella, Virginia, and Mercy Amba Oduyoye, eds. *With Passion and Compassion: Third World Women Doing Theology*. Maryknoll, NY: Orbis Books, 1988
- Schüssler Fiorenza, Elisabeth. *In Memory of Her: A Feminist Theological Reconstruction of Christian Origins*.Crossroad, 1983
- Williams, Delores. *Sisters in the Wilderness: The Challenge of Womanist God-Talk*. Orbis Books, 1993

World Christianity and Missiology

- Fulton, Brent. *China's Urban Christians: A Light That Cannot Be Hidden*. Eugene, OR: Pickwick Publications, 2015
- Kim, Sebastian C.H. *Theology in the Public Sphere: Public Theology as a Catalyst for Open Debate*. London: SCM Press, 2011
- Robert, Dana L. *Christian Mission: How Christianity Became a World Religion*. Oxford: Wiley-Blackwell, 2009
- Sugirtharajah, R.S. *The Bible and the Third World: Precolonial, Colonial and Postcolonial Encounters*. Cambridge: Cambridge University Press, 2001
- Suh, Nam-dong. "Towards a Theology of Han." In *Minjung Theology: People as the Subjects of History*, edited by Commission on Theological Concerns of the Christian Conference of Asia, 51-65. Maryknoll, NY: Orbis Books, 1983
- Walls, Andrew F. *The Cross-Cultural Process in Christian History*. Maryknoll, NY: Orbis Books, 2002

Monastic and Spiritual Formation Studies

- Harmless, William. *Desert Christians: An Introduction to the Literature of Early Monasticism*. New York: Oxford University Press, 2004
- McGinn, Bernard. *The Foundations of Mysticism: Origins to the Fifth Century*. New York: Crossroad, 1991

Eastern Christianity

- Brock, Sebastian P. *The Luminous Eye: The Spiritual World Vision of Saint Ephrem the Syrian*. Kalamazoo: Cistercian Publications, 1992
- Ibrahim, Vivian. *The Copts of Egypt: The Challenges of Modernisation and Identity*. London: I.B. Tauris, 2011
- Meyendorff, John. *Byzantine Theology: Historical Trends and Doctrinal Themes*. New York: Fordham University Press, 1974

Spiritual Formation and Contemporary Applications

Catholic Spirituality

- Day, Dorothy. *The Long Loneliness*. HarperOne, 1952
- Manning, Brennan. *The Ragamuffin Gospel*. Multnomah, 2005
- Moltmann, Jürgen. *The Crucified God: The Cross of Christ as the Foundation and Criticism of Christian Theology*. Minneapolis: Fortress Press, 1993

- Nouwen, Henri J.M. *A Letter of Consolation.* Harper & Row, 1982
- Nouwen, Henri J.M. *The Return of the Prodigal Son.* New York: Doubleday, 1992
- Palmer, Parker J. *Let Your Life Speak: Listening for the Voice of Vocation.* San Francisco: Jossey-Bass, 2000
- Rohr, Richard. *Falling Upward: A Spirituality for the Two Halves of Life.* Jossey-Bass, 2011
- Vanier, Jean. *Becoming Human.* Paulist Press, 1998
- Weil, Simone. *Waiting for God.* Harper Perennial, 2009
- Willard, Dallas. *The Divine Conspiracy: Rediscovering Our Hidden Life in God.* San Francisco: HarperSanFrancisco, 1998

Protestant Spirituality

- Bonhoeffer, Dietrich. *The Cost of Discipleship.* Touchstone, 1995
- Kierkegaard, Søren. *Purity of Heart Is to Will One Thing.* Harper Torchbooks, 1956
- Ware, Kallistos. *The Inner Kingdom.* Crestwood, NY: St. Vladimir's Seminary Press, 2000

Contemporary Spiritual Writers

- Beck, Richard. *The Slavery of Death.* Cascade Books, 2013
- Wilken, Robert Louis. *The Spirit of Early Christian Thought: Seeking the Face of God.* New Haven: Yale University Press, 2003

- Young, Frances M. *From Nicaea to Chalcedon: A Guide to the Literature and Its Background.* 2nd ed. Grand Rapids: Baker Academic, 2010

Biographies and Memoirs

Christian Leaders

- Forest, Jim. *All Is Grace: A Biography of Dorothy Day.* Orbis Books, 2011
- Kagawa, Toyohiko. *Before the Dawn.* Friendship Press, 1925

Global Leaders

- Easwaran, Eknath. *Gandhi the Man.* Nilgiri Press, 2011
- Gandhi, Mahatma. *An Autobiography: The Story of My Experiments with Truth.* Beacon Press, 1993
- King Jr., Martin Luther. *Strength to Love.* Minneapolis: Fortress Press, 2010
- Maathai, Wangari. *Unbowed: A Memoir.* New York: Knopf, 2006
- Mandela, Nelson. *Long Walk to Freedom.* Little, Brown, 1994
- Tutu, Desmond. *No Future Without Forgiveness.* New York: Doubleday, 1999
- Yousafzai, Malala. *I Am Malala.* Little, Brown, 2013

Psychology and Grief Studies

Grief and Loss

- Devine, Megan. *It's OK That You're Not OK: Meeting Grief and Loss in a Culture That Doesn't Understand.* Sounds True, 2017
- Didion, Joan. *The Year of Magical Thinking.* Vintage Books, 2007
- Lewis, C.S. *A Grief Observed.* Bantam Books, 1976
- Wolterstorff, Nicholas. *Lament for a Son.* Eerdmans, 1987

Psychology of Religion

- Fowler, James. *Stages of Faith.* Harper & Row, 1981

Peace Studies and Conflict Resolution

Peace and Reconciliation

- Lederach, John Paul. *The Little Book of Conflict Transformation.* Good Books, 2003
- Stassen, Glen H. *Just Peacemaking: The New Paradigm for the Ethics of Peace and War.* Pilgrim Press, 2008

Environmental Ethics

Religion and Ecology

- Gottlieb, Roger S. *A Greener Faith: Religious Environmentalism and Our Planet's Future.* Oxford University Press, 2006
- Tucker, Mary Evelyn and Grim, John (eds.). *Religion and Ecology: Can the Climate Change?* Daedalus, 2001

Social Justice and Ethics

Civil Rights and Social Movements

- West, Cornel. *Prophesy Deliverance!* Westminster John Knox Press, 1982

Reference Works

- Ellsberg, Robert. *All Saints: Daily Reflections on Saints, Prophets, and Witnesses for Our Time.* Crossroad, 1997

Further Reading

A curated guide to the most accessible and essential works for exploring how the Beatitudes resonate across religious and cultural boundaries.

Starting Points: Understanding the Beatitudes

Dale C. Allison Jr. *The Sermon on the Mount: Inspiring the Moral Imagination* (Yale University Press, 1999)
The most thoughtful and accessible scholarly treatment of the Beatitudes, combining rigorous biblical scholarship with contemporary relevance. Allison shows how these ancient blessings continue to challenge and inspire across religious boundaries.

Glen H. Stassen *Living the Sermon on the Mount* (Jossey-Bass, 2006)
A practical guide that transforms the Beatitudes from abstract ideals into concrete practices for contemporary life. Stassen demonstrates how these teachings can be lived out in families, communities, and society.

Ulrich Luz *Matthew 1-7: A Commentary* (Fortress Press, 2007)
The most comprehensive modern commentary on the Beatitudes, combining historical context with theological insight. Dense but rewarding for serious students.

Jonathan T. Pennington *The Sermon on the Mount and Human Flourishing* (Baker Academic, 2017)
A modern evangelical approach that explores the translation of *makarioi* as "flourishing," showing how the Beatitudes describe comprehensive well-being rather than mere happiness.

Historical Context and Background

Richard A. Horsley *Jesus and Empire* (Fortress Press, 2003)
Essential for understanding the political and economic context in which Jesus spoke the Beatitudes. Horsley shows how these blessings challenged Roman imperial ideology and economic exploitation.

N.T. Wright *Jesus and the Victory of God* (Fortress Press, 1996)
Wright's magisterial work on the historical Jesus provides crucial background for understanding the apocalyptic context of the Beatitudes and their role in Jesus' announcement of God's kingdom.

John J. Collins *The Apocalyptic Imagination* (3rd ed., Eerdmans, 2016)
The definitive introduction to Jewish apocalyptic literature, showing how the Beatitudes fit within broader Second Temple hopes for divine intervention and social reversal.

E.P. Sanders *Jesus and Judaism* (Fortress Press, 1985)
The most influential modern book on the historical Jesus, providing essential context for understanding the Beatitudes within first-century Palestinian Judaism.

Amy-Jill Levine *The Misunderstood Jew: The Church and the Scandal of the Jewish Jesus* (HarperOne, 2006)
A Jewish scholar's perspective on Jesus that helps Christians understand the Jewish roots of the Beatitudes and avoid supersessionist interpretations.

Early Sources and Development

John S. Kloppenborg *Q, the Earliest Gospel* (Westminster John Knox, 2008)
The current standard for Q source scholarship, essential for understanding how the Beatitudes may have appeared in their earliest form before Matthew and Luke's editing.

Geza Vermes *The Complete Dead Sea Scrolls in English* (7th ed., Penguin, 2011)
Provides access to Qumran texts like 4Q525 ("Beatitudes") that show how blessing formulas were used in Second Temple Judaism, revealing important parallels to Jesus' teaching.

Stephen J. Patterson *The Gospel of Thomas and Jesus* (Polebridge Press, 1993)
Explores how early Christian communities outside the mainstream interpreted blessing sayings, showing the diversity of early Beatitude reception.

Liturgical and Devotional Traditions

Paul F. Bradshaw *The Search for the Origins of Christian Worship* (2nd ed., Oxford University Press, 2002)
Foundational for understanding how the Beatitudes functioned

in early Christian worship and spiritual formation rather than merely as ethical instruction.

Robert F. Taft *The Liturgy of the Hours in East and West* (Liturgical Press, 1993)
Shows how Eastern and Western Christian traditions incorporated the Beatitudes into daily prayer and worship, making them living spiritual practices.

John Anthony McGuckin *The Orthodox Church* (Wiley-Blackwell, 2008)
Provides insight into how Eastern Christian traditions have preserved and practiced the Beatitudes as part of comprehensive spiritual formation.

Kallistos Ware *The Inner Kingdom* (St. Vladimir's Seminary Press, 2000)
A master of Orthodox spirituality shows how the Beatitudes function in contemplative practice and mystical theology.

Luke's Gospel and the Blessing/Woe Structure

Joel B. Green *The Gospel of Luke* (NICNT Series, Eerdmans, 1997)
The most comprehensive modern commentary on Luke's Gospel, essential for understanding how the blessings and woes function within Luke's larger theological vision.

Joel B. Green *The Theology of the Gospel of Luke* (Cambridge University Press, 1995)
A focused study of Luke's theological themes, showing how the

pattern of reversal runs throughout the Gospel and culminates in the blessings and woes.

Philip Esler *Community and Gospel in Luke-Acts* (Cambridge University Press, 1987)
A groundbreaking social-science approach to Luke that illuminates the economic and social realities behind the blessings and woes.

N.T. Wright *Luke for Everyone* (SPCK, 2001)
An accessible commentary that helps general readers understand Luke's distinctive emphasis on social justice and economic reversal.

Comparative Religion and World Wisdom

Huston Smith *The World's Religions* (HarperOne, 2009)
The gold standard introduction to world religions, written with remarkable clarity and respect. Smith shows how different traditions approach the same fundamental human questions that the Beatitudes address.

Karen Armstrong *The Great Transformation: The Beginning of Our Religious Traditions* (Knopf, 2006)
A brilliant exploration of the "Axial Age" (800-200 BCE) that produced many of the world's great wisdom traditions. Armstrong demonstrates how different cultures discovered similar insights about compassion, justice, and transcendence.

Mircea Eliade *The Sacred and the Profane* (Harcourt Brace Jovanovich, 1987)

A classic work that helps readers understand how different cultures experience the sacred. Essential for grasping how the Beatitudes function as sacred wisdom across traditions.

Christian Foundations and History

Abraham Joshua Heschel *The Prophets* (Harper & Row, 1962)
Though written by a Jewish scholar, this passionate exploration of Hebrew prophetic tradition illuminates the Jewish roots of the Beatitudes. Heschel shows how concern for justice and mercy runs through both traditions.

Henri J.M. Nouwen *The Return of the Prodigal Son* (Doubleday, 1992)
A deeply personal meditation on grace, forgiveness, and transformation that embodies the spirit of the Beatitudes. Nouwen's vulnerable honesty makes ancient wisdom accessible to modern readers.

Richard Rohr *Falling Upward: A Spirituality for the Two Halves of Life* (Jossey-Bass, 2011)
A wise exploration of how spiritual maturity involves embracing the paradoxes that the Beatitudes celebrate—finding strength in weakness, wisdom in foolishness, life in letting go.

Walter Brueggemann *The Prophetic Imagination* (2nd ed., Fortress Press, 2001)
Essential for understanding how the Beatitudes function as prophetic proclamation, challenging existing power structures while pointing toward God's alternative future.

Islamic Wisdom and Mysticism

Annemarie Schimmel *Mystical Dimensions of Islam* (University of North Carolina Press, 1975)
The definitive scholarly introduction to Sufism, showing how Islamic mysticism developed themes remarkably similar to the Beatitudes—spiritual poverty, divine mercy, and the transformation of suffering.

Rumi *The Essential Rumi*, trans. Coleman Barks (HarperOne, 2004)
The most accessible collection of poetry from Islam's greatest mystical poet. Rumi's celebration of brokenness, divine love, and spiritual poverty echoes the Beatitudes' paradoxical wisdom.

Seyyed Hossein Nasr *The Heart of Islam* (HarperSanFrancisco, 2002)
A clear, respectful introduction to Islamic spirituality that shows how concepts like mercy, submission, and justice function in Muslim thought and practice.

Buddhist and Hindu Perspectives

Thich Nhat Hanh *The Heart of Buddhist Meditation* (Beacon Press, 1975)
A gentle introduction to Buddhist mindfulness that demonstrates how inner peace creates outer compassion—a theme central to the Beatitudes.

The Dhammapada, trans. Eknath Easwaran (Nilgiri Press, 2007)
Easwaran's translation of Buddhism's most beloved text includes helpful commentary that shows how Buddhist ethics align with universal wisdom about non-violence, compassion, and inner transformation.

Barbara Stoler Miller *The Bhagavad-Gita* (Bantam Classics, 1986)
The most accessible scholarly translation of Hinduism's most important ethical text. The Gita's exploration of duty, devotion, and detachment offers fascinating parallels to the Beatitudes.

East Asian Wisdom

Stephen Mitchell *Tao Te Ching* (Harper & Row, 1988)
Mitchell's poetic translation makes Taoist wisdom accessible to Western readers. The Tao Te Ching's celebration of humility, gentleness, and yielding strength resonates deeply with the Beatitudes.

Arthur Waley *The Analects of Confucius* (Vintage, 1989)
The classic translation of Confucius' teachings on virtue, social harmony, and moral cultivation. Shows how different cultures can arrive at similar insights about the good life.

Indigenous and African Wisdom

Vine Deloria Jr. *God Is Red: A Native View of Religion* (Fulcrum Publishing, 2003)
A foundational text that challenges Western assumptions about

spirituality while demonstrating how Indigenous wisdom traditions embody many of the values the Beatitudes celebrate.

Robin Wall Kimmerer *Braiding Sweetgrass: Indigenous Wisdom, Scientific Knowledge and the Teachings of Plants* (Milkweed Editions, 2013)
A beautiful integration of Indigenous knowledge and scientific understanding that shows how reciprocity, gratitude, and reverence for life can guide contemporary living.

Desmond Tutu *No Future Without Forgiveness* (Doubleday, 1999)
Archbishop Tutu's reflection on South Africa's Truth and Reconciliation Commission demonstrates how the Beatitudes' emphasis on mercy and reconciliation can heal even the deepest wounds.

Lamin Sanneh *Whose Religion Is Christianity? The Gospel Beyond the West* (Eerdmans, 2003)
Essential for understanding how Christianity has been received, interpreted, and transformed by non-Western cultures, revealing new dimensions of the Beatitudes' meaning.

Global Church and Liberation Theology

Gustavo Gutiérrez *A Theology of Liberation* (revised ed., Orbis Books, 1988)
The foundational text of liberation theology, showing how the Beatitudes' concern for the poor and oppressed guides contemporary social action and ecclesial commitment.

Jon Sobrino *Spirituality of Liberation* (Orbis Books, 1988)
A Salvadoran Jesuit's reflection on how the Beatitudes sustain communities under persecution and guide the work of justice and reconciliation.

Oscar Romero *The Violence of Love*, compiled by James R. Brockman (Orbis Books, 2004)
Homilies and writings from the martyred archbishop who preached the Beatitudes as both spiritual wisdom and prophetic challenge to structural violence.

Mercy Amba Oduyoye *Daughters of Anowa: African Women and Patriarchy* (Orbis Books, 1995)
A pioneering work in African women's theology that shows how the Beatitudes speak to experiences of oppression and community building from women's perspectives.

James H. Cone *God of the Oppressed* (revised ed., Orbis Books, 1997)
A foundational text in Black theology that shows how the Beatitudes speak to the African American experience of suffering and the struggle for liberation.

Living Examples and Saints

Dorothy Day *The Long Loneliness* (HarperOne, 1952)
Day's autobiography shows how the Beatitudes can be lived out in radical service to the poor and marginalized. Her life embodied the blessings on those who hunger for justice and practice mercy.

Mahatma Gandhi *An Autobiography: The Story of My Experiments with Truth* (Beacon Press, 1993)
Gandhi's spiritual journey demonstrates how the Beatitudes' values can be lived across religious boundaries. His commitment to truth, non-violence, and service to the poor echoes Jesus' teachings.

Martin Luther King Jr. *Strength to Love* (Fortress Press, 2010)
King's sermons show how the Beatitudes can inspire social transformation. His vision of beloved community embodies the reconciliation and justice that the Beatitudes envision.

Nelson Mandela *Long Walk to Freedom* (Little, Brown, 1994)
Mandela's autobiography demonstrates how the Beatitudes' emphasis on forgiveness and reconciliation can overcome even the most entrenched systems of oppression.

Wangari Maathai *Unbowed: A Memoir* (Knopf, 2006)
The Nobel Prize winner's story shows how environmental stewardship can be a form of peacemaking, embodying the Beatitudes' vision of justice and care for creation.

Contemporary Applications

John Paul Lederach *The Little Book of Conflict Transformation* (Good Books, 2003)
A practical guide to peacemaking that shows how the Beatitudes' vision of reconciliation can be applied to contemporary conflicts at every level.

Megan Devine *It's OK That You're Not OK: Meeting Grief and Loss in a Culture That Doesn't Understand* (Sounds True, 2017)
A compassionate guide to grief that embodies the Beatitudes' blessing on those who mourn, offering wisdom for supporting others through loss.

Glen H. Stassen and David P. Gushee *Kingdom Ethics: Following Jesus in Contemporary Context* (InterVarsity Press, 2003)
A comprehensive Christian ethics textbook that shows how the Beatitudes can guide contemporary moral decision-making across a wide range of issues.

Dallas Willard *The Divine Conspiracy: Rediscovering Our Hidden Life in God* (HarperSanFrancisco, 1998)
A profound exploration of how the Beatitudes describe the transformed life available to all who follow Jesus. Willard shows how these aren't just moral ideals but descriptions of spiritual reality.

Spiritual Formation and Practice

Brennan Manning *The Ragamuffin Gospel* (Multnomah, 2005)
A passionate celebration of grace that embodies the Beatitudes' vision of God's love for the broken and marginalized. Manning's personal honesty makes the message accessible to struggling readers.

Simone Weil *Waiting for God* (Harper Perennial, 2009)
The spiritual writings of a brilliant French philosopher who lived the Beatitudes' emphasis on solidarity with the suffering.

Weil's insights into affliction and grace are both challenging and profound.

Parker J. Palmer *Let Your Life Speak: Listening for the Voice of Vocation* (Jossey-Bass, 2000)
A wise exploration of how to discern authentic calling that resonates with the Beatitudes' emphasis on integrity and truth-telling.

Grief and Healing

Nicholas Wolterstorff *Lament for a Son* (Eerdmans, 1987)
A philosopher's honest wrestling with grief after his son's death. Wolterstorff demonstrates how the Beatitudes' blessing on those who mourn can sustain us through profound loss.

C.S. Lewis *A Grief Observed* (Bantam Books, 1976)
Lewis's raw account of grief after his wife's death shows how faith can survive even the deepest sorrow. A powerful example of how mourning can lead to deeper understanding.

Peace and Justice

Walter Rauschenbusch *Christianity and the Social Crisis* (Westminster John Knox Press, 1907)
The foundational text of the Social Gospel movement, showing how the Beatitudes call Christians to work for social justice and economic equality.

Reading Guide by Interest

For those interested in historical context:

- Richard A. Horsley, *Jesus and Empire*
- N.T. Wright, *Jesus and the Victory of God*
- John J. Collins, *The Apocalyptic Imagination*
- Amy-Jill Levine, *The Misunderstood Jew*

For those interested in Luke's distinctive approach:

- Joel B. Green, *The Gospel of Luke*
- Joel B. Green, *The Theology of the Gospel of Luke*
- Philip Esler, *Community and Gospel in Luke-Acts*
- N.T. Wright, *Luke for Everyone*

For those interested in early sources:

- John S. Kloppenborg, *Q, the Earliest Gospel*
- Geza Vermes, *The Complete Dead Sea Scrolls in English*
- Paul F. Bradshaw, *The Search for the Origins of Christian Worship*

For those interested in interfaith dialogue:

- Huston Smith, *The World's Religions*
- Karen Armstrong, *The Great Transformation*
- Abraham Joshua Heschel, *The Prophets*
- Annemarie Schimmel, *Mystical Dimensions of Islam*

For those wanting practical spiritual guidance:

- Glen H. Stassen, *Living the Sermon on the Mount*
- Henri J.M. Nouwen, *The Return of the Prodigal Son*
- Richard Rohr, *Falling Upward*
- Dallas Willard, *The Divine Conspiracy*

For those interested in global Christianity:

- Lamin Sanneh, *Whose Religion Is Christianity?*
- Gustavo Gutiérrez, *A Theology of Liberation*
- Desmond Tutu, *No Future Without Forgiveness*
- Mercy Amba Oduyoye, *Daughters of Anowa*

For those interested in social justice:

- Dorothy Day, *The Long Loneliness*
- Martin Luther King Jr., *Strength to Love*
- Walter Rauschenbusch, *Christianity and the Social Crisis*
- James H. Cone, *God of the Oppressed*

For those dealing with grief and loss:

- Nicholas Wolterstorff, *Lament for a Son*
- C.S. Lewis, *A Grief Observed*
- Megan Devine, *It's OK That You're Not OK*

For those interested in Eastern wisdom:

- Thich Nhat Hanh, *The Heart of Buddhist Meditation*
- Stephen Mitchell, *Tao Te Ching*

- Barbara Stoler Miller, *The Bhagavad-Gita*

For those interested in liturgy and worship:

- Robert F. Taft, *The Liturgy of the Hours in East and West*
- John Anthony McGuckin, *The Orthodox Church*
- Kallistos Ware, *The Inner Kingdom*

For those interested in biblical scholarship:

- Dale C. Allison Jr., *The Sermon on the Mount*
- Ulrich Luz, *Matthew 1-7: A Commentary*
- Jonathan T. Pennington, *The Sermon on the Mount and Human Flourishing*

For those interested in prophetic tradition:

- Walter Brueggemann, *The Prophetic Imagination*
- Abraham Joshua Heschel, *The Prophets*
- Gustavo Gutiérrez, *A Theology of Liberation*

A Note on Reading Across Traditions

When reading works from different religious traditions, approach them with what Buddhist teacher Thich Nhat Hanh calls "beginner's mind"—openness to learning without the need to agree with everything. The goal isn't to create a syncretic blend of all traditions but to discover how different cultures have grappled with the same fundamental questions about meaning, suffering, and transcendence.

The Beatitudes offer a particularly rich lens for this kind of reading because they address universal human experiences—poverty, grief, hunger for justice, the longing for peace—while maintaining their distinctive Christian vision of how God meets us in these experiences. Reading across traditions can deepen rather than diminish our appreciation of what makes each tradition unique while revealing our shared human longing for blessing, meaning, and transformation.

Special Topics for Advanced Study

Apocalyptic Context:

- John J. Collins, *The Apocalyptic Imagination*
- Christopher Rowland, *The Open Heaven*
- Richard Bauckham, *The Jewish World Around the New Testament*

Empire and Power:

- Richard A. Horsley, *Jesus and Empire*
- John Dominic Crossan, *God and Empire*
- Walter Brueggemann, *The Prophetic Imagination*

Luke's Social Vision:

- Joel B. Green, *The Theology of the Gospel of Luke*
- Philip Esler, *Community and Gospel in Luke-Acts*
- Bruce J. Malina and Richard L. Rohrbaugh, *Social-Science Commentary on the Synoptic Gospels*

Greek Language and Translation:

- Jonathan T. Pennington, *The Sermon on the Mount and Human Flourishing*
- Dale C. Allison Jr., *The Sermon on the Mount*
- Ulrich Luz, *Matthew 1-7: A Commentary*

Q Source and Early Traditions:

- John S. Kloppenborg, *Q, the Earliest Gospel*
- James M. Robinson, et al., *The Critical Edition of Q*
- Stephen J. Patterson, *The Gospel of Thomas and Jesus*

Liturgical Development:

- Paul F. Bradshaw, *The Search for the Origins of Christian Worship*
- Robert F. Taft, *The Liturgy of the Hours in East and West*
- Maxwell E. Johnson, *The Rites of Christian Initiation*

These resources provide pathways into the rich tradition of Beatitudes interpretation while opening windows onto the broader human search for meaning, justice, and transcendence that connects all wisdom traditions.

Index

For a comprehensive, electronically searchable index of all terms, concepts, names, biblical references, and cross-cultural parallels discussed in this book, please visit: https://www.beatitudespath.com.

The online index includes detailed entries for:

- *All theological and philosophical terminology*
- *Complete biblical and scriptural references*
- *Historical figures and contemporary voices*
- *Cross-cultural concepts and foreign language terms*
- *Methodological and scholarly references*
- *Geographical and institutional names*
- *Thematic cross-references and related concepts*

Major Topics and Themes

The Eight Beatitudes

- Poor in spirit, 21-28, 385-386
- Those who mourn, 29-38, 387-388
- The meek, 39-48, 389-390
- Hunger and thirst for righteousness, 49-58, 388-389
- The merciful, 59-68, 393
- Pure in heart, 69-80, 391-392
- Peacemakers, 81-92, 393-394
- Those persecuted for righteousness, 93-102, 394-395

Global Wisdom Traditions

- Buddhist perspectives, 24-25, 33-34, 44-45, 53-54, 64, 74-75, 84, 95, 135-144
- Hindu insights, 25, 34-35, 45, 54, 64-65, 75, 85, 95-96, 137-138
- Islamic wisdom, 23, 32-33, 43-44, 52-53, 63, 73-74, 83, 94-95, 117
- Indigenous traditions, 125-134
- East Asian philosophy, 135-144

Living Examples

- Saints and exemplars, 255-272
- Contemporary witnesses, 251-252, 255-260
- Global church voices, 145-163

Complete page references and detailed cross-indexing available online at https://www.beatitudespath.com.

The Beatitudes Path: An 8-Week Journey of Reflection and Practice

A Complete Series for Personal and Group Study

Week 1: Blessed Are the Poor in Spirit

Day 1: The Text

"Blessed are the poor in spirit, for theirs is the kingdom of heaven."
— Matthew 5:3 (New Revised Standard Version)

In Greek: Μακάριοι οἱ πτωχοὶ τῷ πνεύματι, ὅτι αὐτῶν ἐστὶν ἡ βασιλεία τῶν οὐρανῶν. *(Makarioi hoi ptōchoi tō pneumati, hoti autōn estin hē basileia tōn ouranōn.)*

Other translations:

- *"Happy are those who know they are spiritually poor..."* (Good News Translation)
- *"God blesses those who are poor and realize their need for him..."* (New Living Translation)
- *"How blest are those who know their need of God..."* (Revised English Bible)
- *"You're blessed when you're at the end of your rope..."* (The Message)

Reflection Prompt: Read the verse aloud slowly. What does "poor in spirit" evoke in you today—discomfort? relief?

confusion? What might it mean to have "nothing" to offer God, and yet be called blessed?

Day 2: Language and Meaning

"Poor" (πτωχοί) in Greek refers to absolute poverty—those with nothing, who must beg. But Matthew adds *"in spirit" (τῷ πνεύματι)*—qualifying this as poverty of the soul, not the wallet.

This isn't self-hatred, but **radical dependence**. To be poor in spirit is to:

- Stop pretending we are self-sufficient
- Release ego, certainty, and control
- Know ourselves as receivers, not achievers
- Embrace spiritual emptiness that makes room for God

The paradox: The kingdom belongs not to the spiritually strong, but to the empty-handed. Not to those who have it all figured out, but to those honest about their need.

Day 3: Echoes Across Traditions

Most wisdom traditions affirm the blessing of humility and non-attachment:

Islam: The first spiritual station is *faqr* (spiritual poverty)—not material, but surrender before Allah. "And it is He who sends down rain from heaven, and We produce thereby the vegetation of every kind" (Qur'an 6:99). True wealth comes from recognizing our dependence on divine mercy.

Buddhism: *Anattā* (non-self)—awakening begins by letting go of ego-clinging. "The fool who thinks he is wise is indeed a fool" (Dhammapada 63). Liberation comes through releasing the illusion of self-sufficiency.

Taoism: "The highest goodness is like water... It dwells in lowly places that all disdain—this is why it is so near the Tao" (Tao Te Ching 8). True power flows from emptiness and humility.

Common thread: The truly wise are those who release themselves—and discover they're filled by something greater.

Day 4: A Witness — St. Francis of Assisi

St. Francis (1181–1226) was the son of a wealthy merchant, destined for power and prestige. Yet he gave up everything—clothes, family ties, social status—and embraced radical poverty as spiritual freedom.

He called this *"Lady Poverty,"* not as deprivation, but as love—a release of ownership so that God might possess him entirely. Though mocked by many, Francis became a living icon of joy, humility, and belonging to the kingdom.

"What a man is before God, that he is, and nothing more." —St. Francis

He had nothing materially—and found everything spiritually. His poverty of spirit opened him to receive God's abundance and share it with the world through radical hospitality and creation care.

Day 5: In Professional and Public Life

Poverty of spirit is rare in the workplace. We're told to project confidence, mastery, even invincibility. But what if leadership began with **honest limitation**?

Being poor in spirit might mean:

- Admitting "I don't know" and inviting collaboration
- Listening more than speaking in meetings
- Asking for help before pretending to have answers
- Acknowledging failure without spinning or deflecting
- Leading with curiosity rather than false certainty

This doesn't diminish authority—it makes it **authentic**. People follow leaders who are real more readily than those who are perfect.

What might shift in your work life if ego was no longer your first defense?

Day 6: In Personal Life and Relationships

In our closest relationships, pride can poison everything. To be poor in spirit relationally means:

- Saying "I was wrong" without excuse or qualification
- Forgiving more easily because we know our own weakness
- Offering grace instead of judgment when others fail
- Letting go of needing to be "right" in every conversation
- Coming to others with open hands rather than closed fists

Poverty of spirit creates spaciousness—in marriage, friendship, even prayer. It's not weakness; it's the foundation of authentic love that doesn't need to be earned or defended.

Day 7: Contemplative Practice

Breath Prayer: *"Empty me, / fill me with you."*

Sit in stillness for 5–10 minutes. On each inhale, say silently: *"Empty me."* On each exhale: *"Fill me with you."*

Let go of all striving, all roles, all self-descriptions. Rest in the presence of God as one who brings nothing—and lacks nothing. Notice what arises when you stop trying to be impressive, even to yourself.

Alternative practice: Take a walking meditation, repeating: "I am not my achievements, I am not my failures, I am not my reputation. I am beloved."

Weekly Reflection Space

This week, where did you experience the "kingdom"—moments of grace, unexpected blessing, or divine presence?

What areas of your life are you trying to be spiritually "wealthy"? What would it look like to embrace poverty of spirit there?

How did this Beatitude challenge or comfort you? What is one specific way you can practice spiritual poverty in the coming week?

Week 2: Blessed Are Those Who Mourn

Day 1: The Text

"Blessed are those who mourn, for they will be comforted." — Matthew 5:4 (NRSV)

In Greek: Μακάριοι οἱ πενθοῦντες, ὅτι αὐτοὶ παρακληθήσονται. *(Makarioi hoi penthountes, hoti autoi paraklēthēsontai.)*

Other translations:

- *"Happy are those who mourn..."* (GNT)
- *"God blesses those who mourn..."* (NLT)
- *"Blessed are the sorrowful..."* (REB)
- *"You're blessed when you feel you've lost what is most dear to you..."* (MSG)

Reflection Prompt: What are you mourning today—loss, injustice, broken dreams, or the world's pain? How might your grief be not a sign of weakness, but a mark of love with nowhere else to go?

Day 2: Language and Meaning

"Mourn" (πενθοῦντες) is a strong Greek word for deep grief—typically used for mourning the dead. This isn't casual sadness but soul-shaking lament. The present participle suggests ongoing mourning, not just momentary sorrow.

This mourning encompasses:

- **Personal loss**: Death, divorce, dreams that died
- **Moral grief**: Sorrow over sin, failure, and broken relationships
- **Prophetic lament**: Weeping over injustice and the world's brokenness

"**Comforted**" (παρακληθήσονται) means more than emotional soothing. It's *parakaleō*—"to be called alongside." God doesn't just heal our grief; God joins us in it. Divine presence transforms suffering without necessarily removing it.

Day 3: Echoes Across Traditions

Sacred traditions recognize grief's transformative power:

Islam: The Qur'an honors patient endurance (*ṣabr*) through loss: "Give glad tidings to the patient—those who, when disaster strikes them, say, 'Indeed we belong to Allah, and indeed to Him we will return'" (2:155-156). Grief becomes a doorway to deeper trust in divine sovereignty.

Buddhism: The First Noble Truth acknowledges life contains *dukkha* (suffering). But understood properly, suffering teaches compassion. When we truly see that all beings suffer, our personal grief opens us to universal compassion (*karuṇā*).

Jewish tradition: The Psalms don't hide from sorrow—they dive into it. "Those who sow in tears shall reap with shouts of joy"

(Psalm 126:5). Mourning rituals like *shiva* demonstrate that grief shared becomes grief transformed.

Common thread: Authentic grief, honestly faced and communally held, becomes the soil from which compassion grows.

Day 4: A Witness — Henri Nouwen

Henri Nouwen (1932-1996), Dutch Catholic priest and writer, spent his later years living with intellectually disabled people at L'Arche. There he discovered that those society considers "broken" often possess profound spiritual gifts.

Nouwen wrote extensively about his own struggles with depression, loneliness, and self-doubt. Rather than hiding his wounds, he let them become sources of healing for others. His vulnerability in writing about grief made him a trusted spiritual guide for millions.

"The wound is the place where the Light enters you." —Rumi (often quoted by Nouwen)

Nouwen showed that mourning isn't a sign of weak faith but honest humanity. Those who embrace their brokenness often become healers for others' brokenness.

Day 5: In Professional and Public Life

Our culture pathologizes sadness and rushes through grief. But what if mourning well became a leadership strength?

In professional contexts, blessed mourning might mean:

- Acknowledging when projects fail without immediately spinning to the positive
- Creating space for teams to grieve lost colleagues or cancelled initiatives
- Allowing yourself to feel the weight of difficult decisions
- Speaking honestly about systemic problems that cause harm
- Refusing to be constantly upbeat when reality calls for lament

Leaders who can sit with loss—their own and others'—create environments where people feel permission to be human. They build trust through emotional honesty rather than forced optimism.

Day 6: In Personal Life and Relationships

Mourning well transforms relationships by creating space for authentic connection:

- **Don't rush others' grief**: Resist the urge to "fix" someone's sadness. Sometimes presence is the only comfort needed.

- **Share your own losses**: Vulnerability about your grief gives others permission for theirs.
- **Mourn injustice together**: Let yourself feel the world's brokenness. This shared lament often becomes the beginning of shared action.
- **Create rituals for loss**: Light candles, plant trees, write letters. Give grief tangible expression.
- **Welcome tears**: Yours and others'. Tears aren't signs of weakness but love seeking expression.

When we mourn together, we discover we're not alone in our sorrow—and that shared grief often becomes the foundation of deeper love.

Day 7: Contemplative Practice

Lament Prayer: Bring your honest grief to prayer without trying to fix or spiritualize it.

Sit quietly and name what you're mourning—losses, disappointments, the world's pain. Don't rush to find meaning or comfort. Simply offer your sorrow to God as it is.

You might pray: *"God, I am sad about _____. I don't understand why. I don't need answers right now. I just need you to be with me in this."*

Alternative practice: Write a letter to someone you've lost—express what you miss, what you're grateful for, what you wish you'd said. No need to send it. The writing itself becomes prayer.

Weekly Reflection Space

What losses are you carrying right now—personal, communal, or global? How has mourning changed you or taught you?

Where have you experienced God's comfort—through people, nature, prayer, or unexpected grace? How might your grief become a gift to others?

What would it look like to mourn more honestly and receive comfort more openly in the coming week?

Week 3: Blessed Are the Meek

Day 1: The Text

"Blessed are the meek, for they will inherit the earth." — Matthew 5:5 (NRSV)

In Greek: Μακάριοι οἱ πραεῖς, ὅτι αὐτοὶ κληρονομήσουσιν τὴν γῆν. *(Makarioi hoi praeis, hoti autoi klēronomēsousin tēn gēn.)*

Other translations:

- *"Happy are the meek..."* (GNT)
- *"God blesses those who are humble..."* (NLT)
- *"How blest are those of a gentle spirit..."* (REB)
- *"You're blessed when you're content with just who you are..."* (MSG)

Reflection Prompt: What comes to mind when you hear "meek"? How might this word describe not weakness, but strength under control—like a trained war horse, powerful but responsive to guidance?

Day 2: Language and Meaning

"Meek" (πραεῖς) doesn't mean weak or passive. In Greek, it described a wild animal that had been tamed—power under control. Aristotle used it for someone who is angry at the right time, in the right way, for the right reasons, but never ruled by anger.

Biblical meekness includes:

- **Gentleness with strength**: Like Moses, called "very meek" (Numbers 12:3) yet powerful enough to confront Pharaoh
- **Humility without weakness**: Refusing to dominate others while maintaining inner strength
- **Trust over force**: Choosing patience and wisdom over aggressive action
- **Responsive rather than reactive**: Taking time to respond thoughtfully rather than react defensively

"**Inherit the earth**" echoes Psalm 37:11. The meek receive what cannot be seized by force—lasting influence, genuine respect, sustainable relationships.

Day 3: Echoes Across Traditions

Wisdom traditions value strength-through-restraint:

Islam: The Prophet Muhammad exemplified *hilm* (forbearance)—being mild-tempered and forgiving even to enemies. The Qur'an praises those who "walk humbly on the earth" and respond to ignorance with peace (25:63). True strength lies in restraining the ego, not asserting it.

Hinduism: The Bhagavad Gita lists *ahimsa* (nonviolence) and self-restraint as signs of wisdom. Krishna praises those "free from pride and delusion" (13:7-8). This demonstrates *atma-vinigraha* (self-mastery)—not being a doormat, but not needing to dominate others to feel secure.

Taoism: "The soft overcomes the hard; the gentle overcomes the rigid" (Tao Te Ching 36). Like water, the highest good "benefits all things but never seeks status," dwelling in lowly places others disdain (8).

Common thread: True power serves love rather than ego. The gentle inherit what the aggressive exhaust themselves trying to seize.

Day 4: A Witness — Mahatma Gandhi

Though Hindu, Gandhi drew deeply from the Sermon on the Mount, calling it "the essence of Christianity." His *satyagraha* (truth-force) embodied meekness—nonviolent resistance that was neither passive nor aggressive.

Gandhi renounced wealth, privilege, and caste status, choosing to live among the poorest. He fought tirelessly for justice yet refused to hate his oppressors. When attacked, he didn't retaliate; when imprisoned, he continued to pray for his captors.

"In a gentle way, you can shake the world." —Gandhi

His meekness was strategic and powerful. By refusing to respond to violence with violence, he exposed the moral bankruptcy of oppressive systems and ultimately helped liberate a nation. His gentle strength inspired global movements for justice.

Day 5: In Professional and Public Life

Meekness challenges our cultural assumptions about leadership and success:

In professional contexts, meekness might mean:

- **Leading without dominating**: Influencing through character rather than position
- **Listening before speaking**: Especially when power dynamics are involved
- **Accepting feedback gracefully**: Saying "thank you" when someone points out mistakes
- **Choosing collaboration over competition**: Looking for win-win solutions rather than zero-sum victories
- **Defusing rather than escalating conflict**: Using calm strength to lower the temperature in tense situations

Meek leaders create environments where others feel safe to contribute ideas, admit mistakes, and take creative risks. Their strength shows up in restraint, their power in service to others.

Day 6: In Personal Life and Relationships

Meekness transforms how we navigate conflict and intimacy:

- **Pause before reacting**: Take the sacred pause between trigger and response
- **Let strength serve love**: Direct your gifts toward others' flourishing rather than your own advancement
- **Choose relationship over being right**: Release the need to win every argument
- **Practice the gentle answer**: Respond to hostility with calm strength rather than defensive reaction
- **Lead quietly in your family**: Influence through consistent character rather than loud demands

Meekness in relationships doesn't mean becoming a doormat. It means being strong enough to be gentle, secure enough to listen, and confident enough to apologize when wrong.

Day 7: Contemplative Practice

Gentle Strength Meditation: Sit quietly and bring to mind a recent situation where you felt the urge to defend, control, or dominate.

Breathe deeply and imagine responding with meek strength instead—calm, present, responsive rather than reactive. What would that look like? How would it feel in your body?

Practice this prayer: *"God, give me strength to be gentle, power to serve love, and wisdom to respond rather than react."*

Alternative practice: During conversations today, practice listening twice as much as you speak. Notice the urge to interrupt or formulate your response while others are talking. Can you simply be present to what they're saying?

Weekly Reflection Space

Where in your life do you struggle with the balance between strength and gentleness? When has meekness been mistaken for weakness?

Think of someone you admire for their gentle strength. What makes their meekness powerful rather than passive?

How might you practice meekness in one specific relationship or situation this week?

Week 4: Blessed Are Those Who Hunger and Thirst for Righteousness

Day 1: The Text

"Blessed are those who hunger and thirst for righteousness, for they will be filled." — Matthew 5:6 (NRSV)

In Greek: Μακάριοι οἱ πεινῶντες καὶ διψῶντες τὴν δικαιοσύνην, ὅτι αὐτοὶ χορτασθήσονται. *(Makarioi hoi peinōntes kai dipsōntes tēn dikaiosynēn, hoti autoi chortasthēsontai.)*

Other translations:

- *"Happy are those whose greatest desire is to do what God requires..."* (GNT)
- *"God blesses those who hunger and thirst for justice..."* (NLT)
- *"How blest are those who hunger and thirst to see right prevail..."* (REB)
- *"You're blessed when you've worked up a good appetite for God..."* (MSG)

Reflection Prompt: What are you genuinely hungry for in life? What injustice makes your heart ache? How might spiritual hunger be different from spiritual satisfaction?

Day 2: Language and Meaning

"Hunger and thirst" (πεινῶντες καὶ διψῶντες) are visceral, present-tense verbs suggesting ongoing, active craving—not casual interest but consuming desire. This echoes the Psalmic tradition of thirsting for God (Psalm 42:1-2).

"Righteousness" (δικαιοσύνη) encompasses both personal integrity and social justice. In Hebrew, *tzedakah* includes legal justice, ethical behavior, and covenantal faithfulness. It's both being right with God and making things right in the world.

This hunger includes:

- **Personal transformation**: Longing to live with integrity and moral clarity
- **Social justice**: Aching for systems that protect the vulnerable
- **Restorative relationships**: Desiring healing for broken connections
- **Cosmic healing**: Yearning for God's reign of peace and justice

"Filled" (χορτασθήσονται) literally means satisfied like animals after feeding—surprisingly earthy language for spiritual fulfillment.

Day 3: Echoes Across Traditions

The hunger for justice and righteousness appears across wisdom traditions:

Islam: Righteousness (*birr*) encompasses belief, kindness, prayer, charity, and perseverance (Qur'an 2:177). "Indeed, those who have believed and done righteous deeds... their Lord will guide them because of their faith" (10:9). Islamic tradition balances personal piety with social justice through divine law.

Buddhism: The Noble Eightfold Path includes right action, speech, and livelihood—forms of righteousness that align with the Dharma. The Bodhisattva ideal transforms personal yearning into service to others' liberation from suffering.

Judaism: The prophets cried out for righteousness to flow "like a mighty stream" (Amos 5:24). Hunger for justice isn't weakness but spiritual health—the sign of a heart aligned with God's desires.

Common thread: The morally mature aren't those who've achieved perfection, but those who remain deeply dissatisfied with injustice. Holy hunger drives both personal and social transformation.

Day 4: A Witness — Dorothy Day

Dorothy Day (1897-1980), co-founder of the Catholic Worker Movement, embodied hungry pursuit of justice. She lived among the poor not as charity but as solidarity, welcomed the marginalized, and resisted war and systemic injustice.

Day's "revolution of the heart" flowed from her hunger for a world where everyone had enough. She opened houses of hospitality, protested nuclear weapons, and chose voluntary poverty to stand with those who had no choice.

"The mystery of the poor is this: That they are Jesus." —Dorothy Day

Her hunger for righteousness led to a lifetime of uncomfortable choices—jail cells, criticism from church hierarchy, and the daily grind of serving soup to society's outcasts. Yet she found deep satisfaction in aligning her life with gospel values, even when it cost her comfort and reputation.

Day 5: In Professional and Public Life

Hunger for righteousness transforms how we approach work and public engagement:

In professional contexts, this might mean:

- **Questioning systems that harm**: Speaking up about policies that damage people or environment
- **Pursuing ethical business practices**: Even when they're more costly or complex
- **Advocating for fair compensation**: Working toward living wages and equitable treatment
- **Creating inclusive environments**: Building workplaces where everyone can flourish
- **Using your platform for justice**: Leveraging influence to address inequality

This isn't about being the office activist, but about letting moral hunger inform your choices. When you ache for justice, you naturally notice where systems need healing and work toward positive change.

Day 6: In Personal Life and Relationships

Righteousness hunger affects intimate relationships and daily choices:

- **Practice restorative rather than retributive responses**: When hurt, seek healing rather than payback
- **Address family systems that harm**: Gently challenge patterns of favoritism, scapegoating, or abuse
- **Seek justice in your community**: Vote, volunteer, donate—let your values shape your civic engagement
- **Consume ethically**: Let hunger for justice influence spending choices and lifestyle decisions
- **Pursue reconciliation**: In broken relationships, work toward healing rather than simply walking away

Personal righteousness and social justice reinforce each other. Those who hunger for justice in the world often start by pursuing honesty and fairness in their closest relationships.

Day 7: Contemplative Practice

Justice Examination: Spend time reflecting on what makes your heart ache in the world. What injustices stir your soul? Where do you see brokenness that calls for healing?

Ask: *"God, what are you calling me to hunger for? How might my longing for justice serve your kingdom?"*

Don't rush to action plans. Simply sit with your hunger and let it deepen your prayer.

Alternative practice: Walk through your neighborhood or community, paying attention to signs of both flourishing and struggle. Pray for God's justice and peace to flow through these streets. Notice what stirs your heart toward action.

Weekly Reflection Space

What injustices make your heart ache? Where do you experience holy dissatisfaction with the way things are?

How do you balance working for justice with finding peace? Where have you experienced God's "filling" in response to your righteous hunger?

What is one concrete way you can pursue righteousness—personally or socially—in the coming week?

Week 5: Blessed Are the Merciful

Day 1: The Text

"Blessed are the merciful, for they will receive mercy." — Matthew 5:7 (NRSV)

In Greek: Μακάριοι οἱ ἐλεήμονες, ὅτι αὐτοὶ ἐλεηθήσονται. *(Makarioi hoi eleēmones, hoti autoi eleēthēsontai.)*

Other translations:

- *"Happy are those who are merciful to others..."* (GNT)
- *"God blesses those who are merciful..."* (NLT)
- *"How blest are those who show mercy..."* (REB)
- *"You're blessed when you care..."* (MSG)

Reflection Prompt: When have you most needed mercy? When has showing mercy to someone else surprised you with its power to heal? How might mercy be love with its sleeves rolled up?

Day 2: Language and Meaning

"Merciful" (ἐλεήμονες) describes not just feeling compassion but acting on it. This rare Greek word in the New Testament carries the profound sense of divine mercy made manifest in human action—love that moves toward suffering even when justice would allow you to stand back.

Mercy includes:

- **Compassionate action**: Meeting people where they are, not where you think they should be
- **Forgiveness beyond earning**: Offering grace to those who haven't "deserved" it
- **Restoration over punishment**: Choosing healing over retribution when possible
- **Presence in pain**: Staying with people in their suffering rather than offering quick fixes

The reciprocal promise: "They will receive mercy"—not as transaction but as spiritual coherence. Mercy shapes the heart of both giver and receiver. With the measure you use, it will be measured to you (Luke 6:38).

Mercy doesn't erase justice—it transfigures it.

Day 3: Echoes Across Traditions

Mercy as transformative power appears across spiritual traditions:

Islam: God's mercy (*rahmah*) defines divine relationship to creation. "My mercy encompasses all things" (Qur'an 7:156). The Prophet taught: "He who does not show mercy to others will not be shown mercy." Every chapter (except one) begins: "In the name of Allah, the Most Gracious, the Most Merciful."

Buddhism: *Karuṇā* (compassion) lies at the heart of the spiritual path. The Bodhisattva ideal exemplifies this—beings who remain in the world of suffering to assist others. Compassion flows from insight into the interconnectedness of all life and universality of suffering.

Judaism: Mercy interweaves *chesed* (steadfast lovingkindness) and *rachamim* (womb-like compassion). "The Lord is merciful and gracious, slow to anger and abounding in steadfast love" (Psalm 103:8). God's mercy becomes the template for human relationships.

Common thread: In showing mercy, we participate in the fundamental nature of reality itself—the love that holds the universe together.

Day 4: A Witness — Archbishop Desmond Tutu

Archbishop Desmond Tutu (1931-2021) embodied merciful justice throughout South Africa's transition from apartheid. As chair of the Truth and Reconciliation Commission, he chose healing over revenge for his wounded nation.

Tutu's approach was revolutionary: rather than trials and punishments, the Commission offered a path where perpetrators could confess their crimes and receive amnesty, while victims could tell their stories and receive acknowledgment of their suffering.

"Forgiving is not forgetting; it's actually remembering—remembering and not using your right to hit back." —Desmond Tutu

His mercy wasn't soft—it was fierce love that refused to let hatred have the last word. He showed that mercy and justice aren't opposites but partners in the work of restoration. His laughter in the face of evil demonstrated mercy's transformative power.

Day 5: In Professional and Public Life

Mercy transforms workplace culture and public engagement:

In professional contexts, mercy might mean:

- **Second chances for those who fail**: Creating space for learning from mistakes rather than just punishing them
- **Assuming good intent**: Starting with curiosity about others' motivations rather than judgment
- **Flexible policies for human struggles**: Accommodating family emergencies, mental health needs, and life crises
- **Restorative rather than punitive management**: Focusing on future improvement rather than past failures
- **Grace under pressure**: Remaining kind even when deadlines loom and stress mounts

Merciful leaders create environments where people feel safe to take risks, admit mistakes, and grow. This builds loyalty and innovation because team members know their humanity will be honored.

Day 6: In Personal Life and Relationships

Mercy revolutionizes intimate relationships:

- **Choose understanding over winning**: In conflicts, seek to understand the other person's pain rather than prove your point
- **Offer grace for repeated failures**: Remember how often you need forgiveness yourself
- **Practice emotional generosity**: Give the benefit of the doubt when others are struggling
- **Create safe spaces for confession**: Let people know they can bring you their failures without fear of rejection
- **Forgive quickly, apologize readily**: Keep short accounts and clean slates

Mercy in relationships doesn't mean accepting abuse or having no boundaries. It means responding to human frailty with compassion while maintaining healthy limits.

Day 7: Contemplative Practice

Mercy Meditation: Bring to mind someone who has hurt or disappointed you. Without rushing to forgiveness, simply hold them in prayer.

Pray: *"God, help me see this person as you see them—flawed but beloved, struggling but not beyond hope. Give me the grace to respond with mercy."*

Notice what resistance arises. Don't force feelings you don't have, but ask God to soften your heart over time.

Alternative practice: Throughout the day, practice "mercy moments"—choosing compassion over judgment in small encounters. The slow cashier, the distracted colleague, the demanding family member. Each choice to respond with grace is practice for larger mercies.

Weekly Reflection Space

Where in your life do you struggle to show mercy? What makes it difficult to respond with grace to certain people or situations?

When have you experienced unexpected mercy from others? How did receiving grace change you?

How might you practice mercy more intentionally in one specific relationship this week?

Week 6: Blessed Are the Pure in Heart

Day 1: The Text

"Blessed are the pure in heart, for they will see God." — Matthew 5:8 (NRSV)

In Greek: Μακάριοι οἱ καθαροὶ τῇ καρδίᾳ, ὅτι αὐτοὶ τὸν θεὸν ὄψονται. *(Makarioi hoi katharoi tē kardia, hoti autoi ton theon opsontai.)*

Other translations:

- *"Happy are those whose hearts are pure..."* (GNT)
- *"God blesses those whose hearts are pure..."* (NLT)
- *"How blest are those whose hearts are pure..."* (REB)
- *"You're blessed when you get your inside world—your mind and heart—put right..."* (MSG)

Reflection Prompt: What does it mean to have a "pure" heart in a world of mixed motives and competing loyalties? How might purity be about wholeness rather than perfection?

Day 2: Language and Meaning

"Pure" (καθαροὶ) means clean, clear, or unadulterated—free from pollution, cloudiness, or debris. Applied to the heart, it describes not sinlessness but *singleness*—an undivided heart unified in its loves and loyalties.

"Heart" (καρδίᾳ) in Hebrew thought encompasses far more than emotion. It's the seat of thought, will, and moral choice—the center of the entire person. A pure heart has unified moral purpose, clear intention, and transparent motive.

Purity of heart includes:

- **Undivided loyalty**: Not torn between competing allegiances
- **Transparent motivation**: No hidden agendas or ulterior motives
- **Integrated living**: Private life and public witness aligned
- **Single-minded devotion**: As Kierkegaard said, "Purity of heart is to will one thing"

"See God" (τὸν θεὸν ὄψονται) promises spiritual perception—the ability to recognize divine presence in the world, in others, and in the depths of experience. Clear hearts see clearly because they're not looking through the fog of divided loyalties.

Day 3: Echoes Across Traditions

The connection between inner purity and spiritual vision appears across traditions:

Islam: *Ikhlas* (sincerity of intention) forms the foundation of all spiritual practice. "God does not look at your forms or wealth, but He looks at your hearts and your deeds" (Sahih Muslim). The pure heart becomes a mirror reflecting divine light, enabling spiritual insight.

Buddhism: Mental purification (*vipassana*) clears away the *kilesa* (mental pollutants) that cloud clear seeing. "All things arise from mind. When the mind is pure, joy follows like a shadow that never leaves" (Dhammapada). Purity leads to awakened insight into reality's true nature.

Hinduism: *Chitta-shuddhi* (purification of consciousness) is essential for *darshan* (divine vision). "When all desires that cling to the heart are surrendered, the mortal becomes immortal" (Bhagavad Gita 15:51). Various yogic paths clear ego's obscurations to reveal one's divine nature.

Common thread: Inner transparency creates outer perception. When the heart is undivided, we see clearly—both human truth and divine presence.

Day 4: A Witness — Jean Vanier

Jean Vanier (1928-2019) founded L'Arche, creating communities where people with and without intellectual disabilities lived together in mutual respect and friendship. His life demonstrated purity of heart through radical simplicity and transparency.

Vanier saw greatness in vulnerability, not achievement. He discovered profound spiritual truths by sharing daily life with those society often overlooks. His writings reflect deep authenticity and spiritual clarity born from years of simple presence with broken people.

"We are not called by God to do extraordinary things, but to do ordinary things with extraordinary love." —Jean Vanier

Though his legacy was later complicated by posthumous revelations, his work at L'Arche continues to demonstrate how purity of heart recognizes God's presence in the most unexpected places—especially among the vulnerable and marginalized.

Day 5: In Professional and Public Life

Purity of heart transforms how we navigate work and public engagement:

In professional contexts, this might mean:

- **Aligning actions with values**: Refusing to compromise core principles for advancement
- **Transparent communication**: Speaking honestly even when it's inconvenient
- **Single-minded focus on mission**: Keeping the organization's true purpose central
- **Integrated leadership**: Being the same person in the boardroom and the break room
- **Clear decision-making**: Choosing based on what's right rather than what's popular or profitable

Pure-hearted leaders create trust through consistency. People sense when someone has nothing to hide and no ulterior motives. This authenticity becomes magnetic and builds lasting influence.

Day 6: In Personal Life and Relationships

Purity of heart revolutionizes intimate relationships:

- **Practice emotional honesty**: Let your inner reality and outer expression align
- **Simplify your desires**: Notice what clutters your heart with competing loyalties
- **Choose presence over performance**: Be fully present rather than managing impressions
- **Embrace correction gracefully**: Welcome feedback as pathway to greater clarity
- **Return to silence regularly**: Let stillness reveal what noise conceals

In relationships, purity of heart means having nothing to hide, nothing to prove, and nothing to fear. That kind of transparency creates safety for others' vulnerability and enables deeper intimacy.

Day 7: Contemplative Practice

Heart Examination: Sit quietly and ask: "What am I really wanting in this season of life? What desires are driving my choices?"

Notice where your loyalties are divided or your motivations are mixed. Without judgment, simply observe. Then pray: *"God, create in me a clean heart and give me an undivided will to love you and serve others."*

Alternative practice: Throughout the day, practice "one-thing living"—in each activity, conversation, or decision, ask "What is the one thing that matters most here?" Let that single focus simplify your response and clarify your presence.

Weekly Reflection Space

Where do you experience divided loyalty or mixed motives? What would it look like to simplify your desires and "will one thing"?

When have you experienced seeing God—recognizing divine presence in people, nature, or circumstances? What enabled that clarity?

How might you practice greater integration between your inner life and outer expression in the coming week?

Week 7: Blessed Are the Peacemakers

Day 1: The Text

"Blessed are the peacemakers, for they will be called children of God." — Matthew 5:9 (NRSV)

In Greek: Μακάριοι οἱ εἰρηνοποιοί, ὅτι υἱοὶ θεοῦ κληθήσονται. *(Makarioi hoi eirēnopoioi, hoti huioi theou klēthēsontai.)*

Other translations:

- *"Happy are those who work for peace..."* (GNT)
- *"God blesses those who work for peace..."* (NLT)
- *"How blest are the peacemakers..."* (REB)
- *"You're blessed when you can show people how to cooperate instead of compete or fight..."* (MSG)

Reflection Prompt: What's the difference between peacekeeping and peacemaking? When have you stepped into conflict to create healing rather than simply avoiding confrontation?

Day 2: Language and Meaning

"Peacemakers" (εἰρηνοποιοί) is a remarkably rare word—found nowhere else in the New Testament. It's a compound of *eirēnē* (peace) and *poieō* (to make or do). This isn't about those who enjoy calm but those who actively create it, often at personal cost.

Biblical peace (*shalom*) encompasses:

- **Wholeness**: Not just absence of conflict but presence of right relationship
- **Justice**: True peace requires addressing systemic causes of division
- **Restoration**: Healing broken relationships and communities
- **Reconciliation**: Bringing together what has been separated

"Children of God" (υἱοὶ θεοῦ) means bearing God's essential character. In Hebrew thought, being called someone's child meant sharing their nature. Peacemakers resemble the God of peace—they participate in divine character by doing divine work.

This isn't passive peacekeeping but active peace-creating through costly reconciliation.

Day 3: Echoes Across Traditions

Active peacemaking appears across wisdom traditions:

Islam: Reconciliation (*sulh*) is highly esteemed in Islamic law and ethics. "Reconciliation is best" (Qur'an 4:128). The Prophet Muhammad was known as a skilled mediator even before his prophetic mission. *As-Salam* (The Source of Peace) is one of God's names, making peacemaking a divine quality humans can embody.

Buddhism: *Ahimsa* (non-harming) and *karuṇā* (compassion) root peacemaking in inner transformation. "All tremble at violence; all fear death. Putting oneself in the place of another, one should not kill nor cause another to kill" (Dhammapada 129). Peace begins with a peaceful heart.

Hinduism: The spiritually mature remain "the same to friend and foe... calm in mind" (Bhagavad Gita 12:18-19). Inner equanimity becomes the foundation for outer peacemaking. Sometimes maintaining cosmic order (*dharma*) requires confronting injustice rather than maintaining surface harmony.

Common thread: Authentic peace requires addressing root causes of conflict, not just managing symptoms. True peacemakers transform rather than avoid tension.

Day 4: A Witness — Nelson Mandela

Nelson Mandela (1918-2013) endured 27 years of imprisonment under apartheid. When released, he could have sought vengeance. Instead, he chose reconciliation, leading South Africa through transition with grace rather than retribution.

Mandela's approach was revolutionary: the Truth and Reconciliation Commission offered a path where acknowledgment and restoration replaced punishment and revenge. He showed that justice and forgiveness aren't opposites but partners in healing.

"If you want to make peace with your enemy, you have to work with your enemy. Then he becomes your partner." —Nelson Mandela

His peacemaking wasn't weakness but fierce strength—the courage to break cycles of violence and model a different way forward. His restraint and wisdom demonstrated that meek strength can change the world.

Day 5: In Professional and Public Life

Peacemaking transforms workplace culture and public engagement:

In professional contexts, this might mean:

- **Mediating conflicts**: Stepping into tension to facilitate understanding rather than choosing sides
- **Building bridges across divisions**: Creating opportunities for diverse perspectives to engage constructively
- **Addressing systemic issues**: Working to change policies and practices that create recurring conflict
- **Facilitating difficult conversations**: Creating safe spaces for people to air grievances and find solutions

- **Modeling nonreactive responses**: Staying calm and thoughtful when others become defensive or aggressive

Peacemaking leaders don't avoid conflict—they transform it. They understand that sustainable progress requires patient reconciliation work, not forced agreement.

Day 6: In Personal Life and Relationships

Peacemaking revolutionizes how we handle family and community tensions:

- **Become a bridge-builder**: Introduce people across divides; help them discover common ground
- **Practice difficult conversations**: Learn to discuss contentious topics without attacking persons or positions
- **Address root causes**: Look beneath surface disputes to underlying needs, fears, and values
- **Stay present in conflict**: Resist the urge to flee tension; remain physically and emotionally available
- **Seek justice, not just comfort**: Remember that true peace sometimes requires disrupting unjust situations

In families, peacemakers often become the ones others trust with sensitive information and difficult decisions because their motives are clear and their care is genuine.

Day 7: Contemplative Practice

Peace-Breathing: Sit quietly and breathe slowly. On each inhale, pray: *"God, fill me with your peace."* On each exhale: *"Let your peace flow through me to others."*

Bring to mind a specific conflict in your life. Without trying to solve it, simply hold all parties involved in prayer. Ask God to show you how to be a healing presence in this situation.

Alternative practice: Identify one relationship where there's tension or misunderstanding. Commit to taking one small step toward reconciliation this week—a phone call, an honest conversation, or simply changing how you pray for that person.

Weekly Reflection Space

Where do you see yourself as more of a peacekeeper (avoiding conflict) versus a peacemaker (transforming conflict)? What's the difference?

Think of someone you admire for their peacemaking abilities. What makes them effective at creating reconciliation?

What is one specific way you can practice peacemaking in your family, workplace, or community this week?

Week 8: Blessed Are Those Who Are Persecuted for Righteousness' Sake

Day 1: The Text

"Blessed are those who are persecuted for righteousness' sake, for theirs is the kingdom of heaven. Blessed are you when people revile you and persecute you and utter all kinds of evil against you falsely on my account." — Matthew 5:10-11 (NRSV)

In Greek: Μακάριοι οἱ δεδιωγμένοι ἕνεκεν δικαιοσύνης, ὅτι αὐτῶν ἐστιν ἡ βασιλεία τῶν οὐρανῶν. μακάριοί ἐστε ὅταν ὀνειδίσωσιν ὑμᾶς καὶ διώξωσιν...

Other translations:

- *"Happy are those who are persecuted because they do what God requires..."* (GNT)
- *"God blesses those who are persecuted for doing right..."* (NLT)
- *"How blest are those who have suffered persecution for the cause of right..."* (REB)
- *"You're blessed when your commitment to God provokes persecution..."* (MSG)

Reflection Prompt: What has your commitment to righteousness cost you? When has doing the right thing brought unexpected opposition or misunderstanding?

Day 2: Language and Meaning

"Persecuted" (δεδιωγμένοι) implies persistent harassment or pursuit—active, intentional opposition. The perfect tense suggests ongoing effects of past persecution.

"For righteousness' sake" (ἕνεκεν δικαιοσύνης) specifies the reason: not suffering for our own poor choices, but opposition that comes from pursuing justice and integrity. This recalls all we've learned about *dikaiosynē*—both personal integrity and social justice.

The personal turn: Verse 11 shifts from third person ("those") to second person ("you"), making this suddenly direct and intimate. The persecution comes not just from general righteousness but specifically "on my account"—because of allegiance to Jesus.

The promise returns to where we began: "theirs is the kingdom of heaven." This creates an *inclusio* (literary bracket) with the first Beatitude, framing the entire series around the kingdom's surprising citizens.

The cost of kingdom living: Following Jesus and embodying these values will sometimes provoke resistance. The blessing comes not from suffering itself but from what the suffering reveals—a life aligned with God's purposes.

Day 3: Echoes Across Traditions

Standing for truth in the face of power appears across wisdom traditions:

Islam: "Do people think they will be left alone after saying 'We believe' without being put to the test?" (Qur'an 29:2). The concept of *shahāda* (bearing witness) encompasses truthful testimony even under threat. Patient perseverance (*ṣabr*) and truthfulness (*ṣidq*) become twin pillars of dignity under pressure.

Buddhism: Bodhisattvas continue compassionate action even when misunderstood or maligned. Their strength comes not from retaliation but from nonviolent integrity. "Hatred is never appeased by hatred. By non-hatred alone is hatred appeased" (Dhammapada 1.5).

Judaism: The prophets—Amos, Jeremiah, Isaiah—were not honored in their time but slandered, imprisoned, exiled, or executed for speaking uncomfortable truths. Hebrew Scripture repeatedly links righteousness with prophetic witness, even when costly.

Common thread: Those who embody truth and justice often face opposition from systems that benefit from the status quo. This opposition becomes a mark of faithfulness rather than failure.

Day 4: A Witness — Martin Luther King Jr.

Dr. King (1929-1968) explicitly preached the Beatitudes as the spiritual foundation of the Civil Rights Movement. He embodied the dangerous mercy of seeking reconciliation while refusing to ignore systemic injustice.

His commitment to nonviolent resistance came directly from the Sermon on the Mount. He faced imprisonment, death threats, and ultimately assassination for his prophetic witness to racial justice and economic equality.

"I want to be on the right side of the Beatitudes." —Martin Luther King Jr.

King demonstrated that peacemaking sometimes requires confronting injustice. His persecution came not from being divisive but from being truthful about America's failures to live up to its ideals. His suffering revealed the cost of loving enemies while demanding justice.

Day 5: In Professional and Public Life

Persecution for righteousness often appears in subtle forms in professional contexts:

This might include:

- **Whistleblowing consequences**: Facing retaliation for exposing unethical practices

- **Principled stands**: Losing opportunities because you won't compromise core values
- **Advocacy costs**: Being labeled "difficult" for speaking up for marginalized colleagues
- **Moral leadership**: Facing resistance when you challenge harmful but profitable practices
- **Uncomfortable truth-telling**: Being marginalized for naming systemic problems

The key question: Is the opposition coming because you're living with integrity, or because you're being self-righteous? The blessing applies specifically to persecution that results from genuine righteousness, not from our own character flaws.

Day 6: In Personal Life and Relationships

Righteous living can bring unexpected relational costs:

- **Family opposition**: Living differently than family expectations or traditions
- **Social ostracism**: Being excluded because you won't participate in harmful behaviors
- **Misunderstanding**: Having pure motives questioned or misinterpreted
- **Friendship tensions**: Relationships strained when you hold to principles others find inconvenient
- **Community pressure**: Facing criticism for standing with unpopular but just causes

Remember: Not all suffering is redemptive. But when it's the cost of love, integrity, or justice—it becomes sacred. The goal isn't to seek persecution but to remain faithful regardless of consequences.

Day 7: Contemplative Practice

Courage Prayer: Reflect on areas where you feel called to greater righteousness—personally, professionally, or socially. What fears arise? What might faithfulness cost?

Pray: *"God, give me courage to do what is right, even when it's costly. Help me discern between righteous suffering and unnecessary martyrdom. Strengthen me to love my enemies and work for justice."*

Alternative practice: Read about modern witnesses who have faced persecution for righteousness—Malala Yousafzai, Rosa Parks, Dietrich Bonhoeffer, or local heroes in your community. Let their courage inspire your own commitment to costly discipleship.

Weekly Reflection Space

Where do you experience tension between righteousness and acceptance? What has your commitment to justice cost you?

How do you distinguish between righteous suffering and unnecessary conflict? When is persecution a sign of faithfulness versus our own character issues?

What is one area where you sense God calling you to greater courage in living out your values, even if it brings opposition?

Integration: Days 1-3

Day 1: The Beatitudes as a Way of Life

"Blessed are the poor in spirit... Blessed are those who are persecuted for righteousness' sake, for theirs is the kingdom of heaven."

After eight weeks of reflection, we see that the Beatitudes aren't random virtues but a complete vision of human flourishing. They form a **spiritual progression**:

The Foundation: Poor in spirit (Week 1) and mourning (Week 2) empty us of false securities and surface satisfactions, creating space for God.

The Character: Meekness (Week 3) and hunger for righteousness (Week 4) shape how we engage the world—with gentle strength and holy dissatisfaction with injustice.

The Relationships: Mercy (Week 5) and purity of heart (Week 6) transform how we connect with others—offering grace and living with transparency.

The Mission: Peacemaking (Week 7) and persecution (Week 8) reveal the cost and calling of kingdom citizenship—actively reconciling and willingly suffering for righteousness.

These aren't eight separate goals but **one integrated way of life**. The poor in spirit naturally become peacemakers. Those who mourn injustice hunger for righteousness. The pure in heart show mercy because they know their own need for grace.

Jesus doesn't call us to choose our favorite Beatitudes but to embody them all as citizens of his upside-down kingdom.

Reflection Questions:

Which Beatitudes feel most natural to you? Which ones challenge you most?

How do you see the eight working together as a complete vision rather than separate virtues?

What patterns of growth have you noticed over these eight weeks?

Day 2: Creating Your Rule of Life

"For theirs is the kingdom of heaven... they will be comforted... they will inherit the earth... they will be filled... they will receive mercy... they will see God... they will be called children of God."

The Beatitudes aren't just inspiring ideals—they're practical pathways for spiritual formation. As you conclude this journey, consider how to continue living into these blessings through intentional practices.

A Rule of Life is a rhythm of spiritual practices that helps you remain open to God's transforming work. Based on your eight weeks with the Beatitudes, create your own rule:

Daily Practices:

- Which contemplative practices from these weeks were most meaningful? (Breath prayer, walking meditation, examination of conscience?)
- How will you maintain the rhythm of reflection that this series created?

Weekly Practices:

- What will help you remember and integrate these teachings? (Reviewing one Beatitude per week? Monthly retreats?)
- How will you stay connected to community around these values?

Monthly/Seasonal Practices:

- What will deepen your growth in areas where you struggle most?
- How will you evaluate and adjust your practices over time?

Relationships and Service:

- How will you live out mercy, peacemaking, and hunger for justice in practical ways?
- What communities or causes will help you embody these values beyond personal devotion?

Remember: A rule of life serves love, not legalism. It should create freedom for spiritual growth, not burden.

Creating Your Rule:

Choose 1-2 practices from each category that feel sustainable and life-giving:

Daily:
_____

Weekly:
_____

Monthly:
_____

Service/Relationships: _____

Day 3: Blessed Community in a Broken World

"Rejoice and be glad, for your reward is great in heaven, for in the same way they persecuted the prophets who were before you."

The Beatitudes aren't meant for solo spirituality. They describe a **community**—a people shaped by these values together. As you continue this journey, consider how to find or create "Beatitudes communities."

Characteristics of Beatitudes Communities:

- **Honest about brokenness**: No pretending to have it all together (poor in spirit)
- **Safe for grief**: Space to mourn losses, failures, and injustice without rushing to fix or cheer up
- **Gentle with power**: Leaders who serve rather than dominate (meek)
- **Committed to justice**: Not content with personal piety while ignoring systemic problems
- **Practicing mercy**: Quick to forgive, slow to judge, generous with second chances
- **Authentic and transparent**: No performance or image management required
- **Actively reconciling**: Working across differences to heal divisions
- **Willing to be countercultural**: Supporting each other when righteousness brings opposition

Finding Community: You might find these qualities in:

- Churches committed to both spiritual formation and social justice
- Interfaith groups working for peace and reconciliation
- Service organizations addressing root causes of injustice
- Small groups dedicated to spiritual growth and mutual accountability
- Professional networks committed to ethical practices
- Neighborhood initiatives building bridges across differences

Creating Community: If you can't find what you're looking for:

- Start a small group studying these teachings together
- Organize service projects that embody Beatitudes values
- Practice hospitality that welcomes the marginalized
- Model these qualities in existing communities
- Mentor others in this way of life

The Promise: Communities that embody the Beatitudes become signs of God's kingdom—glimpses of the world as God intends it. They offer hope to a divided world and strength for the long work of transformation.

Final Commitment:

How will you continue growing in the Beatitudes way of life?

What community will support and challenge you in this journey?

What is your prayer as you conclude this eight-week path?

Blessing for the Journey Ahead:

May you be poor in spirit and rich in grace, May you mourn with hope and comfort others, May you be meek and inherit the earth's beauty, May you hunger for justice and be satisfied, May you show mercy and receive it abundantly, May you be pure in heart and see God everywhere, May you make peace and be called God's child, May you be faithful in persecution and know the kingdom is yours.

Go in peace to love and serve, Walking the Beatitudes path each day.

The journey continues...

About the Author

Kevin Meyer is a retired executive and lifelong student of subjects that challenge conventional thinking. Trained as a chemical engineer, he spent most of his career in executive roles in medical device manufacturing, where he developed a deep appreciation for the intersection of rigorous methodology and human-centered problem solving.

Meyer cofounded an e-learning company focused on continuous improvement methods, which he successfully grew and eventually sold. This experience reinforced his belief in the power of making complex ideas accessible to broader audiences—a principle that guides his current writing projects.

Born in the United States but raised for seven formative years in Peru, Meyer has traveled to over sixty-five countries, always with an eye toward understanding how different cultures approach fundamental questions about meaning, truth, and human flourishing. This global perspective shapes his approach to exploring diverse intellectual traditions with both curiosity and respect.

For nearly thirty years, Meyer has practiced *bhāvanā*—disciplined cultivation of understanding through deep, intentional study of subjects ranging from marathon running and scuba diving to philosophy, spirituality, and history. Each year, he embraces a new area of inquiry that pushes him beyond his comfort zone and challenges his assumptions.

Now retired and living in Morro Bay, California, Meyer finally has the time to fully explore the wildly divergent topics that have always fascinated him. He remains active in the local biotech startup community, bringing his experience in scaling complex operations to emerging companies.

This book represents Meyer's continued exploration of how human communities preserve and transmit their most treasured wisdom across centuries and cultures. While making no claim to scholarly expertise, he brings to this inquiry the same methodical curiosity and respect for evidence that guided his business career, combined with a deep appreciation for the spiritual significance these questions hold for millions of people worldwide.

Meyer can be reached through his website at KevinMeyer.com.

Other Books by Kevin Meyer

Sacred Editors Series

Sacred Editors: How Power, Politics, and Interpretation Shaped the Christian Scriptures
The remarkable human story behind the formation of the Bible, tracing how scribes, bishops, emperors, and competing Christian communities shaped the New Testament canon through centuries of copying, translating, and theological debate.

Sacred Editors: The Evolution of Jewish Sacred Texts Through Exile, Law, and Dialogue
An exploration of how the Hebrew Bible and Talmud came to be, examining the human decisions, political pressures, and scholarly debates that shaped Jewish sacred texts across centuries of transmission and interpretation.

Sacred Editors: How Preservation and Authority Defined Islamic Sacred Texts
The fascinating story behind the compilation of the Quran and the development of Islamic textual traditions, revealing the complex historical processes through which Muslim communities preserved and codified their foundational texts.

Leadership and Personal Development

The Simple Leader: Personal and Professional Leadership at the Nexus of Lean and Zen

Filled with personal stories, practices, and insights from a thirty-year leadership journey, this book reveals the surprising connections between Lean manufacturing principles and Zen wisdom. Organized into eight practical parts—from reconnecting with your inner self to growing your organization—it shows leaders in any industry how to become more organized, effective, and balanced by integrating concepts like simplicity, flow, respect, and beginner's mind into their daily practice.

Biography

Harleigh Knott: Christmas Greetings From a Remarkable Life

A celebration of Harleigh Thayer Knott (1929-2019), a remarkable woman who lived her entire life in Morro Bay, California, while developing interests ranging from opera to history, polo to Indy car racing. Compiled from sixty years of her captivating and humorous annual Christmas letters, this book preserves the memory of an extraordinary life filled with Stanford education, world travel, and an insatiable curiosity about everything from frogs to the human condition.

www.ingramcontent.com/pod-product-compliance
Lightning Source LLC
Chambersburg PA
CBHW021138160426
43194CB00007B/621